SERIES EDITORS:
Stewart R. Clegg &
Ralph Stablein

Silvia Gherardi
Barbara Poggio

ADVANCES IN ORGANIZATION STUDIES

Gendertelling in Organizations:
Narratives from male-dominated environments

Liber
Copenhagen Business School Press
Universitetsforlaget

Gender Telling in Organizations:
Narratives from male-dominated environments

ISBN 978-91-47-08670-X (Sweden)
ISBN 978-82-15-01216-2 (Norway)
ISBN 978-87-630-0212-7 (Rest of the world)
© 2007 Silvia Gherardi, Barbara Poggio and Liber AB

Publisher's editor: Ola Håkansson
Series editor: Stewart Clegg and Ralph Stablein
Typeset: LundaText AB

1:1

Printed in Slovenia by
Korotan Ljubljana, Slovenien 2007

Distribution:
Sweden
Liber AB, Baltzarsgatan 4
S-205 10 Malmö, Sweden
tel +46 40-25 86 00, fax +46 40-97 05 50
http://www.liber.se
Kundtjänst tel +46 8-690 93 30, fax +46 8-690 93 01

Norway
Universitetsforlaget AS
Postboks 508
NO-0105 Oslo, Norway
phone: +47 14 75 00, fax: +47 24 14 75 01
post@universitetsforlaget.no www.universitetsforlaget.no

Denmark
DBK Logistics, Mimersvej 4
DK-4600 Koege, Denmark
phone: +45 3269 7788, fax: +45 3269 7789
www.cbspress.dk

North America
International Specialized Book Services
920 NE 58th Ave., Suite 300
Portland, OR 97213, USA
phone: +1 800 944 6190
fax: +1 503 280 8832

Rest of the World
Marston Book Services, P.O. Box 269
Abingdon, Oxfordshire, OX14 4YN, UK
phone: +44 (0) 1235 465500, fax: +44 (0) 1235 465555
E-mail Direct Customers: direct.order@marston.co.uk
E-mail Booksellers: trade.order@marston.co.uk

Advances in Organization Studies

Series Editors:
Stewart Clegg
Professor, University of
Technology, Sydney, Australia

Ralph E. Stablein
Professor, Massey University,
New Zealand

Advances in Organization Studies
is a channel for cutting edge theoretical and empirical works of high
quality that contributes to the field
of organizational studies. The series welcomes thought-provoking
ideas, new perspectives and neglected topics from researchers within a
wide range of disciplines and geographical locations.

www.organizationstudies.org

Editorial Board

Professor David Courpasson
Ecole de Management de Lyon
Professor Barbara Czarniawska
Gothenburg Research Institute, Gothenburg
University
Professor Martha Feldman
Department of Planning, Policy, & Design,
University of California, Irvine
Professor Peter Fleming
Judge Business School, University of
Cambridge
Professor Mary Jo Hatch
McIntire School of Commerce, University of
Virginia
Professor Kristian Kreiner
Department of Organization & Industrial
Sociology, Copenhagen Business School
Professor Gideon Kunda
Tel Aviv University
Professor Walter Nord
Department of Management & Organization,
University of South Florida
Professor Kjell Arne Røvik
University of Tromsø, Department of Political
and Organization Science
Professor Majken Schultz
Department of Organization,
Copenhagen Business School

Acknowledgements

This book would not have been possible without the helpfulness of our women and men interviewees and the time that they dedicated to telling us their stories; it is above all to them that we owe a debt of gratitude.

We wish also to thank all those who took part in the research work: Gabriele Ballarino, Clara Barbieri, Paola De Benedet, Paolo Bonfatti, Francesca Decimo, Francesca Odella, and Marco Trentini, who conducted the interviews.

We especially wish to thank Adrian Belton for his generous assistance in translating the text, and to the reviewers for their careful reading and perceptive comments.

We finally express our gratitude to all those who have read the books or parts of it, and made such constructive suggestions: Attila Bruni, Barbara Czarniawska, Joanne Martin and Patricia Martin.

Overall responsibility for this work is shared by the authors. Silvia Gherardi wrote the Introduction, Chapters 1, 5 and the Conclusions; Barbara Poggio wrote Chapters, 2, 3, 4 and 6.

Table of Contents

Introduction

This book gathers the stories told by men and women about a particular event. With a play on words sometimes used by feminists in the past, it could have been entitled *His/story and Her/story*, in order to convey from the outset a banal, but sometimes overlooked, fact: the contents of stories depend on the voice telling them, and the experience recounted in first person differs according to the gender of the narrator. The voice springs from the body, from a subjectivity that is also materiality. Going through the world in the body of a woman or a man entails differing experiences of reality, and therefore the production of differing accounts of that reality. Feminist studies sought to show that history was a story written by men, and that it recounted only part of human experience. The rest was excluded or marginalized; above all the history of women, both as personal experience and as a dimension of everyday life – a life, that is to say, which does not 'make history'.

The main difference between men and women is that they have bodies which expose them to different experiences of the same world; or better, which differently mediate the way in which their relationship with the world is socially constructed. As we recount our experience of the world, we make it intelligible both to ourselves and others. Hence language is a form of mediation among ourselves, our experience of the world, and the others in the world. When the narrating voice talks to the Other, it describes, explains, justifies, constructs discourse objects, transmits emotions, creates intimacy or distance, theorizes, builds a moral and aesthetic order, and constructs the identities of the speaker and the listener. Recounting is therefore a social practice: a discursive practice, in fact, which together with other material practices like working, constructing artifacts, objects of use and complex technologies, constructs social relations and the world as we know it and therefore meaningfully endowed with sense. The knowledge preserved and transmitted by narratives – the practical knowledge about how things are done, and done together, which derives from experience and transmits its flavour and warmth – is defined as narrative knowledge. Opposed to it is the analytical knowledge, also called paradigmatic or scientific, which seeks to formulate universal laws.

The book therefore explores the kind of situated knowledge comprised in the experience – in a Northern region of Italy – of men and women and transmitted through reflection on their work experiences and those of the persons closest to them. We are fully aware of the locally embedded character of the study, and we hope that it will enhance a comparative reflection on cultural similarities and differences among European countries.

The book examines stories about work constructed around a particular event: the entry of a She into a predominantly male work group. She does a job which tradition defines as typically male, or She has a position of organizational responsibility occupied by few or no other women. The He of the story is a colleague of She. He has seen Her join the group and usually has a similar or superior job grade.

We sought to elicit reflexive accounts about a gender-connoted experience shared by a Her and a Him. He represented the gender dominant in the group, while She represented the minority gender. The organizational culture of the work group therefore consisted of male terrain in which the woman's 'alien' presence had to be accommodated. We collected the accounts of thirty work pairs – thirty 'Shes' and thirty 'Hes' – whom we asked to recount how they had come to occupy their present jobs, and then how She had been welcomed, or otherwise, by the work group. As social scientists, we were interested in understanding and describing the experiences of women in occupations where they are traditionally under-represented. But we were especially interested in the intersubjective experience of gender. For this reason we elicited what we call a 'retrospective gaze' from Her and Him on their past experiences.

What we mean by 'retrospective gaze' can be illustrated by Karen Blixen's story of the stork, which Adriana Cavarero (1997) recounts in the introduction to her book on female narrative.

As the story of the stork was being narrated, a drawing of the bird appeared before the eyes of the listener. The narrator began by telling the story of an old man who lived in a small house near a pond full of fish. One night he was woken up by a terrible noise. He ran out of his house to the pond, and in the darkness repeatedly tripped, fell, and got to his feet again. It is at this point of the story that the narrator begins drawing a map of the man's footsteps as he rushed hither and thither to repair a large breach in the pond wall. When he had finished, the man went back to bed. When he looked out of the window the next morning, what did he see? A stork! His footsteps had drawn the outline of a stork on the ground. "He must have laughed out loud", writes Karen Blixen (1937), and then asks: "When the design of my life is complete, shall I, shall other people see a stork?"

The retrospective gaze is metaphorically represented by the man looking out of the window when his night-time work had finished; and it was only *a posteriori*, from the marks on the ground, that he made sense of his labours, discerned a pattern, gave shape to his experience. It is in narrating that signs, traces of events, are assembled to acquire complete sense. The design of a life or of an event arises from hindsight, when thought becomes reflexive, turning back upon itself to compose a narrative and give shape to what was indistinct. A narrative is a gift: it is the drawing given to the little girl at the end of the stork story; and the drawing concretized the volatility of the words. The drawing and the story are inseparable in this case, just as the discursive practices which construct gender are inseparable from the material practices that embody the meaning of gender in artifacts, in technologies, in the physical settings of organizations, in rewards and incentives systems, in presence and in absence. Donna Harraway (1996) has accordingly talked of 'material-semiotic practices', and we emphasise here that feminist practice has always set great value on narrative knowledge, and on the endeavour to make sense of female experience and to historicize it. The retrospective gaze is not a banal methodological expedient used by feminist research, for it induces reflexive thought to appropriate or re-appropriate personal history, and it thus stimulates 'memory work'.

In the 1980s a group of German women in Hamburg published a collected volume which was later translated into English (Haug, 1987) with the title *Memory Work*. The book recounted the work of a women's group in reconstructing, on the basis of individual experiences, the social processes that construct female sexuality. The methodology of memory work was then transferred to other contexts: for instance, the socialization of women to academic work, or the therapeutic treatment of women victims of abuse. Put briefly, the expression 'memory work' refers to the process by which the historical-cultural self is interwoven with practical/social relations, and for which

- the self is a *historical product*, an ongoing trajectory;
- the self is a cultural product (discourse form) and a social product (relational practice).

It is therefore a *methodology* which situates the present self within the relational organization of the process of socialization to work, and which consists in remembering one's body as situated and historical, and in identifying experiences as memories which infiltrate the present. It is based on the assumption that some change in the present can only be produced if the past is subjected to 'dispassionate' analysis. It is therefore evident that memory work is both a methodology for collecting and interpreting life-stories, as it is used in this book, and a methodology for action-research. Indeed, memory work as a research technique focuses on how awareness and identity take shape in relation to modalities of involvement in work. It does so by identifying:

- the ways in which people construct themselves within existing structures;
- the ways in which they reproduce the social system;
- the points/moments when change is possible, that is, when relational bonds are stronger/weaker, when a new equilibrium has been reached (in action-research).

We are particularly interested in how men and women construct, reproduce and change gender relations within male cultural settings. People position themselves as sexed persons, and in doing so, they also position others as sexed persons. Gender is therefore a relational concept (Lorber and Farrell, 1991; Gherardi, 1994) and a social practice. In other words, gender is something that one *does*, not something that one *has*. Gender is a term still 'in the making' (Scott, 1986; Calás and Smirchich, 2006), and it reflects all the social practices of its making.

In social practice, therefore, gender is 'done' by both men and women, in their reciprocal relations and in the relations among women and in those among men, in the institutions that shape social relations, and in the organizations that produce both material goods and social meanings. The pervasiveness of gender practices is demonstrated by the difficulty we have in relating to someone if we cannot attribute a gender to them; unless, that is, we know whether the other person is a man or a woman. In this sense we can consider gender an elementary social practice of the kind that Ann Swidler (2001) has described as "a practice that anchors other practices". To provide a concrete example: in many countries gender still produces a form of social division of labour whereby men have prime responsibility for production, work, and maintaining the family, while women have prime responsibility for care and reproduction. Anchored in this practice is the organization of the school system (children's entry/exit times), the social welfare delivery of elderly care-taking (hiring somebody as a home carer), the state bureaucracy (which employs women to discipline its clients), and other social practices which configure a recipient with a male or female body, and therefore a social organization consistent with gender as a social practice in the division of labour. Gender is consequently a practice which anchors social times, as well as the design of material artifacts like car accessories, or other instruments designed for sexed bodies. Within these kinds of social practices – indeed, within any type of social practice enacted by sexed persons – there occurs the everyday reproduction of a symbolic gender order which expresses social beliefs about what is and what is not appropriate for differently sexed persons and for their social relations. Consequently, those wishing to study gender as a social practice must ask both men and women how gender results from the social gender relations and their institutionalization.

The symbolic gender order is a historical-social product which arises in public, and which for precisely this reason goes unnoticed. It is most evident in its breach, when disorder threatens order, when prescriptions are disobeyed. Social collaboration then repairs the breach and restores at least the appearance of order. For example, work by women can be considered as infringing the symbolic gender order which categorizes between private (female) and public (male). But when women work in care or service occupations, and do so 'discreetly', they restore coherence between work and the female work inscribed in the symbolic universe of the female. The new symbolic order differs from the previous one, but it seems that the breach has been invisibly mended. A more severe rupture occurs when women work in traditionally male settings. The social work which enables repair of the symbolic gender order is the social practice that, with time, is going to affect occupational segregation and the social conception of gender relationships.

It is useful for social scientists to understand the processes that re-establish order, because it is at the moment of transgression that the norms and social usages violated are most evident. It is then that those involved seek to explain to themselves and others which behaviours and values are appropriate to social situations. The contexts of these situations helps define both meanings and behaviours. Hence organizational cultures express a sense of what we term 'gender citizenship': the extent to which a culture accepts differently sexed persons and allows them to participate. The stories by She and He will depict work settings openly hostile to women, settings more traditional in their conception of gender relationships, and ones which are largely paritarian. We shall thus see that entering male territory has a wide variety of meanings. We shall also see that those who garrison those territories vary in their hospitality to women newcomers and in their readiness to accept the novelties that those women bring with them. From these concrete situations we shall extract the rules and customs used by organizations to socialize women into supposedly male occupations, and to maintain and reproduce the masculinity of 'male' work.

The women's stories are woven around a common theme: a challenge raised by a woman aware that she has taken an unconventional path and who, with hindsight, feels satisfaction at what she has done, or sees it as a battle, or even as a quest to fulfil a passion or a desire for self-affirmation. The men's stories are instead marked by a defensiveness which wavers between denial of all difference and recognition that women must struggle to accomplish what men take for granted. But most apparent is scant awareness that men too are caught in the 'gender trap', that they too are gender constructed. However, we shall not anticipate further the accounts of the direct protagonists, whose voices we seek to reproduce as much as possible in what follows.

The structure of the book reflects the main findings of our analysis of the stories. The first chapter establishes a theoretical and analytical framework within which to treat gender as a narrative performance. It is followed by a description of the different narrative forms used by men and women, and the different ways in which they construct the narrating self. Chance and coincidence seem to have conditioned the choices made by the women, and volition those by the men. In this second chapter we argue that men and women communicate differently, not because they are born men and women, but because gender constructs their discursive positionings differently. The third chapter analyses the stories recounted by She, and the fourth analyses those by He. If we were to draw a cartoon depicting a She and a He talking to each other, the bubble over Her head would say something like 'It was tough, but I managed it', while that above His head would say 'We welcomed her with open arms, there were no problems!" This cartoon expresses the sense of the fourth chapter, in which a He and a She talk about their workplace, describing organizations that seem entirely different. Finally, the last chapter before the conclusions analyses the practical knowledge required for everyday survival: the rules that both women and men recognize as expressing organizational norms, and which require both to put their jobs first and to dedicate their time to the organization. Besides these universal rules, there are the 'recipes' suggested to women so that they can integrate better, as well as the tactics employed by the women, and which are often at odds with the rules and the recipes. Tactics in fact, as Michel de Certeau (1984) defines them, are the territory of the Other.

The conclusions centre on the image used by two women to depict their doubt and their question: 'Was it worth it?' This doubt is personified by Don Quixote; or better, by fear of behaving like him and tilting at windmills.

Chapter 1

Gendering narratives and narrating gender

The horizontal segregation of professions and occupations is diminishing in all the developed countries, and the optimistic view now prevails that it will slowly but surely disappear. It may therefore seem perverse to ask *how* male jobs continue to be such, and *how* this prerogative is still preserved. However, although certain of the barriers that used to fence off male work – like physical fatigue, poor working conditions, or danger – have gone because work has become safer and less physically burdensome, and more abstract, other barriers and rhetorics still justify the distinction between male and female work. We may therefore ask what symbols, narratives and discursive practices are deployed in the contemporary world of work to defend the masculinity of occupations against further erosion, and how men and women negotiate gender relations when they work in male-dominated environments.

To this end, we shall examine the experience of women 'pioneers' in strictly or largely male occupations or work settings. We shall thus continue research on women 'travellers in a male world' (Gherardi, 1996), but we shall do so by including the voices of their male work companions, and by focusing – as suggested by the title of this chapter – on gendering narratives and the discursive practices of narrating gender.

To answer the above questions it is not enough to postulate a generic relation between language and gender. Instead, one must construct a theoretical framework which takes account of the relations among organization, gender, and discursive practices. The task is not a simple one, because both organization studies and feminist studies have carefully studied these relations over the past thirty years (Gherardi, 2003a), finding that organizations are not static entities; that gender is not a stable identity, but instead the product of social, organizational and institutional practices; and that discourses constitute, rather than merely reflect, gender, organization, and the relation between them.

In this chapter we briefly describe the interactions among discourse, gender and organization so that we can argue that gender is a social practice and an institution. We then propose a methodology based on the assumption that narrating is organizing (Czarniawska, 1997; 2004).

1.1. Gender, discourse and organizations

We can draw a map of the relations among gender, discourse and organizations by referring to Ashcraft and Mumby (2004: 3–23), who set out what they call a "feminist communicology of organizations". They describe four ways whereby these relations are established and which are particularly useful in summarizing various epistemological positions. We now briefly analyse them:

a) Gender organizes discourse

Within this framework, gender is a socialized individual identity and cultural membership organized around biological difference and which foster predictable communicative habits. Organizations are seen as contexts in which gendered discourses are performed, and they are conceived as settings of power in which gender differences are perceived and valued or devalued. The literature on gender difference illustrates this framework with its emphasis on the 'women's way' or 'feminine styles' of being, saying and doing (Tannen, 1990; 1994). According to its basic image of gendered discourse, women engage in communication as a means to build and maintain relationships, while men view interaction as an instrumental activity. These differences in approach give rise to particular discursive practices. And in organizational settings these discursive differences may erect barriers against women's advancement. Within this framework, gender is the prime producer of discursive practices, and organizations are merely the impartial containers of such differences.

b) Discourse (dis)organizes gender

Within this framework, gender identity is a partial, unstable gender effect, and in everyday life social actors constantly 'position' themselves and others in terms of available gender narratives which, in turn, facilitate and restrict possibilities for action.

Research conducted within this framework typically asks questions such as: how are societal and organizational narratives of gender invoked by people in particular situations, and how do such performances reproduce or challenge the gender order? Whereas the previous framework examines the expression of gender identity at work, this second frame investigates its organizational formation. Power in this case inheres in the construction of identity through the reproduction of difference. Situated within this framework is the literature on how men and women 'do gender' (West and Zimmerman, 1987), 'craft selves' (Kondo, 1990), produce or resist gender differences and power relations through organizational discourse (Alvesson and Billing, 1997). Gender difference is seen as a situated social and discursive practice whereby each party holds the other accountable.

c) Organizing (en)genders discourse

Within this third framework, organizations are theorized as gendering agents, or as dynamic entities that (en)gender subjects; they are not merely contexts or settings for gendered identities. Senses of self are therefore fashioned in the process of becoming an organizational member, and they can be seen as its outcome. Organizations are regarded as both discursive products and producers. Indeed, discourse is taken to be a collective narrative of gender and power taking the form of an organizational design. At the same time, discourse is a practice by which organizational forms become manifest and meaningful (Acker, 1990). From this perspective, also institutions, and not only individuals, are gendered, and gender is a central control mechanism in organizations and constitutive of organizing. This framework gainsays the popular image of sexist individuals discriminating in gender-neutral organizational settings, and stresses the institutional forces at work in the production of gender difference and identity.

d) Discourse (en)genders Organization

Within this framework, gender, organization, and power are reciprocally constituted in discourse. Hence gender identity, and its relation with being and working, is a discursive effect. The term 'discourse' shifts from a micro to a macro dimension: from its conception as 'engrained personal communication habit' (as in the first framework) to 'mundane interaction process' (as in the second framework) to 'organizational form' (as in the third framework), to 'societal narrative'.

This perspective is concerned with how broad discursive formations find life in particular texts. The notion of 'text' is central, since many authors stress the organizing properties of public discourse as it shapes institutions, and how people participate in them and come to understand what work is.

Not only is Ashcraft and Mumby's outline of possible frameworks particularly valuable for its clarity and simplicity, but it offers a useful definition of 'a discourse' as a "broader societal narrative embedded in systems of representation, which offer predictable yet elastic, lucid yet contradictory images of possible subjectivities, relations among them, and attendant disciplinary practices" (Ashcraft and Mumby, 2004: 18). The first two frameworks show that the relation between gender and discourse is produced by the latter through the former, but also that the latter organizes, or better dis-organizes, the former. The organization is largely absent from these two frameworks, in that it figures mainly as the container of gender and discourse practices. In the other two frameworks, however, the organization is viewed as an organizing process, and once again there is a reciprocal shaping between the organizing that produces gender and inscribes it in discourse, and the discourse which, in being institutionalized, produces gender and inscribes it in organizational practices.

The four frameworks are complementary if they are used to represent the various levels at which difference is produced. They helped us when writing this book by situating the discursive production of gender and organization at the following levels:

- in the texts produced by men and women narrating a organizational event: the entry by a She into male territory;
- the co-construction of the gender culture of the organization in which She and He work;
- the institutional discourse that sustains the masculinity of male jobs and, by doing so, regulates the gender relationships between men and women.

These three levels closely interweave in the act of narrating: that is, in the activity performed for another and in the presence of another, and which makes the theme recounted intelligible to the self and to the other. Through the story, the relation with work and the organization is described, the narrator's discursive identity is performed, and a world is made intelligible. However, before we begin analysis of the narrative construction of gender, we must briefly illustrate the theoretical framework in which gender is conceived as a material-discursive practice (Bruni, Gherardi and Poggio, 2005; Poggio, 2006).

1.2 Gender as practice and institution

The literature on the relationship between gender and organizations is too abundant to be summarized here, and numerous excellent surveys are in any case available (Ely and Meyerson, 2000; Calás and Smircich, 2006; Gherardi, 2003a). Here we shall only be concerned with the strand of theoretical analysis which conceives gender as a social practice and which has been applied in organizational studies on the relationship between 'doing gender' and 'doing organization'.

This strand of analysis first arose from symbolic interactionism and ethnomethodology, with the landmark study by West and Zimmerman (1987): *Doing Gender*. This article continued the Goffmanian tradition which treated gender as a practical accomplishment involving a gender display appropriate to a particular situation (Goffman, 1976). The anthropological tradition comprises the study by Kondo (1990), whose ethnography of work in a Japanese factory focuses on the inter-relations among work, identity and gender. Kondo described gendered identity as a "strategic narrative assertion", and she was the first to analyse gender as a 'performance' enacted in speech and action. This performance is situated within the gender system of a particular society, so that gender identity is always shifting, fluid, and contested, rather than being a fixed essence. Kondo anticipated the work of both Butler (1993) and Connell (1995).

Judith Butler is a postmodern feminist philosopher, who, following Derrida, Lacan, and Foucault, explores how the material body is gendered through discourse and how individual action produces and is produced by a constructivist gender system. She emphasises the need to take account of the dynamic of *performativity* in conceptualizing gender. "Performativity is not a singular 'act,' for it is always a reiteration of a norm or set of norms, and to the extent that it acquires an act-like status in the present, it conceals or dissimulates the conventions of which it is a repetition" (or "citation"; Butler, 1993: 12). In fact performativity is construed as the power of discourse to produce effects through reiteration.

Within sociology, Connell (1995) focuses on the practices/practising of masculinity/ies rather than on the generic dynamic of doing gender. He defines masculinities as "a configuration of practice within a system of gender relations" (1995: 84) and masculinity displays its distinctive feature – namely its claim to be 'hegemonic' – along three main dimensions:

1) *Power relations*, principal among which is the subordination of women to men and the supremacy of particular groups of men over others. In this respect, masculinity is 'hegemonic' in that it reconstitutes gender relations as a scenario within which dominance is generated.
2) *Production relations*, constituted by the gender division of labour with its economic consequences and its definition of some forms of work as 'more masculine' than others. The 'hegemony' of masculinity acts here as a direct link between the gender order and the class order, creating economic incentives for acceptance of the patriarchal organization of family and labour.
3) *Cathexis*, or discourse based on the dominant model of sexual practices and desire. In this case, masculinity achieves its 'hegemonic' position through the organization and institutionalization of heterosexual relations between people.

Practices are the core feature of Connell's definition, and, influenced by Connell's work, many sociologists of work are now focusing on the practising of masculinities and femininities in work organizations (Bird, 1996; Britton, 1999; Dellinger and Williams, 2002; Fletcher, 1999; Quinn, 2002; Wharton, Rotolo and Bird, 2000).

Within sociology and within organizational symbolism, Gherardi (1994; 1995) talks of 'the gender we think, the gender we do'. Gender is assumed to be the symbol of difference that permeates organizational cultures and gender relations at the interactional and institutional levels. The symbolic order of gender that separates the symbolic universes of the female and the male sanctions a difference whereby what is affirmed by the One is denied by the Other. The One and the Other draw meaning from this binary opposition, which forms a contrast created *ad hoc* which maintains a hierarchical interdependence (Derrida, 1967; 1972). The interdependence-based symbolic order is a relational order which rests upon difference and the impossibility of its definition. Male and female are undecidable, their meaning is indeterminate and constantly deferred.

The origins of the widely-used concept of 'difference' (Derrida, 1972) warrant examination. By 'difference' is meant a form of self-reference "in which terms contain their own opposites and thus refuse any singular grasp of their meanings" (Cooper and Burrell, 1988). In order to stress the processual nature of difference, Derrida invented the term *différance*, which in French is pronounced the same as *différence* and incorporates the two meanings of the verb *différer*: defer in time, and differ in space. Male and female are not only different from each other (static difference) but they constantly defer each other (processual difference), in the sense that the latter, the momentarily deferred term, is waiting to return because, at a profound level, it is united with the former. The difference separates, but it also unites because it represents the unity of the process of division. Because of their multi-individual dimension and supra-individual duration, male and female as symbolic systems possess a static aspect, which creates a social perception of immutability, of social structure and institution. But male and female is also a social relation dynamic whereby meaning is processually enucleated within society and individual and collective phenomena. The symbolic order of gender is static difference and processual difference. Put better, it is the product of their interdependence: the impossibility of fixing meaning once and for all sanctions the transitoriness of every interpretation and exposes the political nature of every discourse on gender.

In sum, bodies and activities are constituted in gendered practices, and this conception of gender bypasses the initial location of difference either in the body, or in society, or in language. Gender may be defined as a social accomplishment, learned and enacted on appropriate occasions and organized around shared practical understanding of its performance.

An influential article on gender as practice is Patricia Martin's "*'Said and Done' Versus 'Saying and Doing': Gendering Practices, Practicing Gender at Work*" (2003), where she argues that men and women socially construct each other at work (a) by means of a two-sided dynamic of *gendering practices* and *practising gender*; (b) this dynamic significantly affects both women's and men's work experiences; (c) gendering practices produced through interaction impair women workers' identities and confidence; and (d) attention to the practising of gender will produce insights into how inequalities are created in the workplace.

For Martin, behaviour is gendered *only* because and when it is enacted within a gender order (or institution) that gives it meaning as gendered. In other words, gender is a social practice and an institution (Martin, 2004). Nevertheless people practise particular kinds of gender, not generic forms. For this reason, Martin advocates focusing on practising femininity/ies and practising masculinity/ies, rather than on practising gender.

In Martin's study on masculinities (2001), she showed that men mobilized some forms of masculinities *for* women, some *for* men, and some *for* both genders. For example, men targeted peacocking and self-promoting masculinities only on men, but they targeted dominating and expropriating masculinities on both women and men. They directed affiliating masculinities only at men, and they frequented men in search of resources, 'sucked up' to men, and offered other men protection and support; but they did not act in these ways towards women. The audience(s) to whom/which men hold themselves accountable at work relative to gender is primarily other men (Martin, P.Y., 1996; 2001).

Performing gender re-constructs gendering practices in a way that stabilizes gender as an institution, but it also provides material for future gendering practices/practising of gender (Campbell, 2000). Analysis of 'doing gender' has increasingly focused on situated practices of doing gender and institutionalizing specific forms of gender (Martin, J.; 1994; Collinson and Collinson, 1996; Kerfoot and Knights, 1996; 1998; Bruni, Gherardi and Poggio, 2005).

With regard to the classic analysis of 'doing gender', which focuses on deliberate action, Patricia Martin (2005) suggests that 'gender in practice' should be viewed as produced by both voluntary and involuntary actions, because: "improved understanding of *non-reflexivity* can reveal how and why well-intentioned 'good people' practice gender in ways that do harm. Unintentional/non-reflexive practicing of gender is more prevalent at work than intentional practicing is". Martin notes how blatant sexism and gender bias are viewed as illicit in workplaces (and elsewhere), but sexism and bias in their subtle forms, constituted through non-reflexive practising, are rarely recognized or condemned. We need to know more about how such practices are created and sustained, and also about how they are resisted and challenged.

Now that we are more aware of the pervasiveness of gender as social practice and more aware of the power of language and discourses in gendering practices, we can also stress the unintended consequences of using the term 'doing gender'. As Deutsch (2007) noted, the use of the verb 'doing' refers to something that is accomplished, or brought about, and the commonsense use of the expression brings to mind the accomplishment of gender difference rather than its dismantling. She argues that, notwithstanding West and Zimmerman's definition that comprises both conformity and resistance, doing gender has become a theory of gender persistence and the inevitability of inequality. She reframes the programme in terms of 'undoing gender' in order to focus on: (a) when and how social interactions become less gendered, (b) whether gender can be irrelevant in interaction, (c) whether gendered interactions always underwrite inequality, (d) how the institutional and interactional levels work together to produce change, and (e) interaction as the locus of change.

In fact, the phrase 'doing gender' should be accompanied by a longer sentence stating 'in order to do it differently', or as Deutsch proposes, 'doing and undoing gender'. In any case what is worthy of note is the legacy that West and Zimmerman's article has left for the foundation of a study of practising gender.

Appreciating the significance of *practising gender* urges us to seek more effective strategies and methods with which to unveil gender dynamics in organizations.

A special issue of the journal *Gender, Work, and Organization*, devoted to gender as a social practice, emphasised that gender research itself is a practice, and that the shift of perspective in gender studies entails a radical rethinking of research methods and programmes (Poggio, 2006). New research tools with which to grasp the fluidity, the situated, unreflexive and tacit nature of processes and new perspectives are needed to transform dominant practices, given that every research process is a gendered and a gendering process, and that every researcher is inevitably involved in the production of gender.

One way to make the practising of gender more visible and available to scholars is to collect *stories*. Letting people describe their work experiences – requests to answer the telephone, calling out ratings, making policies, tossing underpants – can provide access, although far from perfect, to gender dynamics otherwise hidden from view (Gherardi and Poggio, 2001). It is for this reason that we decided to privilege the narrative analysis of gender.

1.3 Gender as organizational narrative

One of the most fruitful ways to study gender as a discourse, practice and institution is to examine stories and the narrative practices with which they are constructed. Narratives, in fact, are on the one hand the sole access channel to material practices and the way in which they are interpreted by organizational actors; on the other, they themselves are specific practices for the production of meaning and identity (Poggio, 2004a).

In recent years, numerous studies have been conducted on organizational narratives (Czarniawska, 1997; Gabriel, 2000; Boje, 2001), understood not only as organizational artifacts, but also as organization instruments and processes (Czarniawska and Gagliardi, 2003). People in organizations use narratives to make sense of the organizational reality around them, to find a place in it, and to craft an organizational self within it. Furthermore the use of a narrative approach allows one to highlight the polyphony of voices present in every organization and to give voice to the silenced stories (Boje, 1995; Brown, 2006)

These considerations apply in particular when attention focuses on the reproduction of gender relations (Hanappi-Egger and Hofmann, 2005). Analysis of story-telling, in fact, uncovers the patterns whereby symbolic gender orders are constructed and reproduced, showing that the organizational environment is permeated by asymmetrical gender relations (Silberstein, 1988), and by the powerful discourse of 'male narrative' concealed by its hegemonic nature.

The central importance of narratives in gender construction processes can be highlighted by concentrating on certain aspects in particular: the construction of a gendered self, the sense-making process, and the configuration of careers.

The construction of a gendered self

Many scholars claim that narrative is the prime locus for the creation of identity, understood as a relational construct produced and reproduced in interactions, and as a constantly negotiated reciprocal process (Gergen, 1991; Czarniawska, 1997a), something created at the moment when it is acted (Butler, 1990). The construction of gender identity takes place through positioning: "the discursive process whereby selves are located in conversations as observably and subjectively coherent participants in jointly produced story lines" (Davies and Harré, 1990: 48). The concept of positioning goes beyond a unitary idea of subjectivity by acknowledging the multiplicity of the subjects' positions and of the narrative strategies available to them. It is mainly through narrative practices that the positioning process take place and individuals are able to negotiate new positions. The story-teller constructs his/her identity within the narrative process, assuming a particular positioning with regard to the characters in the story and his/her interlocutors. Every narrative implies the positioning of the narrating self according to how the listeners are interpreted. The concept of positioning is particularly efficacious for analysis of how a gendered self is constructed. Gender, in fact, can be viewed as a relational construct produced through a process of positioning where male and female are defined as alternative categories, so that membership of one entails non-membership of the other.

For example, a study on the stories of men and women in political roles (Poggio, 2004b) has shown how women are positioned as the Other *vis-à-vis* the narrator and more generally the political system, and how this process comes about through rhetorical strategies like negation and exclusion, the blaming of women themselves for their exclusion, an emphasis on the exceptional nature of women in politics, the impossibility of reconciling family commitments and politics, and the delegitimation of laws designed to facilitate the entry of women into politics. These strategies reflect and reproduce citizenship models in which gender differences are simultaneously denied and exploited, and in which otherness also entails marginalization and/or subordination.

Socialization to the organizational culture

Narratives have often been studied as forms of expression adopted by the organizational culture (Gabriel, 1992; 2000), and as devices for socialization (Louis, 1980; Trice and Beyer, 1993).

What is transmitted by stories – argues Lyotard (1979) – is the set of pragmatic rules that constitute social knowledge: what one must know how to say, what one must know how to understand, and what one must know how to do. In recounting the exploits of their characters, narrators describe concrete and situated examples of action, giving their listeners concrete instructions and strategies for action applicable to new situations by analogy (Suleiman, 1983; Witten, 1993).

Every culture has a repertoire of legitimated narratives – or as Bruner puts it a "tool kit" of "canonical life narratives" with "combinal formal constituents" on which members can draw to construct their stories (Bruner, 1987: 15). Every culture favours certain narrative identities and disfavours others, so that every actor has access to a repertoire of culturally available narratives with which to express or depict particular aspects of reality.

All this obviously applies to gender as well. Just as fairy stories in infancy socialize children to specific roles and tasks in the family and society, so in organizations anecdotes, jokes and exemplary stories define gender-appropriate behaviours and norms. Narratives can therefore be considered expedients used to reproduce and maintain the dominant symbolic gender order. They are social practices whereby values and ideologies are produced and reproduced. By means of repetition, connections among events are reified: they are made fixed and immutable so that the *status quo* is legitimated and alternative interpretations are precluded (Mumby, 1987; Silberstein, 1988).

Narratives and organizational learning

Narratives are channels for learning in and about organizations. Various authors have stressed that the bulk of organizational learning takes place through the circulation of stories (Czarniawska-Joerges, 1997b; Orr, 1990). Approaches which treat organizations as communities of practices (Lave and Wenger, 1991; Wenger, 1998) have highlighted that organizing is a practice based on a system of distributed knowledge, and that learning is a process by which people become members of a group by learning its stories. Penelope Eckert and Sally McConnell-Ginet (1992) showed that gender is produced and performed through membership of particular communities of practice. They emphasised the need for a methodological redefinition of gender studies so that attention would focus in particular on usually neglected aspects like "people's active engagement in the reproduction of or resistance to gender arrangements in their communities" (Eckert and McConnell-Ginet, 1992: 472). Rather than taking gender differences as its point of departure, the 'community of practice' concept emphasises the dimension of learning (through shared practices) and the variability of linguistic manifestations in different groups (Bergvall, 1999). In short, it shifts the focus from gender differences to "the difference gender makes" (Cameron, 1992: 13). Research thus concentrates on how gender is constructed through shared social and linguistic practices situated within a specific community. In an ethnographic study of the learning trajectory of a female novice in an branch office of a male-dominated organization, Attila Bruni and Silvia Gherardi (2001) describe how a young woman learns how to enact a gendered identity while learning how to master professional practices.

Defining careers

Career paths are certainly among the phenomena that lend themselves to analysis through narratives collected in organizations. Every culture has paradigmatic narratives on professional experience, or representations of an ideal career path comprising study, work experiences, and personal relations which is normatively regulated by the timing of events (Elder, 1964; Hogan, 1978). People's accounts of their work histories, and also those of others, tend to follow an ideal sequence and to justify divergences from it. Careers themselves tend to develop according to an isomorphic pattern whose main stages are defined by the dominant narratives. The analysis of the life-story patterns of some professional women conducted by Ina Wagner and Ruth Wodak (2006) has shown the existence of a relation between the narrators' self-representation strategies and the sectors and organizations to which they belong.

A particularly interesting category of career stories comprises the narratives of entrepreneurs. These usually take the form of heroic stories which – through celebration of the entrepreneur-hero – propose implicit and personal theories of managerial action (Pitt, 1998). One of the principal features of such action is its coincidence with a model of hegemonic masculinity. In an ethnographic study which collected stories of entrepreneurship from women and men, the present authors showed the persistence of discursive practices intended to safeguard traditional gender models and to represent entrepreneurship as male activity, both 'naturalizing' the social destiny of women and 'socializing' the practices that construct them as less reliable (Bruni, Gherardi and Poggio, 2005).

Organizational change

Stories do not only describe events; they also produce them. They are not just instruments for the reproduction of gender inequality, since they may also be resources for change (Hanappi-Egger and Hofmann, 2005). They can transform themselves into autopoietic instruments, changing reality and the organization and opening the way for new models and understandings (Davies, 1992; Rhodes and Brown, 2005). Narrating requires the intellectual capacity to imagine alternatives. It therefore develops the competence of organizational actors in producing new visions and generating new assumptions.

Edeltraud Hanappl-Egger and Roswitha Hofman (2005) have stressed that the creation of new stories may be crucial for the transformation of gender relations in organizations. Such transformation is engendered by a disruptive event which clashes with the dominant reference system, undermining the 'naturalized' gender model. The actors respond to this event with a process of enactment which, according to Weick's (1995) theory of sense-making, may either prompt an attempt to incorporate the event into existing patterns of meaning or produce actual transformation in the dominant social order.

There are several studies in the organizational literature which stress the efficacy of narratives for training purposes. Narrative methodology gives the participants a chance to conduct retrospective analysis of their past work experiences (individual and organizational), and it generates different interpretative perspectives and new meaning configurations in order to cope with working life and organizational dynamics. For instance, the present authors used a training methodology founded on memory work and narrative potential to stimulate an individual and group reworking of the gender and leadership relationship, in narrative workshops conducted with women working in managerial positions (Gherardi and Poggio, 2007). Narrative stimuli were given to the participants in order to prompt more general reflection about male and female modes of power management (and about the connected practices of domination/exclusion). The purpose was to highlight the social and cultural factors that influence these differences, and to offer perspectives alternative to dominant patterns.

1.4 Gender and narrative: a methodological framework

One way to analyse how gender is constructed in organizations, and how the symbolic gender order is reproduced, is to examine the narrative constructions and practices of the men and women who work in them (Gherardi, 1996). Narratives can be treated as 'artifacts' by means of which cultures can be understood and interpreted, and their dominant values and norms identified (Piccardo, Varchetta and Zanarini, 1990; Czarniawska, 1997). Alternatively, narratives, or better narrating, can be regarded as processes of 'practising gender', where gender is produced non-reflexively and interactively with other actors (Martin, P.Y., 2003; 2006).

Corresponding to these various ways to consider narratives are diverse analytical approaches and research questions (Poggio, 2004a). A first approach, the one most widely used, concentrates on the narrative as an 'object' or 'text', on the general concepts emerging from the stories, and on how they embody and reflect specific gender orders. The question that we seek to answer concerns the 'what': what is being said (and done) by the story. Therefore, our analysis sought firstly to bring out the gender subtext embedded in the stories recounted, to identify and classify themes, situations and characters, and to draw conclusions that enable reflection on the various ways in which people live and give meaning to their experiences from a gender perspective.

A second approach, which more specifically characterizes narrative analysis, focuses on the structural and contextual dimensions of the narrative. Conducting a narrative analysis, in fact, requires us to look not only at 'what' is recounted, but also and especially at 'how' people "impose order on the flow of experience to make sense of events and actions in their lives" (Riessman, 1993: 2). As argued by Polkinghorne (1995), narrative analysis is concerned to identify the plot and the rhetorical devices that act retrospectively to combine the elements of a story and give them meaningfulness, producing nexuses of sequentiality and causality as parts of a temporal development which culminates in the finale of the story. For our research, therefore, investigating how narratives are organized meant reconstructing narrative sequences, demonstrating how they produced and reproduced a specific symbolic gender order. It also required us to show how the narrative scheme defined specific nexuses of causality between events and actors' responsibilities for them, and how the plot served to confer plausibility and sense on unexpected situations – for example, a woman's entry into a typically male context.

A third approach ensues from a further research question, this one concerning 'why' the story has been recounted in that particular way (Riessman, 2001; Poggio, 2004a). When considering a story, in fact, it is important not only to identify its content dimensions or structural parameters, but also to examine culturally problematic aspects: those, that is, which may produce silences and contradictions. Investigating the 'why' of a story's construction is to recognize that there may exist numerous other ways to produce and elaborate the text. This is one of the assumptions of the deconstructionist strategy which seeks to show the ambivalence of every discursive practice, but especially those to do with dichotomous orders, and then unmask their hegemonic character (Martin, J. 1990; Calás and Smircich, 1991). This approach is particularly fruitful when research is being conducted on gender practices within organizations, because it demonstrates the artificiality of aspects that the narrative depicts as pertaining to a naturally existing order. Moreover, it reveals rhetorics used to justify consolidated forms of segregation or discrimination, and it highlights how man and women cooperate to produce and reproduce a symbolic order which then becomes binding upon both. Recognition that there exists a generative and interpretative polysemy of stories also makes it possible to highlight the 'conjunctive' dimension of narrative (Bruner, 1986), which is the necessary condition for the production of alternative versions (Good, 1994) and therefore the essential basis for change.

1.5 Gendertelling in traditionally male contexts

Our interest in how gender is normatively constructed within organizations induced us to focus on narratives of gender, on the assumption that gender is a cultural practice. We analysed the ways in which narratives are gendered, and gender is narrated in organizations, by collecting the narratives of men and women working in male-dominated professions, and describing their reactions to the entry of women into traditionally male jobs.

Our purpose was to analyse the narrative construction of gender in organizations where maleness occupies a hegemonic position. We decided to consider situations in which women had managed for the first time to enter occupations hitherto regarded by organizations to be male preserves. This would enable us to conduct simultaneous analysis of 'successful women' (those who managed to remain in a male dominated context) and of segregated organizational settings: a combination that sheds particularly interesting light on the organizational construction of gender. In fact it is above all 'extraordinary' situations that yield better understanding of how gender positioning is narratively constructed. To this end, therefore, we identified contexts and jobs in which the entry of women was (still) a novelty for the organization.

It should be pointed out that other studies have examined women working in traditionally male settings, as well as men working in typically female ones (Williams, 1989; 1995; Kvande and Rasmussen, 1994; Sjørup, 2005). However, our study differs from these others in both its methodology and its object of analysis, which in our case is the *narrative of entry* of women into such settings, rather than the gendered nature of the work within them. For every woman selected, an interview was conducted with a male co-worker already present when the woman entered the organization. Therefore we had *his-story* and *her-story*.

We formed our sample after mapping gender segregation in the labour market and conducting interviews with key informants that enabled us to select 34 cases of 'women pioneers' in organizations: that is, women in traditionally male jobs. The research was carried out in the Italian province of Trentino, a socio-economic context in which the labour-market entry of women was initially somewhat belated, compared with other Western countries, but has nevertheless accelerated substantially in recent decades.[1] We selected a set of workplaces characterized by female segregation, both horizontal and vertical. And therein we collected the narratives of 34 women occupying traditionally male roles and positions, and those of an equal number of their male colleagues (see Appendix).

The cases selected pertained to a variety of sectors: agriculture, the environment, industry (food, chemicals, textiles, engineering), building, information and communication technologies, banking, and retail. Among the female interviewees working in typically male settings and occupations there were, for example, a cattle veterinary surgeon, a surveyor on a construction site, an agricultural technician supervising the activities of the members of a farming consortium, an electrical engineer working for a large electricity transformation company, and an engineer working as a designer for a mechanical engineering company. Among those who instead worked in not typically male organizations, but in jobs mainly (and previously) occupied by men, there were, for example, a bank manager, a bank inspector, a newspaper editor, a television company executive, a customer relations and marketing manager at an IT company, the head of telephony at a large telecommunications company, the head of the chemicals department of a food company.

---

[1] The Province of Trento is located in the North-East of Italy. It is a province with a special statute of autonomy, with a good level of welfare, and a low rate of unemployment. Employment is mainly in services, tourism and light industry. The female activity rate in 2002 was 53%, slightly higher than the national average (48%), but below the European average (61%). The gender segregation index (16.6% in 2000) does not differ significantly from the Italian (15.4%) and European (17.8%) averages. The fact that the research was conducted in a small geographical area restricts its generalizability. But this is not among the concerns of narrative research. Our intention, in fact, was not to obtain a systematic and objective picture of the problem of segregation, but rather to take a different perspective on the way in which gender is constructed in organizations.

The ages of the interviewees ranged from 21 to 59. Just under half the interviewees belonged to the 30-to-39 age cohort, and around one quarter to the subsequent one (40–49 years old), The shares of men and women in these two cohorts were similar, whilst there was a larger number of women in the 21-to-29 age cohort (9 women against 2 men), and a smaller one in the last cohort (aged 50 and above).

The interviewees were conducted by a group of six expert interviewers: three men and three women. The research design maintained gender uniformity between interviewers and interviewees so as to favour gender 'complicity'.

Interviews began with an open-ended stimulus question asking the respondents to recount their work histories, focusing in particular on: 'What happened when She (or You) entered the group?' While men were asked to describe the entry of their woman colleague, the women described their own entry experience. The main aim of the interview was therefore to elicit a narrative about how the women joined their current organizations and how they had been received in a male dominated organizational culture.

Each interview was recorded and transcribed. We read and analyzed the transcripts, asking the following questions: what does the story say and do? How did the interviewees plot the stories to make sense of events and actions? Why did they recount the story in that particular way? In trying to answer these questions we focused on the following more specific objects:

• The formal and structural characteristics of the narratives. We examined the stories of the female and male interviewees, focusing in particular on the incipit and plot of the story, in order to show how the subject positions were rhetorically constructed;
• The plot of the women's narratives in describing their careers in traditionally male roles and jobs. Women's stories were stories of challenges. We thus focused on how the challenge was differently represented and thematized in the stories;
• The organizational gender culture as described by the stories of men and women working for the same organization, or in the same sector, trying to highlight and compare the different emerging conceptions of gender citizenship;
• Finally, the implicit and explicit rules, relative to success at work, produced and reproduced through the interviewees' discourses, and the ambivalence that characterized them.

In the chapters we devoted considerable space to excerpts from the interviews, not because we thought that they "spoke for themselves", but because they show the discursive construction of the accounts used to make sense of personal gender experiences.

Before beginning our analysis, we would stress that ours too is a narrative; and therefore one way amongst others to make sense of our research experience, and where our narrating voices interweave with those of our interviewees.[2]

---

[2] Indeed, one of the features that most markedly distinguishes narrative analysis from other research methodologies is that it seeks to produce new stories (Polkinghorne, 1995) by generating a new order and new meanings through the interpreting and writing process (van Maanen, 1998).

Chapter 2

The Discursive Production of Selves

"Let those who are setting out with me raise their right hands for the pact of fidelity. The others may go off to other stories, other storytellers. I do not tell stories simply to pass the time. My stories come to me, inhabit me, and transform me."

(Tahar Ben Jelloun, The Sand Child)

The main questions addressed by narrative analysis do not concern 'what' is recounted, but rather 'how' people impose order on the flow of experience to make sense of events and actions (Riessman, 1993: 2), and 'why' a story has been told in a particular way. Even if we had not started with these questions, our reading of the interview transcripts would have steered us in this direction. In fact, when we read the professional and organizational stories told by the men and women interviewed, we were immediately struck by significant differences between male and female accounts. Although the men and women interviewees worked side by side in the same organizational settings and had the same professional roles, they employed diametrically different narrative styles. The males told linear and uninterrupted stories, with active and strong-willed protagonists, and with relatively stylized storylines; the women told much more complex and self-reflexive stories characterized by obstacles, impasses, and unexpected coincidences. To give a holistic image of the difference, female narrative resembles a cobweb where each part is related to the whole, while male narrative unfolds through a linear sequence of events.

The first questions that we decided to address in our analysis – and which form the core of this chapter – concerned identification of (i) how narrative selves are constructed, and (ii) what plots are mobilised in order to produce them as a discursive outcome. We investigated in particular whether the diversity of narrative modes was due to a more general gender specificity of communicative models, or whether a more composite interpretation taking account of social construction processes within organizations was possible.

Support for the former hypothesis was seemingly provided by Deborah

Tannen's analysis of the sociolinguistic development of gender identity (Tannen, 1990), which describes people's communicative modalities as variables ascribed to sexual membership. Tannen argues that there is an intrinsic difference between men and women in their perception and recounting of experiences. Linguistic diversity between the two sexes is already evident in the games and interactions of childhood, and in adulthood it gives rise to different communicative styles (dependence/independence, intimacy/separateness, etc.) which if not recognized and brought to awareness, may generate misunderstandings and conflict. Like other scholars (Chodorow, 1978; Gilligan, 1982), Tannen attributes behavioural differences – in this case communicative – between men and women to the differing psychological dynamics that characterize the relationship between mother and son, and between mother and daughter. The main problem with this interpretation is its inherent determinism, which holds that attitudes acquired in early childhood determine people's gender identities throughout their lifetimes, regardless of the social and structural context and of changes that may take place in them. From this perspective communicative abilities and styles are considered as constants of gender, as traits acquired once and for all; but not as features constructed and reconstructed in interactions, and according to the different contexts in which people find themselves during their lives. So this view tends to reinforce gender polarization, presenting female and male language as two distinct categories and not as an overlapping continuum (Freed, 1992; Bing and Bergvall, 1996).

In this work we prefer to opt for a different interpretation: patterns of communication cannot be systematically associated with gender membership; rather, they are the interactive medium through which gender is constructed. Consequently, it is not gender that determines communication, but rather the reverse. Gender thus assumes the form of a relational performance produced and enacted within inter-actor relations, and in particular through discursive practices (Poggio, 2006).

Support for this thesis is provided by the many studies of recent decades which have problematized the notion of individual identity (McIntyre, 1980), replacing it with a view of identity connected with the concepts of performativity (Butler, 1990), positioning (Davies and Harré, 1990), and narrative (Giddens, 1991; Czarniawska, 2000). These approaches yield a view of the individual, not as an essential entity or the unitary and definitive product of a process of social construction, but as a performance constantly constructed and reconstructed by the multiple discursive practices of society (Davies and Harré, 1990; Kerfoot, 1999; Dent and Whitehead, 2001); a performance whose situated and relational nature is paramount. The concept of 'positioning' stresses that identity is constructed through a process whereby individuals position themselves in accordance with the discursive practices that society imposes upon them, aligning or contraposing themselves with the positionings of others (Davies, 1989; Gherardi, 1996). Identities are therefore performed in conversations, and selves are rhetorical assertions, produced by our linguistic conventions, which we narrate and perform for each other (Kondo, 1990: 307) against the background of a plot which is negotiated by those taking part in the conversation.

On this view, communicative styles are not the necessary consequences of manhood or womanhood; rather, they are the media through which individuals construct their identities by difference. Hence gender identity – and a gendered self – is not given once and for all. It is instead re-constructed through the discursive practices that characterize relations among social actors.

Storytelling is indubitably one of the most significant of these practices. Patterns of behaviour and explanations of gender relationships are often established and tacitly reproduced through narrative. Every story describes particular social and organizational practices, explaining them on the basis of beliefs and cultural models, and legitimating their presence and transmission in social relations. Storytelling may therefore be an implicit way to define the gender characteristics that persons possess, or must possess, to be deemed competent members of a specific gender culture.

In what follows we shall accordingly examine the stories collected by considering them as texts. We shall focus here on the discursive strategies and other signifying practices around which meaning – through difference – is constructed not only in the written text but in our society in order to bring out the different (and often complementary) ways in which gendered selves are positioned in the narratives. We shall analyse and compare the forms taken by the narrative in female and male accounts – or in other words, the modalities in which accounts are constructed and developed. The different narrative modes identified will evince the different patterns of professional and organizational positioning of the men and women in their storytelling.

2.1 Narrative selves and gender positionings

Accounts of men and women relative to female entry into traditionally male organizations and roles constitute the texts that we analyse. All the interviews began by asking the interviewees (both men and women) to tell their professional story and to recount their entry into the organization where they worked. Comparison of the stories brought out various differences in narrative style related to how the narrative selves were positioned. One of the most evident of them concerned the length and complexity of the account: the men furnished rather short and linear stories; the women told ones which were more intricate and lengthy. When analysing the incipits of the stories we identified the main story-opening moves and the identity-positioning process subtending them:

(a) *the volitional self* – In the first type of opening move, the narrative – often beginning with an expression like 'I have done' or 'I am' – embarked on a linear story in which they described their education and first entry into employment, of which the protagonist was always the narrating self. This type of attack was most common in the male interviews, while in female interviews it mainly characterized those with younger interviewees.[1] This incipit sustained a narrative construction of self in which the professional dimension was paramount and events were represented as stages in a necessary sequence, although intentionality also played a fundamental role. The narrators were therefore the absolute protagonists of the story: they often occupied new roles tailor-made for them and developed by them with autonomy and enterprise. The first-person beginning emphasised the assumption of responsibility and initiative by the storyteller:

> "This job didn't exist before I arrived. I came in as the commercial manager for the region. Previously I worked with this company and another one, in Milan. They were two companies with image problems. They needed someone who could promote them as companies rather than working on sales. I've done this work for a year now and the results are coming in" (Man, 37, public relations manager in a wine production company[2]).

> "I graduated quite quickly. By the end of the fourth year I'd completed all my examination requirements and I was looking for somewhere to do my degree thesis. All the places in the faculty that interested me had been taken, and I didn't want to wait. Hanging around would have been absurd because I was right on schedule, so I looked for a place where I could do an external degree thesis" (Woman, 28, marketing manager in a wine production company).

(b) *the historical-processual self* – The second type of incipit referred to the narrator's historical-social context. In this case the self emerged as the historical product of a linear series of transitions. Like the previous story beginning, this one too mainly typified male interviews. These accounts frequently made reference to the timing of events, and the first words often served to establish the time interval of the story. The account's contextualization and the historicization of the account implied a discursive identity less self-centred than the previous one The narrators were still the protagonists of their stories, but these reflected events and circumstances surrounding the storytellers. For this reason, unlike in the previous case, experience and expectations did not always coincide.

---

[1] A similar result is reported by Isabelle Bertaux-Wiame, who in her study on life histories of internal migrants in France found that men tended to speak with the active "I", putting themselves at the centre of the story, while women tended more to use impersonal or plural pronouns (Bertaux-Wiame, 1982).

[2] From now on we use M and W to denotethe sex of the interviewee, and a number to identify the couple of persons working for the same organization.

"I graduated in architecture in 1985. I wanted to work outside my region. I immediately, and unthinkingly, accepted a proposal by ex-university colleagues, and we set up a small engineering company in Rome. Three years later a referendum was held which banned nuclear energy. The site closed down, our company collapsed, and I came back here. I got a study grant to do a postgraduate course. In the end my colleagues went off to jobs in the public sector, only I stayed in the private sector. I was taken on by this company to start up a new department. Things have developed from there…" (Man, 38, survey manager in an environmental services cooperative).

"I … did the standard curriculum until the end of middle school … but perhaps it'd be useful if I say where I was brought up. Almost forty years ago I was living in a small village in Calabria, small but close to a town, so I was able to go to school in the town and not in the village" (Woman, 41, customer relations and marketing manager in an IT company).

(c) *the fortuitous self* – The third type of narrative started from an incomplete action or condition (usually expressed with a verb in the imperfect tense) and then recounted entry into work as resulting from a coincidence, or anyway from an unplanned event. Here the narrative did not follow a linear and consequential sequence but began by immediately describing obstacles and incidents. The self was therefore represented as a contingent 'evenemential' product situated in a discontinuous temporal framework punctuated by events which disrupted its linearity. This kind of incipit occurred mainly in the interviews with women, especially older ones. Unlike those of the males, the stories of these women proceeded in fits and starts, with unforeseen interruptions, changes of direction, and haphazard choices.

"I was studying at university when a company approached me looking for someone to fill a senior position in the personnel department of one of its subsidiaries. So I applied, just to see what was involved, without really intending to start work. But since my application went well, and at that particular moment of my life I felt like setting my studies aside for a while, I gave it a try" (Woman, 35, production unit manager in a telecommunications company).

"So I chose engineering without being really sure about what I was doing. I didn't realize what I was getting into" (Woman, 37, head of commercial office in a processing company).

(d) *The sidelong self* – In a final group of narratives the narrator was introduced through reference to situations and/or people different from the narrator itself. Mainly women, the narrators no longer described themselves as the artificers of their stories but merely as characters involved in them, while their work entry was brought about by colleagues or superiors.

"My employer is a young guy, and I believe that counts for a lot, because otherwise I would never have entered a firm like this one, in such a masculine job, because it's true: the fact there's such a flexible employer helps a great deal, according to me" (Woman, 33, exports manager in a quarrying and exports company).

In this type of incipit – more common among women – the agency of the story was shifted outside the narrator: the account began with the intervention of another protagonist as a *deus ex machina*.

The incipit of the story provides the narrator with an immediate opportunity to position his or her identity. The story represents an opportunity to perform a volitional self, a historical-processual self, a fortuitous self or a sidelong self. The fact that men and women selected different opening moves for their accounts – more assertive and active for men, more passive and dependent for women – can be interpreted in cultural rather than psychological terms. The tendency of women to present a self less central to the development of the story ensued from their need to repair a breakdown in the symbolic gender order due to their entry into traditionally male work contexts. The women responded to this need – which is not inherent to sexual membership but is learnt through social and organizational interactions – by minimizing their agency or contextualizing it in a broader setting. It is as they sought forgiveness for having done something that women do not usually do.

This interpretation is borne out if we look at the narrative development of the stories. The narratives collected from the men displayed a concise and schematic style and a relatively standardized narrative structure (in which the obligatory stages were education, work entry, career). Events were usually recounted as functional to achievement of the narrator's current position. The present was the central dimension of experience in the male accounts; the only key with which they interpreted the past. Not coincidentally, many of the men asked the interviewer to formulate more specific questions, thereby manifesting their difficulty in telling stories unaided. For them, work was something so taken for granted and automatic that it was difficult to transpose into a narrative. Just as it is hard for all of us to describe how certain automatisms first came to condition our everyday actions, so these male interviewees were unable to articulate things that they took for granted into a story.

The women talked more willingly. Their stories had more intricate and complex lines of deployment. Indeed, one may say that the narrative structure of the men's stories recalled the linear style of the fairy tale, or the plain one of the news story, while the women's stories were often reminiscent of the novel in its various genres: from psychological, in which interior aspects, contradictions and intimate dramas were accentuated, to social, with a realistic narrative and emphasis on surrounding events.

The accounts of the younger women were somewhat different, in that many of them were structured similarly to those of the male interviewees. Here too, in fact, the transition from education to career was treated as obvious and almost never problematized. These narratives were more circumscribed than the other stories, not only because the younger women's careers were shorter, but also because their plots were linear.

2.2 The plots of the female stories: choices and coincidences

For a narrative not to be a mere list of significant events there must be something which organizes it into a meaningful whole (Bruner, 1990). This 'something' is usually the plot. It gives the overall sense to the actions and events recounted (Brooks, 1984) and it works as the scheme offered by the narrator to interpret the story.

We therefore wondered how the male and female interviewees constructed the plot of their accounts?

Analysis of women's narratives reveals a continuum where stories about choices lay at one extreme, and stories about coincidences at the other. In the 'choice stories' the female narrators were women who had decided to create their own space in the labour market. They consequently described their lives as marked by a series of choices which had gradually led up to the position that they now occupied.

> "I initially expected to do what I'm doing now. I'm a vet, and I did a veterinary science degree because I wanted to work with cattle. Then, as I got on at university, I decided to be a bovine gynaecologist ... and that's what I do" (Woman, 40, large animal veterinary surgeon in a breeders' consortium).

These stories partly resemble the male ones in their emphasis on volition and determination, but they differ from them because men take work for granted.

> "I can start with an important moment when I was living at home and I decided to go to university, and then of course my choice of job. I'm young, but I'm forty-one years old. If you think about thirty years ago, you can probably imagine how a girl was seen by the mentality of the time: a girl shouldn't really get a degree, she should get a good school certificate instead, and then perhaps marry. I must say that I've always been ... someone whose mind has been made up. I said to my parents – you want me to get a school certificate because you think I'll get married and perhaps quit work, but if you think that I only need a school certificate then you'd better think again: I want to go to lycée and then to university" (Woman, 41, customer relations and marketing manager in a IT company).

Women position themselves as confronted by numerous choices in their life-courses. They are required to select among types of secondary education; then they reach the crossroads between university and work; then they must decide what type of job to look for, with what type of investment, if and how they can keep it; what to do about their family responsibilities; and so on. The women's stories structured around the theme of choice emphasised the intentional and projective dimension of choice among several options – decisions which several times conflicted with the social context.

> "After that I began to realize that there was space for women as well, right? And I began to understand that what women often lack is awareness of their abilities; they tend to give up, they tend to say that we'll never rise to those levels, so we can't keep up careers which are mostly male. I began to see that there were good possibilities, because the staff, because the people working with me ... you know, when you understand the mentality of those people, I began to think that I could do something more. So I made inquiries, I talked to the personnel office and I told them that I wanted to be given the chance to do a bit more" (Woman, 36, branch manager in a bank).

The choice might be made at the beginning of the story and then condition its subsequent development, as in accounts by women who had a vocation for a certain profession and overcame obstacles to enter it. Or it might be the consequence of a later realization: at a certain point, the woman decided to change her life by looking for a job. This choice often entailed a sacrifice: when the women said that they were confronted by a problem of choice, they were positing an alternative between career and family commitments.

At the other extreme of the continuum are stories in which chance seemed to be the true protagonist; stories where words like 'luck' and 'coincidence' were frequently used and gave the impression that the interviewees were defending themselves for achieving a position unusual for women. Sometimes, however, chance and luck in fact resulted from specific management policies: a case in point being the interviewee who had applied for a job "on the off chance" and had been hired mainly because of the company's diversity policy, and therefore as a result of action which was not fortuitous but deliberately undertaken to redress the gender balance. However, even the women's stories with a more unassuming rhetorical style exhibited choice processes concealed beneath an emphasis on randomness.

> "I think that being a woman in a place like that was only an advantage for me. I don't know, probably, if I had been a man, at the beginning they'd have said 'look, we don't care', but instead there was a sort of respect for the fair sex and a kind of initial politeness so that a relationship developed [...] so I believe that it was my good luck to meet their needs, and that they needed someone like me" (Woman, 29, quality manager in a wine-producing company).

"Well, I ended up there, and I'm still there. I went on the off chance, they assessed my abilities and everything ... but I went there by chance" (Woman, 28, shop manager in a supermarket).

"I got promoted to office administrator and I'm really satisfied with everything. I wouldn't have got ahead if it hadn't been for the competitive examination [...] That's my story ... a series of lucky situations because if I hadn't been studying and if the exam hadn't been held at the same time ... Not that I'm particularly career-minded..." (Woman, 59, inspector in a bank).

Although they talked of fortunate coincidences, many of the interviewees fashioned plots in which determination and intentionality were certainly not extraneous. These women called themselves fortunate because they had passed an examination, or because they had been what the company needed, or because someone had placed trust in them. They therefore cited a series of reasons which had very little to do with luck or chance. When these stories are considered carefully, they are just as much characterized by planning and deliberate choices as the previous ones were; what distinguishes them is the type of rhetoric used to present the story.

Just as there was no lack of reference to choice in the women's stories about coincidences, so luck figured largely in the stories about deliberate choice. Consequently, even those women who described their lives in predominantly volitive terms acknowledged their indebtedness to chance, as if determination and ability were not enough to ensure the professional success of women:

"I've wanted what I've created with all my being. I believe that luck certainly plays a part in what happens; I mean, being in the right place at the right time is certainly important, but I believe that luck should sometimes be helped" (Woman, 36 branch manager in a bank).

"I believe that, although my law degree has opened opportunities for me, I've been lucky as well; it's true that as someone said – *quisque faber fortunae suae* – but you also need luck" (Woman, 31, loss adjuster in a insurance company).

There is then a particular kind of 'luck' cited in the female stories: the luck of working with people – men in particular – who have valued the women, and to whom they therefore feel grateful. In various accounts, in fact, the women interviewees tended to minimize their responsibility and above all their merits, instead emphasising the importance of other people – mainly male – in their lives. By paying homage to these others they often achieved greater legitimation than did women who instead stressed their own efforts.

"Lucky coincidences: there was a colleague who was working in this area and she needed help. So a form of collaboration started between us. She asked me if I felt like coming in, I tried it out and it worked, with a series of coincidences (...) I was lucky enough to have a managing director who believed in me, who gave me support, who helped me. And he acted as a barrier in so many situations that I grew as a person. I would say that I've been lucky, because I've got a very helpful husband, so that the housework has been equally divided between us (...) I've been doubly lucky because he has a job which leaves him a lot of free time, so that my daughter has been able to spend a lot of time with her father when I haven't been there" (Woman, 44, brand manager in a bank).

"I've been lucky enough to belong to a work group whose members have mathematics degrees like me, who have an approach to work in its method and content which is, let's say, quite scientific" (Woman, 43, department manager in an IT company).

"With my colleagues ... I work with wonderful people; there too I've been lucky. All my colleagues are male, and they're fantastic" (Woman, large animal veterinary surgery in a breeders' consortium).

Even when substantial elements of deliberate decision-making and determination can be read between the lines of the accounts of professional careers, narrative and rhetorical devices were used to downplay these features by constructing a narrative self more consistent with the socially endorsed image of femaleness – the lucky woman, or the grateful woman (because she has been helped). By constructing plots in which agency was shifted away from their own volition, these woman sought a positioning which expressed 'modesty', rather than flaunting their merits and abilities. Their aim was not to engage in a gender struggle but to obtain the benevolence of the organization to which they belonged, thereby averting possible conflicts.

2.3 The plots of the male stories: the path marked out, and marking out one's own path

When reading the male stories we noticed another pair of meanings which developed around the ideas of the marked-out path, or marking one's path. The men's stories, in fact, were characterized less by the rhetoric of choice or chance than by 'following a path already marked out', or by marking it out for oneself.[3] With respect to the constructs of choice and chance, these two options emphasised the necessary nature of work for men, who enter the labour market and male settings not by chance, nor by choice, but be-

---

[3] Similar findings came from other research conducted in Italy, where Adriana Luciano and Manuela Olagnero identified two different narrative modules in men's stories: conformist (where all the events are considered 'natural', taken for granted) and manipulative (where the the protagonist is the creator of his destiny) (Luciano and Olagnero, 1996).

cause it is *natural* for them to do so. Distinctive of the male interviewees was their tendency to describe themselves as following a route assigned to them by society, or as individuals who had wanted to 'blaze their own trail'. The former category comprised men who not only recounted their professional experiences as taken for granted, but deterministically described a variety of paths, often in the same company. Each of their career advancements followed an automatic, progressive and traditional sequence – as respectively described by the following interview extracts:

> "I've worked for this company since I finished upper secondary school. I started as a temporary replacement for someone on maternity leave. Then they took me on permanently, still in the commercial office. The job has more or less always been the same. I haven't got anything particular to say: there have been few significant stages because the career is almost automatic" (Man, 38, shift foreman in a telecommunications company).

> "A few weeks after getting my upper-secondary certificate I was called for an interview by the company. Things went well, and some months later, after a brief apprenticeship, I started work here. Then I moved around other posts [...] The company involved me in increasingly important tasks, if you can call them that [...] All this took place over twenty-three years. It wasn't rapid, but gradual" (Man, 39, quality control manager in a wine-producing company).

> "After I graduated in economics and business studies from Milan I started working in *** [a large national bank]. I moved through the various stages of the bank's career structure according to the standard sequence, starting in the front office until I qualified as an executive" (Man, 52, branch manager in a bank).

The second pattern was displayed by accounts in which the narrators described a path where individual effort was much more important: they themselves had marked out their own routes by creating space for their expectations and ambitions, and by seizing the opportunities given to them. The accounts in this group were provided mainly by men from higher social backgrounds and with better educational qualifications.

> "I was offered this opportunity, which I accepted for one reason above all, so that I could take risks. I mean, here I'm the head of personnel, I'm not anyone's assistant. I've had a series of bosses (...) but, I have to say, I've got a lot of leeway for manoeuvre here, because the plants are excessively independent, and I'm personally at risk. This was the choice I made, because I needed to test myself" (Man, 36, personnel manager in a metalworking company).

> "I was teaching at a high school and working as an assistant at the university, on factory automation projects [...] There wasn't much on offer in the Veneto region at the time, especially for people with degrees in engineering, and electronics in particular [...] In '71 I moved to Turin, where I got a job

at the largest research centre in Italy, in the telecommunications field, and I worked there until '80, first as an ordinary researcher and then as a senior researcher. So I made a career for myself, project head and so on, mainly in IT applications for telecommunications. Because of my experience, backed by three patents deposited at international level, and therefore by concrete results, I was contacted by the general management of a large telecommunications company which had opened a new technical division, and they asked me if I wanted to move to their headquarters in Rome. [...] Then they asked me to move up a level and take charge of company-level quality control [...], and after that to coordinate all the company's information technology. Then I was asked, together with the present general manager, to set up this company. We started from scratch, drawing up mission statements and business plans, defining how the company should develop. The company's executive committees approved our proposals, and here I am" (Man, 58, chief executive in a IT company).

In both cases, the plots of the men's stories are linear and predictable. The protagonists steer themselves like navigators along routes which have already been marked out; or at any rate they follow courses across familiar seas towards already-known destinations. By contrast, the stories of their female colleagues describe voyages fraught with difficulties, where it is the sea and the wind that determine the direction. Determination is certainly still important, but so too are luck and the benevolence of the gods.

2.4 The narrative construction of difference

Having considered how the narrative selves are positioned through the incipit of a story and how different plots are mobilized in order to account for agency in working histories, we now analyse two extracts in which a woman and a man narrate their entries into traditionally male work roles or settings. The accounts have been divided into sections in order to evince the processes by which the narrators position their own discursive identities and those of other subjects through narrative reconstruction.

An engineer in the herd

The first narrative was provided by a woman engineer, Vittoria, and describes her entry into the company where she was working as a design technician. Her narrative highlights the process by which a woman is accepted through negation of her femaleness.

Table 2.1

A_1	It's like when a new animal joins a herd, the others must first work out who the newcomer is.
A_2	Then I understood it wasn't going to be easy. I had to show what I knew, then I felt that I was being watched. I had to be careful about what I said. I felt I was being watched as an engineer, as a woman, as a person [...]
B_1	Then, at a certain point they calmed down. They realized what I knew how to do and what I didn't, how far I could go and what I could give. And they also realized that I was no longer a woman, just an engineer. So they stopped at the 'engineer' stage.
B_2	Okay, that was fine by me: they disregarded the fact that I'm a woman and that they are all males. I don't want to say 'I'm a male as well', but we work on an equal footing, we're treated as equals, and that's fine. Only that you can't ignore the fact that I'm a woman.

The first part of the narrative sets the scene and describes the disruptive event (entry by a woman in a male setting).

A_1 (exposition): The narrator describes the situation, highlighting her diversity with respect to the members of the organization, likening them to a herd of animals and thereby emphasising their homogeneity and cohesion as a group. The group adopts a 'wait and see' attitude towards the newcomer: it must first "work out" who the intruder is before accepting her or otherwise. Vittoria therefore describes her entry as disrupting a consolidated equilibrium.

A_2 (complication): Vittoria says that she felt herself being scrutinised as regards not only her professional abilities ("I felt I was being watched as an engineer") but also her personal and gender identity. This was therefore a test of identity performance of the kind often performed on 'token subjects', or people whose diversity from the dominant group makes them more immediately visible, and who therefore tend to become symbols of the minority group (Kanter, 1977). As frequently happens to women in minority situations, Vittoria felt that she had to 'demonstrate' that she measured up to requirements by emphasising her similarities with respect to the group, and thereby reducing distance and difference.

The second part of the narrative (B) instead recounts the process of Vittoria's integration: the group accepts the newcomer, but the cost of that acceptance is denial of her difference.

B_1 (climax): Victoria recounts that when she passed the test, the group "calmed down": it lowered its guard and accepted the newcomer, whose abilities as well as limitations ("what I know how to do and what I don't") were important for the group to ascertain. The account stresses that acceptance into the group entailed attribution to the newcomer of a different status – one based on a male type of professionalism – which implicitly devalued her gender membership ("I was no longer a woman, just an engineer").

B₂ (resolution): In the final extract, the narrator's ambivalent state of mind emerges. On the one hand she expresses her satisfaction with being accepted by the group, and with the fact that her femaleness – and therefore diversity – is disregarded; on the other, she expresses her discomfort at having her gender identity ignored ("you can't ignore that fact that I'm a woman").

Vittoria's narrative therefore describes first a rejection and then a denial of gender difference. In her story, the female newcomer is at first treated with suspicion because of her diversity and then accepted by the group as an 'honorary man', so that her difference is neutralized. The way in which Vittoria constructs her account expresses her frustration with this arrangement and her demand not only for non-discriminatory treatment but also for recognition of her gender membership.

The positioning process that takes place can be compared to a dance, where gender is accentuated and/or denied in a sequence of steps. The gender asymmetry is produced by acceptance practices imbued with the stigma of difference: acceptance as an engineer at the cost of the negation o gender identity. It is a collaborative process (like every dance), where the positions and figures assumed by the dancers reflect the power relations of gender in the organization.

A women shift leader

The second account selected for analysis is taken from the interview with Giorgio, a production manager in a chemicals company. In this case, too, the extract has been divided into sections in which the narrator describes his

Table 2.2

A₁	For me, I won't say it was a trauma, but it was something that had to be dealt with, the fact that the majority of the workers on the shift were women. I've always done everything at the male level ... before they were male contacts; yes, there were some contacts with women, one unit was coordinated by a woman, but I didn't often see her during working hours.
A₂	In this case the contact was different, so that trying to understand the mentality of a male person and a female person was something new.
A₃	It was just the approach, it's not that people themselves are different ... but, I don't know, a woman is better suited to doing repetitive work, a man gets bored more quickly, and other things, so they cause you problems also at managerial level. There was a bit of difference.
B	Anyway, not that I'm boasting, but when I was on shift I was the first to pick a woman as coordinator. I was the first to make me a woman shift leader, so that when I went off shift, I handed over to this girl; who has developed quite successfully, and I've got on very well with these workers.

experience when coordinating a shift largely made up of women within a male-dominated organization.

In the first part, Giorgio defines the context, describing and justifying his reaction to finding women in traditionally male positions.

A$_1$ (exposition): Giorgio begins by stressing his initial difficulty in coping with the exceptional nature of the situation. He felt awkward because he has always worked in male settings ("I've always done everything at the male level"). It is interesting to note that if coordination by a woman is not visible, it is perceived as less disquieting.

A$_2$ (complication): The novelty of the situation lay in the difficulty of handling differences, and Giorgio stresses that he was confronted by two different mentalities, male and female. Although he adds that the difference was not between people, only between their behaviours, then gives some examples which instead highlight a more substantial difference – as when he uses the concept of suitability ("a woman is better suited to doing repetitive work").

In the second part of the narrative (B), Giorgio assumes an active role and represents himself as the sponsor of one of the female workers.

B$_1$ (climax): Giorgio talked about his decision to promote a woman as co-ordinator. Here his positioning is that of a mentor, someone who facilitates the career of someone else.

B$_2$ (conclusion): the story finishes with a happy ending: when he was promoted to a higher position, his position was filled by this woman and he expresses his satisfaction in working with these kinds of women.

The narrator uses this account to position himself as a *mentor*, an attentive superior who supports and encourages the career of a *protégé*. We met this type of positioning in other male narratives, where men expressed pride at promoting the careers of colleagues or described themselves as risk-takers willing to gamble on a female colleague. As in the above extract, when recounting how they had helped female colleagues, these men stressed, somewhat self-satisfiedly, their initial expectations and the results achieved for these women. The protagonist of the above story, however, is not a woman who has advanced through her own efforts, but a man expressing satisfaction at his magnanimity. The language he uses also evinces a sense of ownership *vis-à-vis* the female colleague ("I was the first to make *me* a woman shift leader").

The striking feature of the two stories is the evident asymmetry that they discursively construct. The positionings accomplished by the two accounts – positionings also apparent in most of the other narratives collected – collocate men as 'those playing at home' and the women as 'intruders', or at most 'guests'. Women are the exception, and the men must determine what the women "know how to do and what they don't know how to do" or "the mentality of a female person". In both stories, the order disrupted by difference is restored in an equilibrium functional to the organization and to gender hierarchies. The threat raised by a woman entrant is diminished if her difference is denied or if incorporated into a frame where the correct order is re-established. In this way not only is the distinction safeguarded but it is harmoniously reinforced within the organization.

2.5 Narrating gender between the exceptional and the ordinary

When people tell stories, they give order and sense to their experience and construct their own identities and those of others. The fact that men and women who work together in similar roles narrate their work histories so differently may therefore be due, not to a gender-ascribed diversity, but to the mechanisms whereby gender is produced and reproduced in social and organizational practices, and in particular through gender competent narratives. In other words, the diversity of narrative genres expresses, and above all constructs, the specificity of gender experienced by people with different bodies. The narrating self thus constructs its subjectivity in accord (or disaccord) with the social attribution of gender.

By initiating and developing their accounts in different ways, and by constructing different plots to connect events in their professional and organizational lives, men and women working in traditionally male organizations and positions produce and reproduce their gender identities within the organization's symbolic order. How is it done? Language, of course, plays a crucial part in constituting social realities and identities, but "meaning is always ambivalent and resonates with the flux of experience" (Hopfl, 1994: 468). In other words, language is metaphorical and indeterminate and language and meaning are an embodied practice. Moreover, their use of narrative is epistemic because they communicate knowledge through everyday, imaginative ways of talking, metaphors, storytelling and gestural statements (Cunliffe, 2002).

In order to explain how the differences between male and female are accounted for, we may refer to Jerome Bruner's (1990) analysis of what a narrative 'does'. Bruner argues that narrative renders events comprehensible against the background of the ordinary, which is what people consider to be the fundamental condition of life. Narrative helps to restore order, to repair breakdowns, and to adjust erroneous courses of action. At the basis of every narrative there is an overturning of an initial canonical order which must consequently be reconstructed or replaced (White, 1981; Turner, 1982). Once a breakdown has been identified, the task of narrative is to make it comprehensible. Storytelling seeks to make the ordinary not only prevalent but compulsory, whilst it presents the extraordinary as optional and as a matter of choice. In telling a story the narrator gives a retrospective justifi-

45

cation for what has been done or could have been done and, in constructing plausibility and accountability, makes sense of the current situation, especially when it is unexpected (Weick, 1995).

In this light, therefore, it is possible to account for the meaning of some of the differences performed by the male and female work stories. We have said that the male interviewees produced shorter and more standardized stories, and that they sometimes asked the interviewer to rephrase questions. Every good story is able to surprise the audience with the disruption of an initial equilibrium, and to reassure it by eventually restoring that equilibrium. Because the men failed to see any breakdown of equilibrium in their life-courses, only a linear and uninterrupted sequence, they thought that they did not have good stories to tell and therefore preferred more structured questions (and answers).

Women's narratives were different. Because they did not take work – and especially traditionally male work – for granted, either for themselves or their colleagues, in order to describe it they resorted to more elaborate rhetorical devices which served not only to describe events but also to justify them, to furnish a harmonious image, and to produce a coherent narrative self. In the case of the female interviewees, narrative was therefore a formidable instrument with which to repair the breakdown in the symbolic gender order caused by their career choices, and therefore to establish connections between the exceptional and the ordinary, thus justifying departures from the norm (Bruner, 1990).

It is not just the greater complexity of female life-courses (due to multi-location in diverse and sometimes conflicting environments) that produces more intricate narrative models; it is also the greater difficulty with which work experience is recounted, especially when it is of central importance to a person's life. When commenting on the results of a study which suggested the existence of two different styles of autobiographical narrative – a more linear and conflictual male model, and a more discontinuous and compliant female one (Freccero, 1986) – Norman Denzin (1989) recommended that these differences be contextualized historically, arguing that if the professional paths of women become more similar to those of men, the differences of narrative will probably disappear. This recommendation helps us understand why the accounts of the younger women more closely resembled those of the men than of the other women. It corroborates the hypothesis that narrative style is a difference not ascribed to sex, but rather to social and – in our case – organizational features. These women had personal and professional experiences which more closely resembled those of their male colleagues. They belonged to the generation of women who had made large investments in education and therefore had high expectations regarding their careers. When these women did not belong to weaker social groups, work and a career had lost the transgressive connotations that they had for previous generations, and they felt no need to justify their position or to make amends. Moreover, unlike older women, they could usually rely on their families of origin, which constituted a resource rather than a constraint as they did for their male colleagues sustained by the domestic work and care of their wives.

In this chapter we have analysed only some of the narrative devices by which gender is produced and reproduced in organizations. They are certainly not the only modalities of gender performance. In different ways, men and women deployed processes and strategies by which, on the basis of their experiences and expectations – but also the organizational constraints and rules imposed upon them – defined their reciprocal gender positioning at work. In the next chapters we shall concentrate on how men and women cooperate to delineate gendered selves in organizations when they recount entry by one or more women in a male dominated environment.

Chapter 3

Women Tell Their Stories: Challenges and Windmills

*"What giants?" asked Sancho Panza. "Those that you see there",
answered his master, "with the long arms, which
according to some are nearly two leagues in length."*

*"Look, my lord", said Sancho. "What we see there are not giants
but windmills, and what seem to be their arms are the vanes that,
turned by the wind, make the millstone go."*

*"It is clear", replied Don Quixote, "that you are not used
to this business of adventures. Those are giants, and if you are afraid,
away with you from here and betake yourself to prayer,
while I engage them in fierce and unequal combat."*

(Miguel de Cervantes, Don Quixote)

The literature on gender and organizations offers various metaphors with which to describe women who enter traditionally male contexts and occupations: women as intruders (McIntosh, 1985, Kvande and Rassmussen, 1994), as strangers (Gherardi, 1995), or as travellers (Marshall, 1984), these are some of the most evocative images of the experience of women as outsiders in male organizational cultures. In this chapter we propose a further image which represents the theme underlying the story of 'when She joins a group of men'. The image of the challenger is the leitmotif of the women's stories that follow.

This is a challenge raised against the organization's symbolic gender order: that is, the way in which the members of the organization define and understand specific domains of gender reference, and on the basis of which attributions and stereotypes relative to sexual membership are produced and maintained – the expectations that men will be male and women will be female, that the former will invest in the public sphere and the latter in the private sphere, that the former will undertake productive tasks and the latter reproductive tasks. Further on we intend to argue that the challenge to the symbolic gender order is a *twofold challenge*. In fact, by investing significant amounts of time and resources in their work, women in male contexts belie the expectations of the traditional female model. But at the same time, as women in the midst of – and in the place of – men, they challenge the traditional allocation of roles within organizations. The challenge is therefore predicated on diversity: women in traditionally male settings and positions display a twofold difference, for they are different from men but also from other women.

3.1 The twofold challenge: different from men but also from other women

The twofold challenge highlights the ambivalent positioning of the female narrator: on the one hand women emphasised their differences from their male colleagues; on the other, they stressed their similarities to them, thereby distinguishing themselves from what they cast as *the other women*.

'Casting the Other' (Czarniawska and Höpfl, 2002) is a concept proposed to shed light on the attribution of otherness/difference, that is, on the practices which forcefully impose gender. The metaphor has various origins: a theatrical one (as being cast in a role, and with the implications for required performances), a material one (a cast not only imposes a shape but it is also concerned with immobilization, as in the case of a broken arm); a spatial one (the action of casting, as in the act of throwing forward, defining a trajectory a point of arrival, or in forecasting and prediction). The process of otherness attribution is therefore a process which tends to fix the performance or identity or the path. We shall see that always implicit in the positioning of the One is a positioning of the Other, and that interaction always involves the negotiation of reciprocal positionings.

Whilst identity is discursively constructed through identification and distinction, the outcome of the interaction between the two processes is in a certain sense contradictory: our women interviewees asserted at the same time their distinction from, and identification with, both men and women, and thus straddled the gender boundaries defined by the dominant symbolic order.

In what follows we shall discuss the features of the twofold challenge by considering the ways in which the narratives of our women in male roles constructed their difference from the 'other women'; that is, from those who fulfilled the expectations of the symbolic gender order. We shall then examine how disruptive elements were introduced into the narratives and how the female narrators differentiated them from their male colleagues.

We took as a starting point the assumption that narratives are *loci* in which personal and organizational identities are constructed, and that in storytelling narrators activate a process of social comparison by which they define their reference groups. Rosabeth Moss Kanter has pointed out that when women form the minority in male cultures and want to avoid isolation, they often seek to become members of the dominant group (Kanter, 1977).

In their narrative positioning, our female narrators asserted their difference from colleagues who occupied traditional female roles (secretary, switchboard operator, and similar gender segregated occupations) and who seemingly displayed less organizational commitment (Marshall, 1995). The 'other women' thus became the negative reference group, the one with respect to which the narrators stressed their difference by rejecting their values and behaviours.

> "I'm talking about a certain kind of woman who wants to achieve something in the world of work, because for example I have lots of colleagues who don't want to follow a schedule from morning to evening, they finish at four o'clock and think no more about it" (Woman, 44, brand manager in a bank).

> "The others don't really care, they're married so they already find it difficult to keep working … […] the others, I'm talking about my situation, are all happy to have a good job … Yes, they don't have careers because they don't want them…" (Woman, 59, inspector in a bank).

In this positioning, the 'other women' are those 'from 9 to 5', with priorities other than work, and who adjust to a more traditional division of roles. They are cast as women content with secondary positions and roles, who shun responsibilities, who are more concerned with appearance than with job content, who seek to reduce their investment of time and resources in work to the minimum, and who put their own interests before those of the company.

> "I certainly believe that those who are getting ahead, who've managed to create their own space, I believe are women with an extra gear compared with other women: they've got character. Because if a woman doesn't have a tough character, suited to getting on in a world of work made up of men, for men, by men, she'll certainly soon cave in, or let it drop, or do something else (…) I'll give you a banal example: we've got two secretaries; of these two, since I've been here the one who's married I've seen for about a year, because in the meantime she's had two children, with two pregnancies at risk … and I don't see how she could have two pregnancies at risk, I mean, doing office work!" (Woman, 33, agricultural technician in a agricultural consortium).

> "But to be honest, there were thirty-five people in this office and only five women; the boss has always been against women, and, sincerely, in the world of work with the people that I've had to deal with … I'm a woman, but I think he's right, because I've had some colleagues, not surveyors but accountants or office-workers, who messed things up… […] I had clear cases where I worked, in the world of work, where women screwed us all; I don't want to be mean, but…" (Woman, 30, site surveyor in a construction company).

The difference is mobilized, on the one hand, by describing other women in unflattering terms and stigmatizing their femaleness, and on the other, by emphasising closer affinities and similarities with their male colleagues, minimizing their femaleness in order to construct a discursive self – women with character – which fits with the male culture of their organizations.

> "The others are dreadful … I include them in the 'cutie-pie' category, I call them all that, or 'milady'" (Woman, 29, environmental operator in a environmental services cooperative).

> "Technical production is totally different from what an office-worker or administrator does, I mean, varnished nails, short skirts (…) the mindset and the attitude are completely different, so I say that … I don't know, they dial the phone with a pencil so that they won't ruin their nails, they're things that make me laugh, but for me it's different, so I say that I'm a bit more masculine, a bit more down-to-earth, come on, we're here to work" (Woman, 30, production manager in a textiles company).

Some narratives linked this affinity with the male to the woman's childhood, or at any rate to her early socialization. They thus produced a sense of continuity over time and strengthened identity. If the past was re-read in light of a present where the narrator had a male job, the life-story tended to emphasise the male elements in identity construction.

> "I was the tomboy in the family. I started at thirteen with my grandfather; I did the wiring with my grandfather when I was thirteen, there were three of us females, my grandfather needed some help, and I … with a chisel and a hammer we laid the cables, wires, we installed the light fittings, the switches; when I was five he taught me how to change the wheel on my bike, I was with him and handed him the spanners. When I made my choice my mama burst into tears; I remember my first year at technical school, with sticking plasters on my hands, when we did machine tuning, I got blisters because I wasn't used to it, and I remember that I cried, that they told me I should change schools, that it didn't matter if I lost a year" (Woman, 30, leak detector in a metalworking company).

The sense of continuity in a life-cycle was retrospectively constructed, mobilising the past at the service of the present, in which males were therefore represented as an aspirational reference group; that is, a group to which the women wanted to belong, or which they wanted to resemble.

> "Me personally, I'm certainly one of those many women who wish they'd been born a man, even if this doesn't cause me any problems, but that's how it is … probably it's the way I was brought up by my mother, or things have made me think this way. Perhaps it's an excuse, I use it as an alibi because I haven't got much determination, sometimes I wish I had more grit, I always

think – if I'd been born a man I'd be much surer of myself" (Woman, 28, marketing manager in a wine-producing company).

The narrators' desire not to fall victim to a gender stereotype (that women are unable to do men's work) induced them to strengthen that stereotype by discursively constructing a difference and an otherness based on mobilization of a desired masculinity. They thus produced texts in which women's devaluation was in fact reaffirmed. This process of devaluation – which we call second-sexing in order to stress its active dimension – recalls the one described by Simone De Beauvoir (1949) in *The Second Sex*: although recognition of otherness plays a fundamental part in the construction of a person's identity, the Other is also reciprocally constructed. However, De Beauvoir argues, in the case of the relationship between men and women this does not happen, because the woman is a 'residual other' to whom full subjectivity is denied. By representing women engaged in more traditionally female tasks and roles as 'other' with respect to a self likened to male subjectivity, our women interviewees consolidated the symbolic devaluation of femaleness.

It should be noted how second-sexing was done by the stories told by the women: a sort of devaluation, or at any rate non-recognition, of their role by the female colleagues, whom they labelled 'the others'. As in a mirror game (Schutz, 1962; Gherardi and Strati, 1990), or what narratologists call *mise-en-abyme,* the 'other colleagues' were positioned as those who showed little or no solidarity with the narrator, who felt criticised or even ostracised by them. The argument mobilised was that women are less willing to legitimate the authority of women colleagues than the authority of men.

> "There's still a reluctance to accept women in certain roles: you experience it even from below ... the secretary, if I ask her something, she grumbles, but if my male colleague asks, she's more helpful. Level remaining equal, a man has more authority ... I'm friendly with the secretaries, so every so often I joke about their different attitude towards men ... and they agree, they say it's true" (Woman, 36, bank executive).

The fact that women in traditionally female positions tend to be better disposed towards male superiors than towards other women can be read as a consequence of the unequal distribution of power between men and women in organizations: the preference for men – as Kanter (1977) points out – is an option towards power. However, rather than greater consideration towards men, the narratives revealed the presence of a negative – indeed hostile – attitude towards women in positions of responsibility:

> "The funny thing is that if some woman achieves something extra, it's women themselves who obstruct it" (Woman, 29, environmental operator in a environmental services cooperative).

"It's not that there's been a specific episode, but you feel these things, I mean, you live them in a certain way: you feel in the background that if you do something extra the others don't like it; they comment 'But who does she think she is?'" (Woman, 30, leak detector in a metalworking company).

This attitude of the 'others' towards women occupying typical male positions did not resemble 'the happy act of surrender' which – Melania Klein (1957) argues – characterizes admiration of someone who has achieved a difficult goal. Nor did it belong to the more neutral category of competition, where more dynamic comparison is possible. Rather, it resembled the sense of envy where satisfaction at the Other's achievement is subordinate to its debasement (Pajardi, 1998). The onset of envy appears tied to the organizational context, and in particular to the meanings attributed within it to relational dynamics and opportunities for individual development. Organizational contexts where career prospects display gender segregation, and where professional growth paths are less fluid, are more fertile terrain for envy to grow. At the same time, as the next chapter will argue in more detail, the attribution of envy to women is often a rhetorical device used to delegitimate the assumption by women of competitive and aggressive behaviour not socially recognized as competent gender behaviour.

Colleagues in typically female positions were not the only *others* cast in the narratives. In fact, there emerged various *other* female figures who responded better than the narrator to the expectations of society and organizations *vis-à-vis* women. Among them were the wives of many of the male interviewees. The majority of these women had first gone out to work, but then, as their husband's workloads increased and with the birth of children, they had left their jobs or reduced their work commitments. Like the previous group, they followed what Benshop and Dooreward (1998) call the 'mommy track': that is, they deviated from the normal career path and took the 'atypical' (with respect to the organizational norm) route of greater dedication to the family.

Both the male and female narratives talk about wives. The later stressed that a wife's support enabled their male colleagues to devote themselves more time and effort to work:

"One thing that makes me very weak is the problem of working hours, even more so now that I've got a small child, because my hours are crucial for me; so they're a weapon that they use against me, because almost all my colleagues have wives at home, so they don't have problems" (Woman, 43, editor at a television station).

As we shall see in the next chapter, the men's argument instead tended to emphasise the need for wives to sacrifice their jobs for the good of the family.

Finally, also belonging to the group of *others* were those women who – although they had initially invested in work and therefore had stories similar to those of the interviewees – had subsequently quit their jobs or reduced their work commitments, and had therefore complied with expectations about female behaviour.

> "One of the biologists here had a child around two years ago, the girl's one and a half, and before she was vice-president of the cooperative, but when she started a family, she resigned" (Woman, 36, chemical sector manager in an environmental services cooperative).

All the narrative positionings examined in this first part have displayed a process whereby the women compared (and constructed) diverse reference groups and made value judgments: the women who had invested in professional careers compared themselves with those who, although they worked, had priorities other than their jobs, with those who had quit their extra-domestic work, and with their male colleagues. But above all, this process of comparison enabled the women to stage a plot in which their positioning challenge "female stereotypes, but in so doing reproduce" them. Three main types of rhetoric are used for casting *the other*: one has to do with working hours (the 'other women' do not accept extended working schedules), one with maternity (which the 'other women' are not willing to forgo), and the third with authority (the 'other women' do not comply with female authority) – these being the main challenges faced by women in male-dominated environments. The challenging positioning is constructed by resorting to three rhetorics: one attributes to oneself a tough character, the second tells a story which naturalizes or socializes a masculine character since the childhood; and the third highlights the rent position that men enjoy by virtue of their sex, like having a wife at home (free domestic work) or an aura of power.

3.2 Stories of challenge and challengers

At the symbolic level the main challenge is women's entry into mainly male environments. This was a challenge which arose from the novelty that these women represented for organizations which had always been exclusively male – or at least ones in which positions of responsibility were occupied by males. The entry of women into these positions not only disrupted a tradition cherished by the organization's members, it also undermined the practices, norms, language and values of the male organization. We shall argue that the entry of these women was a challenge against the organization's symbolic gender order, although it was a challenge which took various forms.

On analysing the stories around challenging the symbolic gender order,

54

we may identify three distinctive features characterizing the women's narratives: intentionality, awareness, and success.

The degree of intentionality. Not always was the challenge raised intentionally: in the majority of cases, the challenge against (and the breach of) the organization's rules was an implicit, though unwitting, outcome of choices made and actions undertaken by the interviewees in their work careers. These women often came to occupy certain roles as a natural consequence of their training, or because only they possessed (as the assistants of previous incumbents) particular expertise. The frequent use of the concept of randomness emphasised the interviewees' desire to play down their challenges.

The degree of awareness. There were various levels of awareness among the women concerning the type of disruption or threat that their entry caused to the dominant symbolic order. They sometimes made choices or undertook actions without being fully aware of the consequences within the organizational culture.

The degree of success. The challenge could be successful to varying extents. When was it successful? When the challenger assumed behavioural styles, performed actions, or occupied spaces in contrast with the rules (and threatened their existence) and obtained some sort of recognition or legitimacy within the organization.

Bearing these differences in mind, and also considering the different social and organization backgrounds of the women, together with their commitment to work and their organization, and their behavioural responses to the organizational culture, we identified five types of challenge:

– challenge as symbolic presence;
– challenge as struggle;
– challenge as adventure;
– challenge as affirmation;
– challenge as gender denial.

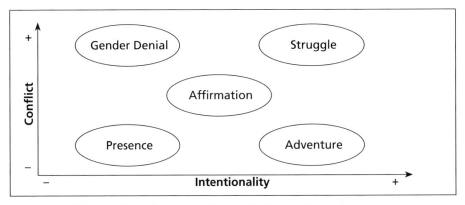

Figure 3.1 *Types of challenge to the symbolic gender order.*

55

We now present five idealtypical stories which exemplify each of these types of challenge. These stories do not correspond to any singular story collected in the research, but they summarize some of the main elements featuring different plots.

Challenge as symbolic presence

Belonging to this first group were stories by women who challenged the organizational culture only by being present in male settings. Theirs was a presence, however, which they sought to conceal, and above all to make non-conflictual. These stories evinced calm awareness by the narrator that she was exceptional, that she had 'made it' – but not by opposing or seeking to change the organization's gender culture.

Anna is 50 years old; she has worked for the same company for more then thirty years since she was forced to leave school because of economic problems at home. She has always worked very hard, and only once – at the beginning – has she had to insist on having her work recognized. Since then, her commitment has always been appreciated, and she was one of the first women to be promoted to a senior post in the organization. Over the years, despite her position of importance, she has never flaunted her achievements, being helpful and cooperative with her colleagues rather than asserting her hierarchical superiority over them. This has created a conflict-free working environment, where her colleagues have never felt humiliated.

Despite Anna's large personal investment in her job, she has had three children, and she has been able to look after them with her family's help. During her first two pregnancies she worked until the last moment and then returned to work as soon as she could. She has also tried to be absent from work as little as possible. This double workload – family and job – has been extremely burdensome, and today, worn out and worried that she has neglected her family, Anna asks herself whether it has all been worth it.

With the birth of Anna's third child, the company retrenched her position and replaced her with a man. She understands the company's reasons for doing so, and makes no criticism of the organization's decisions and strategies.

In Anna's story, as in the other narratives which configured challenge in the form of symbolic presence, simply asserting the woman's right to 'be there' – in a job where there are few other women – and legitimating her presence in a male organizational culture constitute challenges in themselves. Stories of this kind exhibited awareness by the women that they were exceptions or 'tokens' (Laws, 1975), although the intentionality of the challenge was rather muted.

"They invited applications for the post. I wasn't particularly interested because I've never been ambitious; all I'd wanted was recognition, doing my work with the proper grade (...) But my mother insisted that I should apply, and I said 'yes, you're right', because I was still up with my studies, and I came equal first with an external candidate, and the contract said that in the case of a tie precedence was to be given to internal candidates, so willy-nilly the Board had to appoint me the first female executive officer in the region I remember I got phone calls because I was the first woman executive" (Woman, 59, inspector in a bank).

The plot of challenge as symbolic presence was constructed by older women, mainly with lower-secondary school educations, and most of whom had always worked for the same organization. Their stories almost always included marriage and children, and they highlighted the difficulty of balancing family responsibilities and work, as well as the need to make choices.

"You're always busy, that's why I do it, even neglecting my family sometimes, when I was charge nurse the schedule didn't give me enough time to go home in the evening, and someone in the family always took over ... because with the girls being born only two years apart ... and then I'd just caught my breath and the boy was born ... and he was incredibly demanding, but I stuck to it, because with two salaries you don't have to cut down on your spending, and so I said 'Okay, there'll always be time to quit work, to resign' and then I got up to 36 years of service [...] I managed it, but it was a bit tough, I mean, now I see my colleagues with small children and I say 'God, you've got all that hassle to go through' and then in the end you're worn out and you say, 'But was it worth it? – I don't know'" (Woman, 59, inspector in a bank).

As regards organizational experience, these stories emphasised cooperation and mediation, stressing in particular the attitudes that the symbolic gender order attributes to women.

"After I'd been promoted over these male colleagues who'd previously been my superiors, we always got on well because I never put myself forward ... so people almost always went to my colleague and I let them talk to him, and then on the quiet I decided, it was me who signed ... like that, but I've never imposed my authority and humiliated people, or thrown my weight around, so the atmosphere has always been tranquil" (Woman, 59, inspector in a bank).

But there was no trace of complaint or recrimination against the work environment or against colleagues, whose merits were instead often emphasised.

One notices a certain irony in these stories, and a subtle pleasure at having attained an important role in the organization, without expecting it and probably without seeking it.

"I'd say that what has been given me has always come easily, I've never had to ask, or put myself forward, in the sense that I've always done my work, and my work has been appreciated, I think that it's been fair recognition, I don't like to think that it could have been something else. I do believe that I've been, I won't say overvalued, but fairly valued. So, perhaps I'm a bit conceited, but I think that I've deserved what I've been given, and I'm now in a situation where my professionalism is always available to others. So I presume that I've acquired something" (Woman, 52, section head in a tele-communications company).

The challenge thus became an assertion that women are 'just as good as men': they can compete and win on the same terrain, as testified by their presence in the organization. At the same time, awareness of the costs borne by these women prevents them from crowing over their achievement; rather, they ask themselves 'Was the game worth the candle?'.

Challenge as struggle

In this case, the stories recounted battles against discriminatory practices in the workplace. The storytellers saw their experiences in male contexts as struggles for self-assertion. They tended to portray themselves as proud Amazons ready to assume masculine postures in order to combat on equal terms against the hostility of male colleagues and the organizational culture.

> Paola is 37 years old. On graduating, she went to work for an organization which had few female employees, and with no women in senior positions. She immediately noticed the asymmetry in the organization's gender practices and realized that she would have to fight hard to create space for her professional development. She thus began to lay down a career strategy for herself, forging the right alliances, adopting a combative stance, and avoiding traditionally female roles and tasks ('a straitjacket', she said), and showing the organization that she was determined to get ahead. This strategy meant that she could show no weakness and had to adopt relational behaviour marked by uncompromising aggressiveness, rather than meek compliance. She was helped in her battle by her husband, who backed her choice of career and shared domestic responsibilities with her. The birth of her child was planned, however, and it created difficulties with her male colleagues, who instead had no child-rearing responsibilities because their wives did not go out to work. Paola's combativeness won her few friends among her colleagues, but they nevertheless respected her because they thought she was 'like a man'.

In stories like this the principal motivation (beside personal growth) inducing the women narrators to take up work was self-affirmation. Most of these women were graduates who had begun to work immediately on leaving university, mainly moving up internal career structures. In order to impose their presence and to carve out the space necessary for their self-affirmation, they had to struggle against the dominant organizational culture and a symbolic order in which women were denied full citizenship.

> "I must say that the main problem I've had because I'm a woman is I've always had to show that I'm worth at least as much as men, which is stressful in the long term, also because I've probably not gone the right way about it, because I've used aggressiveness (…) My relations with men, which they are for the most part, are difficult for two main reasons: being practically the only women at a certain level of responsibility has piddling advantages, I mean the everyday ones of being a woman, they buy you a coffee, they try to be nice, they moderate their language, they act like gentleman, or they try to be funny, which is annoying, but it doesn't give you any more substantial advantages, because in the end you never stop battling against these people" (Woman, 35, production unit manager in a telecommunications company).

> "I've had some quite nasty experiences of harassment (…) Not sexual harassment, because I'd never allow it, but only for that reason, because otherwise they would certainly have tried it on. And I've also been in a situation where someone with power in the company has sworn at me because I protested against his behaviour with the young women" (Woman, 35, production unit manager in a telecommunications company).

These narratives stressed the dominance of male models and the consequent tendency to exclude women from authority and power. The female narrator therefore recounted how they had to assume the same behaviour as their male colleagues, accepting the organization's male cultural socialization and opting to be aggressive.

> "I'd say that in the past three years I've begun treading on people's toes, especially the senior managers', because I know what I know, and I'm now trying to assert myself much more than I did at the beginning […] You realize that when the time comes for you to show your professionalism, you always have to fight. Now they've changed the organization chart, I'm the only woman with an office and, guess what, when they convened the first meeting for the office heads, they didn't tell me about it: so I went along and asked them, and they said 'Ah, well, you know, there's been a slip-up, we forgot'; it's a constant struggle" (Woman, 43, editor at a television station).

> "I couldn't read the political news, and now, not coincidentally, I'm into politics, and I've fought against what used to be taboos and still are at national level, because women are only conductors and I've always refused that job,

because it's a typical job for women, but for me it was a frigging trap; in fact, one of my colleagues who was department head and conductor never did the work of department head, and I tried to get her to rebel, I incited her; I deliberately rejected the job of conductor because I wanted to become department head" (Woman, 43, editor at a television station).

The expressions most frequently used ('struggle', 'assert yourself', 'determination' 'impose yourself') belonged to the lexicon of overt conflict on gendering practices. The clash with the organization could be more or less overt, or it could involve more or less subtle strategies, but the challenge was always deliberately raised.

Challenge as adventure

Adventure was the dominant theme in this type of challenge: each story recounted the passionate pursuit of an apparently unreachable goal (a traditionally male job) and its hard-won achievement after overcoming a series of obstacles.

Diana, now aged 40, was a 'tomboy' as a girl, and she grew up with a strong desire to enter her grandfather's typically male occupation. Despite pressure by her mother, and also many obstacles at school and humiliations in her first job, she has done everything possible to achieve her goal. Her progress to her present position has been beset by difficulties, and above all characterized by situations in which she has been constantly put to the test by male colleagues and customers – and all this in a predominantly male and uncultured environment. However, her passion for her work has enabled her to cope with her difficulties. Her job is a source of great satisfaction to her. Consequently, she tends to devote more time to her work than is necessary, and often thinks about it during her free time.

Her career choice has also had repercussions on her personal life. She is now separated and lives alone with her daughter, who she is able to look after with the valuable help of her family. After her separation, she decided that marriage was not for her, because most of her time and energy is taken up by her work, and there is no room for a demanding relationship.

The stories in this group are about women driven by a strong commitment to – in some cases an outright vocation for – occupations once exclusively male preserves (site surveyor, agricultural technician, bovine veterinary surgeon). To justify their aspirations, the narrators tended to emphasise their greater affinity with male models, in some cases tracing it back to early socializing experiences.

"I really enjoy it [the job of electrotechnician], but I've paid for my choice, because otherwise I wouldn't be on an assembly line now. I'll tell you straight, I've paid for my choice. But if I went back in time I'd do it again, because I've really happy with it; like, I was the tomboy in the family. I started at thirteen with my grandfather; I did the wiring with my grandfather when I was thirteen, there are three of us females, my grandfather needed some help, and I ... with a chisel and a hammer we laid the cables, wires, we installed the light fittings, the switches; when I was five he taught me how to change the wheel on my bike, I was with him and handed him the spanners. My sisters, one's got a degree in mathematics, the other's an accountant. When I made my choice my mama burst into tears; I remember my first year at technical school, with sticking plasters on my hands, when we did machine tuning, I got blisters because I wasn't used to it, and I remember that I cried, that they told me I should change schools, that it didn't matter if I lost a year" (Woman, 30, leak detector in a metalworking company).

The women in these stories had usually had a rough ride in their jobs. On starting work, some of them had been subjected to initiatory tests of their motivation and resistance.

"There was this person who had a big firm [...] I went to the interview and I told him 'I want to try out as a site surveyor. I can't say whether I'll like it, I just want to try it'. And he said, 'I'll flank you with another surveyor who knows what he's doing, we'll see how it goes.' Those were the worst years of my life [...] It was incredible because there were two surveyors with assistants, me and this guy: it was great to see the other surveyor who looked at this guy when he arrived in the morning and said, 'Hi, do you fancy a coffee?' And mine who cursed and said to me 'Get in the car because we're late'. That was the scene, I was terrified to see him in the morning and hear the first words he spoke to me" (Woman, 30, site surveyor in a construction company).

"They're constantly testing you; I mean, you're always on a knife edge, and then there are the foremen, who aren't foremen but skilled workers, especially the older ones, who are always testing you. And if you're right, if you give the right answer, OK. If you give the wrong one, heaven help you. The day after everyone knows about it. I'm now working for a quarrying firm, and it's my mentality to find out who's in command of the team, who you've got to get on the right side of, who to keep sweet, because at a certain point they might say 'look, I'm the boss, I don't give a toss about you' and you can't do anything" (Woman, 30, site surveyor in a construction company).

More than the others, these narratives stressed the need for strategies to handle male colleagues other than competing with them, given that this was counter-productive.

"[The men] don't feel threatened because I'm not competitive, I wasn't even when I was young, because all that's interested me is my work. It's also because of the experiences I've had, they've taught me a lot about how to handle men. I'm not competitive by nature, and then compete against whom, why, for what…" (Woman, 40, large animal veterinary surgeon in a breeders' consortium).

The narratives of these women also highlighted the incompatibility between work and family. One of the central themes of these stories – whose protagonists were almost all unmarried or divorced – was that of choice.

"I am really committed to my work … you have to make choices in life, I'm convinced of this, and unfortunately a choice of this kind rules out other options. I couldn't work ten-twelve hours a day, come home and find hubby waiting for me, no, because those few hours I have I devote to my son, never again to a man, there wouldn't be enough time, that's the way I am, I'll never change … so I know I mustn't get married … because I prefer to work. It's a choice" (Woman, 40, large animal veterinary surgeon in a breeders' consortium).

Challenge as affirmation

In this fourth plot the narrators were aware of the novelty represented by their presence for the organization, and they also realized its transgressive impact. Yet they refrained from going head-to-head against the dominant organizational culture, but they also lacked the feeling of risk and personal fulfilment that permeates the challenge as adventure. Work was seen as a opportunity for personal growth and fulfilment.

Claudia is 34 years old. She obtained a science degree and then became a teacher. But she left the teaching profession because of the scant opportunities for professional growth offered by the educational system. For reasons she called 'fortuitous' she was contacted by the company where she now works and was offered the demanding job of taking charge of a new sector and developing it. She accepted the challenge enthusiastically; she says, in fact, that she enjoys being stretched. She has been very successful, and the excellence of her work has been recognized by the company, and by her male colleagues, with whom her relations are good. The aspects of her job that she stresses in particular is the autonomy that it gives her and the opportunities for further learning that it affords. However, she does not see her present situation as definitive: when she feels that she can no longer learn and enhance her skills in this company and this job, she may decide to look for something else.

Claudia's organization is prevalently male, especially as regards its senior positions, but she does not complain about discrimination; indeed, she says that she gets on well with her male colleagues, especially compared with other organizations.

Claudia is not married. Her large investment (in terms of time, but not only) in her work means that she cannot devote much time to herself, or start a family.

The stories in the next subgroup are those told by women who had accumulated professional experience in various spheres and achieved evident success in the organizations for which they now worked. The narratives revolve around the concepts of affirmation and a search for space.

"I was at Agency X, and the post of the head of the overseas office fell vacant, and they asked if there was anyone interested in replacing the person taking early retirement. At the time I didn't know much about overseas, I had the basics, but because I'd never worked in that sector, my knowledge was obviously skimpy. I thought for a moment, ten minutes I think, not even that, and then I said, 'All right, I'll do it' (...) You could say I was foolish, but foolishness shouldn't be confused with strength of will; you can say I was foolish, but I've always been convinced, and I'll repeat it, you have to know what you want in order to get it" (Woman, 36, branch manager in a bank).

More salient than in other interviews was the theme of luck and coincidence, even though it apparently conflicted with the determination distinctive of these women's professional paths. However, as we have previously argued, this was a rhetorical device used to play down the magnitude of the challenge represented by the women's professional success.

"Here in this company I really can't complain, given my luck in entering the world of work, let's say, in a job where I've generally been able to express and apply my training in a sector new for this company; I didn't have anyone to guide me, but I've always had the support and cooperation of everyone, so beyond a shadow of a doubt I consider myself lucky (...). The company wanted to obtain certification, and I somehow volunteered to deal with the matter; there was interest, immediate awareness on the management's part, and the idea of this consultancy was put forward, together with my own ideas and some requests by customers, especially abroad. And I was practically the right woman at the right moment, because I had to find my place in the organization, I had the good fortune to have sufficient time to show I was able to handle it, to organize control procedures abroad as well, and so I was given this task" (Woman, 29, quality manager in a wine-producing company).

Although the stories recounted relations with male colleagues marked by collaboration and ease of communication, almost all the women interviewees stressed that they had had to prove their worth to be accepted by their organizations.

> "To be frank, relations were difficult at the beginning, because I was always seen as a woman, and a very young one at that ... A woman must always prove that she's professionally very valid, because that's what it all comes down to in the end (...) I well remember the meetings they held to discuss things and the measures to take, and I remember that very often I wasn't asked to join these groups, which were very informal (...) I reckon that little by little you manage to get the others to understand that a person doesn't only have luck but professionalism as well" (Woman, 36, branch manager in a bank).

> "On the outside, you still realize that a woman must prove that she's worth more than a man to have the same grade and the same recognition as a man ... Yes, sometimes the commercial, so to speak, relationship is difficult ... I mean there are still people who don't understand that if you go out to dinner on business it's only for work ... so that we try ... it's not that I've had serious difficulties ... but there are always these things underneath, which are still difficult to resolve in reality" (Woman, 40, general manager in an environmental services cooperative).

These stories described less arduous professional paths compared with the narratives centred on the concepts of struggle and adventure. Nevertheless, these women had had to create space for themselves in environments that were not always friendly and welcoming. What changed was the stance that they decided to adopt towards their male colleagues and the organization by forgoing direct confrontation and opting instead for a more subtle strategy showing – as the above interviewee put it – that they were "the right women at the right time".

> "I believe we [women] create our own spaces; I mean, we often confuse the spaces that we want to create with those that we want the others to create for us. I'm convinced it's above all through our own efforts that we create spaces (...) I frankly don't believe that this hostility exists, very often it's exaggerated ... I haven't felt any hostility; I believe that if you take a positive attitude, because in the end everyone is looking for cooperation ... and I believe it depends on our abilities, because you obviously see if an obstacle's been raised, consequently it's we who should try to be more sensitive, and sometimes we're better than men in understanding how far we can go, how to behave to achieve our goals" (Woman, 36, branch manager in a bank).

Once again, as in the previous plots, one notes a certain incompatibility between family and work, although in this case it was a 'non-choice' that was recounted, rather than the obligatoriness of an alternative option. The narratives spoke of such a determined commitment to work that no time was left to 'think' about a family.

"I find it difficult to balance the two things because I work very hard and therefore have little time for myself. In fact, my time for myself is limited to the weekend; during the week, yes, I meet people, but I don't have a life ... if we take away my summer holidays and sometimes when I go for a walk at weekends ... I've little time for myself. But you see, it's also because I get home late, I have to cook, I've got the housework, there are so many things to do..." (Woman, 40, general manager in an environmental services cooperative).

"My work influences my private life to some extent, because sometimes my mind's elsewhere [...] The fact that I'm not in a steady relationship is probably because I haven't got time to think about anything really long-term [...] I've realized that my work affected a relationship I once had, of this I'm certain... It's a mental question, this business of the time and energy to devote to myself, I mean, what I want when I'm away from here is peace and quiet and no hassles, see some friends, go out with someone, but without any problems, and this isn't possible in a couple, because problems should also be shared, right? So I believe this lack of energy has also somehow influenced my private life, no doubt about it..." (Woman, 27, chemical section manager in an environmental services cooperative).

These narratives evince a mix of intentionality and conflictuality, but these are moderated by a desire to 'be there', and by a subtle critique of male sociality. Again a recurrent theme is the challenge as struggle: as in the excerpt describing how the woman's male colleagues 'forgot' to tell her about an 'informal' meeting. This was indicative of the broader problem of exclusion from informal networks – and consequently of less access to unofficial information and a lower accumulation of human capital. As a large body of literature has highlighted, the visibility of women, and the work necessary to achieve and maintain it, is an organizational practice. In organizational cultures based largely on informality, on communality, and on casual work procedures, not being one of the 'good old boys' is a form of exclusion which is difficult to struggle against overtly.

Challenge as gender denial

These various kinds of challenge can be conceived as lying along a continuum ranging from the most to the least subjective meaning attributed to membership of a male-dominated working group. The older women, for whom professional work had been a conquest, had experienced in first person the social pressure to choose between work and motherhood. They narrated the weight of their care work, their attachment to work, and their desire to 'be there' and to matter, with great pathos and elements of heroism. The younger women had different experiences of the labour market and society. And different as well was their personal situation if they still lived at home, had worked for only a few years, and had a stable employment relationship.

In the last group of stories now considered the gender aspect seems deliberately suppressed. In fact, all these stories were characterized by the age affinity of their protagonists, who claimed that they had overcome all gender differences in their organizations, and more generally in the labour market.

> Lara is 27 years old. She graduated cum laude from a prestigious private university and was hired by the company where she had previously researched for her degree thesis. Her story is relatively brief because she has only been at the company for three years. She thinks that she has worked well and is appreciated by the company. She feels closer to her male colleagues than to the other women in the company, who occupy typically female roles and make little personal investment in their jobs. She devotes a great deal of time to her work and is willing to travel for it if necessary. She sees other roads opening up for her in the future: he present job is an opportunity to gain experience, but her subsequent career may develop in other directions. She is not married and still lives at home, but she does not see having a family as irreconcilable with her career.

The narratives centred on this kind of plot recount the stories of young women, almost all graduates, who had just entered the world of work and were mostly unmarried, or at any rate did not have children. Some of them had technical-scientific training, and their previous experience of gender minorityship was not unpleasant. Theirs are the narratives which most assertively denied the existence of gender specificities and discrimination in the workplace.

> "I never thought about it … male, female, it never affected me; to be sincere, I was too young … At school there were 14 of us girls in a total enrolment of 1240, there were 7 girls in the class with 18, 19 males, we were certainly in the minority. I realized that there were fewer of us, that we were in the minority, but it seemed normal to me […] I thought it was perhaps because girls preferred other subjects, whereas I liked scientific subjects more" (Woman, 23, chemical surveyor of a wine-producing company).

> "When they tell me about training courses for women, Women's Day, it's as if they're talking about blacks, poor things who can't integrate into society; if they talked about a training course for blacks, I'd say 'What's the difference between blacks and whites, apart from the fact that perhaps they don't speak Italian very well?'" (Woman, 28, marketing manager of a wine-producing company).

These stories tended to assert an entirely asexual and meritocratic view of a labour market in which there was no difference between the treatment of men and women, and the racial question was beyond awareness. At the same time, this kind of narrative challenges a positioning of women as the 'minority' when their presence in society is not minoritarian.

Regardless of sex, their narratives affirm that there is space for all those, like these young protagonists, who were willing to invest in their jobs.

"I reckon that at a certain level these problems don't exist if someone, woman or man, wants to get ahead, to make it somehow, perhaps the problems are more banal, let's say, like a woman's having to stay at home; I know that when my female friends go for job interviews, the first thing they're asked is 'Are you married, do you want to have children?', the usual things which they never ask men. But it's never happened to me, and I've had lots of job interviews. It's probably due to the fact that a person of 24, who went to Bocconi, which rightly or wrongly is seen as a university for men, who's in marketing ... because I don't think that someone who studies for 25 years, spends 5 thousand euros a year on university fees, is going to get married and stay at home" (Woman, 28, marketing manager of a wine-producing company).

At the same time, these accounts evince the need felt by the narrators to emphasise their similarity to male colleagues and their difference from other women, whom they described as making insufficient investment in their work, and consequently as being responsible for their marginality.

"I think I've got quite a masculine character, and that's probably why ... I've got quite a masculine character, I can't help it; I mean I'm very dedicated to my work; it's not that I have my eight-hour timetable, this and that to do, so perhaps it's this that makes me seem different; It's not that I say, 'Okay, I've got to go home, or I've got small children, or a husband waiting for me', things like that, so that my way of doing my job is more typically male than female" (Woman, 30, production manager in a textiles company).

In fact when the professional paths of women become more similar to those of men, either because of changed models of work participation or because they are at early stages in their careers, their narratives challenge the gender construction of the previous generation and the idea of a female 'weakness'. Denying gender difference has an emancipatory value.

The future scenarios described by this group of narratives foresaw not only a carefully-planned and much desired career but also a family as a non-exclusive option. The ideal of the division of roles underlying these narratives does not seem conceivable in any but rigorously paritarian terms.

"I want to have both, I mean not just a job and not just, some day, a marriage, but ... I mean, I enjoy what I do, I want personal gratification from my job, doing certain things, but I want both, and to be able to reconcile them

... [*Do you think that will be possible?*] where there's a will there's a way, it won't be easy, just as it's not easy to handle my present workload. So we'll have to see; it's not easy now, and I don't think it will be any easier later, but if you care about these things, I believe that it always depends on how much you want things" (Woman, 30, production manager in a textiles company).

3.3 Women and windmills

The narratives of how 'women entered male dominated environments' were mainly success stories, also because we interviewed women and men who were still at work. We may therefore have missed the stories of those who had quit work, even if we asked for reported stories of failure.

The 'successfull' protagonists represented themselves as women who had moved into traditionally male jobs, challenging the dominant symbolic gender order as they did so. However, apparent in many narratives was a sense of resigned acceptance that it was impossible to change the gender cultures of the organizations for which the women worked. This concerns the 'sense of the game', what Bourdieu (1994) calls *illusio* or 'interest', recognition that a game is important and is worth playing, and that the stakes are worth contending for.

In order to emphasise this feeling, a number of interviewees cited Cervantes' hero and his battle against the windmills. The metaphor of Don Quixote has various meanings and well represents the ambivalence in voluntaristic imagery and discourse: on the one hand, he represents the romantic ideal of the defence of justice, of errantry, of fighting the impossible fight; on the other, the tragicomic experience of choosing the wrong adversary or obstacle, and the ingenuousness of those who confront life unrealistically. Our narrators cited Don Quixote as a symbol of challenge and its significance: the question posed by use of this reference was whether taking up the challenge made sense and was worthwhile.

> "Do you know something? You're proud of yourself, but every so often, when you say 'This is great!' you realize you're only tilting at windmills like Don Quixote ... because I've fought all right, but for what? For something that was already mine by right, equality with a man. I wasn't asking for the moon..." (Woman, 30, site surveyor in a construction company).

> "That's the way things work, unfortunately, and you have to accept the dynamics you find. You can't act like Don Quixote, otherwise you'll end up cleaning the stairs, cleaning the desks of your colleagues" (Woman, 43, editor at a television station).

Although the two extracts use the image of Don Quixote in different ways – the first emphasises the absurdity of fighting to obtain something that should be yours by right; the second the realism of not mistaking windmills for giants and accepting that adjustment to male behaviour is unavoidable – they evince doubt, self-interrogation, and reflectiveness. These women increasingly relied on work to construct their identities – especially the professionals, and those with managerial responsibilities in organizations where women were under-represented. However, their critical spirit had not abated; work was still not an inevitability or something taken for granted. The women stopped to interrogate themselves, they were afraid of behaving like Don Quixote. They had taken up challenges, but they asked themselves whether they were challenging giants or windmills. Other studies (Marshall, 1995) have reported systematic doubt about the life-meaning of work, and they have documented episodes when women at the height of their careers have quit work to strike off in other directions.

In many narratives there were an overt awareness of the challenge that women represent for the symbolic gender system, and like Don Quixote women position themselves as engaged in "fierce and unequal combat". However, when worn out by their constant combat, they asked themselves whether the battle made sense and who the enemy really was: might they not be tilting impotently against the impassive windmills of the organization? The question was not addressed to themselves alone, nor did the meaning of asking the question reside in its answer. The women's concern that they were mistaking windmills for giant enemies was a way to interrogate them-selves about the allure of the organization and the centrality of work in their lives.

Tilting at windmills is an imaginary battle, but it is also a metaphor for a 'war of the imagination' (Augé, 1997). The anthropologist Marc Augé argues that a colonized people becomes definitively subjugated when it sur-renders to the dreams of the colonizers. Without wishing to overstretch the analogy between women and colonized peoples, it is nevertheless interesting that these women in territories marked by male culture were not completely integrated into that values system. They implicitly disputed it, even when the question 'was it worth it?' was addressed to themselves.

With reference to *Don Quixote*, Alfred Schütz stressed that the novel's central theme is the clash between the two sub-universes of meaning (or 'provinces of reality') of the characters. The epilogue to Don Quixote's story is a surrender to the everyday life-world and to common sense, which shows that the only hope is to compromise with this world, learn to behave like others, and take for granted what others take for granted (Schütz, 1962b). By renouncing his imaginary world, Don Quixote embraced the suspension of doubt typical of commonsense thought, and he abandoned his conviction that different 'realities' exist (Jedlowski, 1995). These are the temptations that entice men and women in organizations, and especially women who have invested heavily in their work: unconditional surrender to the certainties of commonsense and the symbolic gender order that embodies them; acceptance of the 'good sense' which says that truth resides in the dominant interpretation.

Chapter 4

Men Tell Their Stories: Gender Is Not a Problem!

This chapter should more properly be entitled 'men *do not* tell their stories'. The differences in the ways that the women and the men recounted their stories are so striking that we are unsure whether we can convey them to the reader. In quantitative terms, the interviews with the men were around half as long as those with the women, and their structures were very similar. The men usually responded to the initial question on how they came to be in their present jobs with a narrative style reminiscent of a curriculum vitae or a job interview. Their accounts began with a summary of 'education and qualifications' and then moved through a linear sequence of career stages and advancements. The interviewees related almost nothing about their personal lives: there were no anecdotes, unforeseen events, vivid memories or disappointments. They empathically communicated that there was little to say about their entry into work. When the crucial question was asked – what their reaction had been to the advent of Her in a predominantly male group – they rarely recounted significant episodes, or how the relationship had begun and developed. Prevalent instead was defensiveness and denial that problems existed. Significantly, gender was defined as a problem in order to claim that there were no problems; that although the person in question was a woman, the male group had instantly accepted her as competent and therefore as deserving to be where she was. This emphasis on absolute parity between men and women signalled denial, or an inability to handle the theme of gender discursively. Finally, the men interviewees dwelt on the reasons why the job in question was male 'even though' it could be done by a woman. The interviews therefore consisted of opinions, judgements and descriptions of 'facts', while seemingly absent from them was any relish for storytelling or for talking about personal matters.

We were taken aback by this striking difference, and it induced us to doubt the quality of the interviews and the goodness of the methodology. We put these doubts to various colleagues and then asked ourselves why the men had be so reluctant to talk about themselves. We found a first reason in the literature (Jedlowski, 2000) and in our previous experience of conducting qualitative interviews. This explanation centred on gender differences in communicative styles: men generally prefer a more impersonal form of communication, and a vocabulary of action rather than of reflection. A second reason concerned the context of the interviews. Our request to interview men and women about occupations in which women are under-represented may have triggered an implicit mental reference to 'equal opportunities' and possible discrimination. This may have produced a defensive stance which denied discrimination for fear of being accused of prejudice. A third reason, directly connected with the previous one, had to do with familiarity with gender issues and an ability to reflect on one's gender membership. Men have not yet developed a vocabulary with which to reflect on gender and masculinity; nor have they developed a willingness to discuss such matters with interviewers whom they do not know. It may be that men choose different contexts of interaction to talk about themselves, or that they see storytelling as proper to relational situations of intimacy (Giddens, 1994). Added to this is the fact that the sentimental education of men teaches them to control their emotions and to confine relational discourse to the private sphere. Hence, the fact that men are less skilled at relating their intimate experience, or are reluctant to do so on a public occasion like an interview, can be interpreted as a manifestation of the social construction of masculinity. Not only do men not possess a vocabulary for relationality, but their lack of one is due to their socialization into the role of male adult.

Finally, there is the more elementary explanation that links gender with power. The social tendency to make masculinity invisible and to transform male experience into the yardstick for human experience is a covert endeavour by social culture in which both men and women actively and unwittingly collaborate. Our male interviewees were of the 'right gender' for their jobs, and therefore, like fish in water, they were not always aware of the element in which they were swimming. This metaphor recalls the point made in the second chapter when we analysed the gendered modes of storytelling. Because storytelling is a device to reduce the extraordinary to the ordinary, men do not have a great deal to say about their entry into work. An interview paradigmatic of this capacity for synthesis was conducted with a recently retired company manager:

> "My name is …, born in … on …, where I have my permanent residence. So, I went to nursery school in …, elementary school in … [*the account continues for a page, exactly with a further 981 words, and concludes as follows*]. This in brief is my career in the company […] If you have no specific questions, I have nothing to add" (Man, 53, head of customer care in a processing company).

We shall accordingly move directly to the discursive strategies which placed the extraordinary – Her entry – in the ordinary world of 'simply work'.

4.1 How was She welcomed?

The male interviewees were rather reticent in their accounts about Her entry into their world, and they sought to reassure the interviewer concerning the absence of discrimination, their positive attitude towards working women, and their personal conviction that, all in all, She had not encountered major problems. This narrative style is well illustrated by the following excerpt:

> "I believe that equal opportunities exist. I don't think that male chauvinist attitudes predominate" (Man, 47, final products manager in a bank).

The desire immediately to put forward a general judgement dispelling any suspicion of discrimination was backed by a belief that the recounting of minor episodes was nothing but gossip – as several interviewees explicitly stated:

> "From the point of view of being a woman, no, I don't think there's anything specific, unless you want to indulge in gossip, but then … either you know things for certain or you don't … so nothing of importance" (Man, 33, software assistant in an IT company).

Discrimination was perceived as active discrimination, the expression and effect of discriminatory behaviour either by the organization or by a direct superior. Yet there was little awareness of the objective datum that the occupational community was almost entirely male – and in the majority of cases constituted an purportedly male occupation. This suggests that, in homage to a misunderstood principle of equality, difference was denied to the point that numerical disparity was not perceived, or the effect of this disparity on the under-represented was ignored. The danger was that to deny masculinism was also to deny masculinity as a form of sociality which creates bonds among some persons but not among all of them.

However, after the initial reassurances, the interviewees admitted to a certain 'disruption' of routine, although this was soon resolved:

> "As far as I know, when she took responsibility for the department from a male, it caused a bit of a stir. Also because Ms *** has rather a decisive, pragmatic personality. When the changeover happened there was some consternation, fear of the unknown.
>
> Then, seeing that she was very able in running her department, not only technically but also in her relations with people, everything went well. I know that my colleagues get on fine with Ms ***. All in all, I'd say her entry has been viewed positively. And anyway it's always like that: when you get used to working in a certain way, with specific people, and someone of another sex comes in, things are shaken up a bit, and this may be positive or negative. At the beginning there's a moment of … but then things sort themselves

out" (Man, 28, plant and maintenance manager in a telecommunications company).

The following example of how a He saw the entry of a Her, and the interpretation given to the opportunities that She was given, elucidates the expression 'there are no problems':

"[Her entry] caused some commotion and argument among the laddish clique. They said 'Hey, it's a woman, now the women are taking over, in a few years' time they'll be in command', the usual griping. And of course she had to do much more than anyone else to show that she was up to running the branch and doing it well. Why? Because she was being constantly watched, and not only by the general management – because it may also be that someone there was prejudiced against women and clobbered her if something went wrong – but she was also scrutinised by her other colleagues, so that, unlike us, she always had to make maximum effort to get everything right, to achieve the best results, to show that a woman is able to run a section. (…). But she was also an exception, she found herself in the right place at the right time. Someone left, and she was the only person who could run that particular service … so they had to give her the job. This woman, who was in the right place, stepped in for three months and then they automatically had to promote her. And she probably deserved it, but I know that there were doubts at the last moment, they would have liked to move her so as not to promote her, but there wasn't anyone else to put in, so they had to leave her there" (Man, 56, agency manager in a bank).

There were then the tensions caused by age differences. Manufacturing industry is the principal locus of tension due to a combination of gender and age:

"It had perhaps the greatest impact on the older workers, those who'd spent 30 years here or even more, but the mentality in the factory is changing. According to me, there's no difference between a woman and a man. Especially because on my assembly line I've relied on *** [*the She*] because, you know, perhaps change is really a good thing. For me there's no problem, I can't see one. When *** becomes line foreman, according to me it'll be because she's better than lots of men" (Man, 44, skilled worker in a metal-working company).

"I'm really pleased, and I say it with some pride, I'm really pleased that I've put a woman in charge of the assembly line. That's not something which happens every day, because she's not much more than a girl, if you'll pardon the expression, 25, 26, 27 years old, who hassles everyday with old lags who know it all, who are 40, 45 years old and have 20, 25 years of experience, and suddenly find themselves being ordered around by a girl, who tells them 'Look today you've got to do it like this', who says 'Look, today you've messed up a couple of pieces because they've reported a quality defect'. That

74

certainly has an impact. Though it's natural for me to have a woman writing 'a meeting is convened, please come', I reckon it's different for a fifty-year-old, with a wife and children and a paternalistic, even patriarchal, attitude at home, who finds himself being told what to do by a girl, pardon the expression again, of twenty-six, twenty-seven, with five or six years of experience elsewhere, which he finds ridiculous compared to his own twenty-five years of experience" (Man, 36, personnel manager in a metalworking company).

The doubts came to the surface when the men looked at the newcomer and asked themselves: Is she the right person for the job?

"I don't think it was a woman-versus-man issue. In this case there were lots of misgivings, not only within the organization, connected with age, given that she was twenty-six, twenty-seven years old and had practically no work experience. It was this aspect that mattered most, even if somebody perhaps thought about the fact that she was a woman as well. That wasn't the main consideration, though, given this other aspect which was much more important in the assessment. A position of this kind is usually filled by someone much older and with a certain amount of experience. I don't know why the decision was taken ... anyway, since she became director she's changed a lot" (Man, 33, commercial manager in a textiles company).

In fact there is a 'right' way to enter an organization, as exemplified by the following excerpt:

"When *** arrived, she'd only just got her degree. So she had practically zero business knowledge. She came in very timidly, without stuck-up attitudes like 'I've got a degree, I've been to Bocconi University'. My relationship with her was of the type: 'if there's anything you need, don't hesitate to ask'. Also because there was no lack of contact. She entered in the right way, so she settled down very quickly in behavioural and human terms. For me, sincerely, man and woman are the same thing" (Man, 37, public relations manager in a wine-producing company).

"When it was necessary to create a management post, there were probably some doubts about the fact that she was a woman. Then when it happened, it was stressed that she was a woman, so that means that it had an impact, whereas nobody stressed this when it happened to me, as a man. It was emphasised because it was the first time it had happened, and it was a message that they wanted to give to everyone, that no one is excluded" (Man, 43, production manager in an IT company).

Finally, the other side of the denial of difference (i.e. discrimination) was represented by the admiration, sometimes excessive, expressed for women's qualities. There seemed to be general agreement that women are better than men, but are held back by attitudes towards them:

"Women are usually more capable than men. They're more precise, they're better at taking on jobs and seeing them through. They're better able to achieve goals. These are characteristics that make a manager successful. For me, from this point of view they are more capable than men. On the other hand, according to me, men have a different attitude to risk: men tend to take risks and this brings success. Without a spirit of initiative you can't do anything even if you're extremely capable" (Man, 33, commercial manager in a textiles company).

"Women in positions of responsibility get more rapid results than men. This is because of the characteristic I talked about before, dedication to work" (Man, 53, head of customer care office in a processing company).

"In terms of precision, transparency and clarity they're perhaps more conscientious than male personnel" (Man, 47, financial products manager in a bank).

"Yes, I have the preconceived idea that women are more sensitive than men, so they've got an extra gear in human relations" (Man, 34, bank official).

"I think it's very positive that a woman was put in charge of quality certification, because it's the kind of role I think women are better able to perform than men, because they are more conscientious, and today perhaps more motivated than men. This is something which I've noticed and have been pointing out for some time. Today it's easier to find motivated women to fill responsible positions than it is to find men" (Man, 39, quality control manager in a wine-producing company).

"Perhaps women are more peevish than men, but when they have to pull their weight, they do so" (Man, 53, head of customer care office in a processing company).

"When I've dealt with capable women dedicated to their work, I've seen that they have a determination that makes them more tough-minded, and so I'd say that on average they are more reliable than men when they put everything into it, because men have this attitude that they've got little to lose, whereas women don't. If they're intelligent, well-prepared, smart, they're more motivated to use those qualities than men. This is their strength" (Man, 43, production manager of an IT company).

It might be thought that there is a certain amount of flattery in these assessments by men of their female colleagues (female virtues are represented as: precision, dedication, conscientiousness, sensitivity, motivation, reliability). However, if one also considers the sense of challenge and satisfaction that emerged from the women's stories, one gains the impression that for these cohorts of professional females, work is also a source of satisfaction and identity granted to them either admiringly or grudgingly.

Matters are different for younger women, and for various reasons: because they are at the beginning of their careers, because they have grown up in a more egalitarian cultural climate at home and at school, and because work is now being taken for granted in their case as well. In this case, younger men are even more terse in recounting what they see as a non-event, the continuation of experience at school or a hangover from a past masculinist mentality. Career competition between young men and women can be intuited from their replies, but it is not overtly mentioned because men still enjoy situational rent or rely on meritocracy, or still buttress their positions with rhetorics portraying their work as 'male'.

It is now of interest to analyse how, when positioning Her entry into their group, the male interviewees positioned themselves as well, and discursively constructed their narrating self.

4.2 Men's positionings: the detached observer, the risk-taker, the cadet

To understand the narrative positioning constructed by the speaker for himself while narrating Her entry, we must consider not only the interview text as a whole – so that we can go beyond the initial reticence to concrete episodes – but also how the speaker positioned himself in his family's relational life.

We have already implicitly presented the first discursive positioning. It was performed by those men who, for various reasons, seemed largely indifferent to the fact that She was the only woman in their occupation, or wanted to minimize the fact, or at any rate felt uninvolved by the event. The distinctive feature of their narrating self was detachment, and the focus of their discourse shifted easily from the particular (the She entering a workplace in which women were under-represented) to the general (women in their organization, whatever the job).

For example, the younger men quite frequently said that the small number of women in certain professions was simply due to a disparity between girls and boys in access to technical-scientific education, and that with time the gap would close. This enlightened position, which avoided any reference to discrimination, is well represented by the following extract, where the interviewee is replying to a question on why there were so few women in his occupation:

> "I think it's because women started later. Certain professions, like programmer for instance, have only recently come along. When I was at school, between 1980 and 1985, it was a courageous decision for a girl to go to technical institute. So now we're seeing women entering the jobs market, though only a few" (Man, 31, software manager in a IT company).

Hence, because women started belatedly to invest in technical education, they were unable to compete in the market for certain jobs. This claim, which rejects the influence of gender on educational and vocational choices, has also been made by economists who espouse the theory of social capital. However, the 'detached' narrating self expressed confidence in the changes in gender relationships brought about by long-period socio-demographic changes on the macro-scale. Consequently, there was no need for the narrator to make any particular effort, because in any case 'the times are a-changing'.

Very different was the position of the male interviewees who described themselves as placing trust in women, and Her in particular. This was the 'risk-taker' discursive positioning of men who described themselves in proactive terms, who had assumed the risk of selecting or promoting Her, or of somehow assisting her career. These men were often older than Her; they expressed satisfaction at having made a successful investment, and they positioned themselves as pioneers in that they had been the first to bring a woman into a male environment:

> "Not that I'm boasting, but when I was on shift I was the first to pick a woman as coordinator. I was the first to make me a woman shift leader, so that when I went off shift, I handed over to this girl; who has developed quite successfully, and I've got on very well with these workers" (Man, 35, production manager in a metalworking company).

The risk of sponsoring a woman is that consequences may ensue from having challenged socially shared beliefs. Yet none of the interviewees recounted cases in which She had been unable to cope with responsibility and thereby confirm the stereotype of the unreliable woman. A particular case of the risk-taker positioning was represented by 'a paternalistic and protective stance' – as in the relationship now described:

> "She's a bit too laid back in the good sense of the expression. She doesn't get angry, she's patient, sometimes too patient. I intervene when the others take advantage of her good nature and get her to do more than she should. I intervene and I say to her: 'No, you answer him like this, and you tell him where to go.' She's worried that she should do it anyway, when there are things where we can only go so far and no further, it's impossible to do any more. So I have to say to her: 'Tell him to sort it out himself, tell him to call back later.' She's too helpful, she's incapable of saying 'no'. Or perhaps she doesn't know whether to say 'yes' or 'no', in the sense that she perhaps doesn't know the service's policy, so I have to step in. More than anything else to hold her back. She'd do anything they ask" (Man, 33, veterinary coordinator of a breeders' consortium).

This narrating self therefore oscillated between the identity and sentiments of someone who challenged gender stereotypes and invested in a woman's abilities, and someone who watched Her protectively from afar – and as he did so, often assessed her abilities with explicit reference to a wife. We noted, in fact, that in many cases these men had a wife at home, or who worked part time, or who had quit work to assist her husband's career. Comparison of the female professional colleague working in a male occupation with a wife in a more traditional gender situation expressed many of the feelings elicited by these women. Some examples follow:

> "My wife works; fortunately, she works part-time. She's English and she's a teacher. I say 'fortunately' because of what I said previously about my colleague" (Man, 36, economic manager of an environmental services cooperative).

> "Imagine my wife, who has two children. She could never have done what *** has done. Not even if she had twice the intelligence, ambition, etc. Having two children at the age of twenty-five, she devoted five years of her life to them. A woman who wants to have this sort of success, if we can call it that, certainly can't afford motherhood. It's an obvious drawback. If all women had careers, humanity wouldn't exist" (U28).

To be noted here is the discursive positioning *vis-à-vis* motherhood as an exclusive 'competence' of women. It is the narrator's wife who has two children, and maternity and career are a zero sum game which threatens humanity with extinction. It was therefore comparison with the wife – and implicitly or explicitly with the domestic *ménage* – that shaped the attitude towards the female colleague or the assistant who had made a different choice. This comparison became all the more significant when the narrating self positioned itself as the 'cadet': the analogy being with the younger son in an aristocratic family who assumes the principal role among the siblings excluded from rights of primogeniture. 'Cadets' were the men, aged between forty and fifty, who showed greater sensitivity and less ambivalence towards professional women. They often belonged to a two-career couple (Saraceno, 1984) and therefore shared the wife's career problems and family responsibilities on a more egalitarian basis. Understanding of the female colleague thus derived from the wife's experience of similar situations. The narrating self therefore constructed itself as more reflexive and less detached:

> "I have to talk about Ms *** separately, because she's someone who was already here when I arrived. She's a particular case, because she's my assistant, so she has a role which is decidedly important and which I'm enhancing. I mean, when I arrived Ms *** was mainly concerned with communication and training. The first thing I did was create a much more important role for her, so she's now in charge of personnel selection. I give her a hand from time

to time, when we're really in difficulties. And in fact she's now responsible for communication and recruitment, as well as social fund financing, the labour agency, joint courses run with various external bodies, etc." (Man, 36, personnel manager of a metalworking company).

"I personally believe that my wife is very good at her job. I've made every effort to make sure that she's not penalized by the family, we've got two children. I'm the husband, when she was due to go back to work after maternity leave she said:

'I almost think I'll take some time off ...'
'you won't take anything, you'll go back to work'
'but the children'
'we'll get some help, we'll hire a nanny'.

Perhaps I forced my wife, she went back to work on the exact day she was supposed to, without asking for even a day's extension. (...) Both my work problems and hers [the wife's] have always been considered. She knows what it means to work long hours; I know what it means to be a free professional: working until a week before the birth and then resuming five days afterwards. So when I think about those women who take maternity leave for two years, I absolutely do not agree" (Man, 36, public relations manager of a wine-producing company).

"I reckon that women are more reliable than men at work. I say this because I've sometimes been in the minority at men-only meetings. My opinion is backed by the fact that my wife works in the same sector as me, she's a manager and I have great respect for her [...] Women must equip themselves to overcome more problems than men if they want to work; though if they don't want to work that's a different matter" (Man, 43, production manager of an IT company).

In the cadet's construction of the narrating self, the family became the subject of reflection. The wife's work was a variable in the organization of the couple and in the planning of their children, so that the possible sacrifice of the wife's career was regarded as a problematic issue. The difficulties of professional women were assessed, not in relation to a female colleague but in direct relation to the man's experience at home. Figure 4.1 summarizes men's positionings according to their degree of emotional involvement in women's participation and their willingness to take action in relation to their participation. Therefore we can have a discursive position of indifference, in which both involvement and willingness are low, and at the other extreme the cadet position in which both involvement and active participation are high (the colleague is like a sister). The position of risk taker regards a female colleague as an investment, showing a willingness to act and less emotional involvement. Finally, the patriarchal position expresses high emotional involvement, but not a corresponding active attitude.

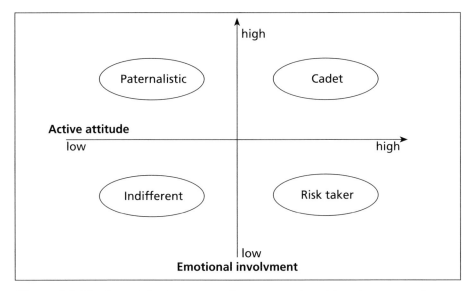

Figure 4.1 *Men's positionings according to emotional involvment and active attitude.*

We may therefore conclude that the men were rather reticent in recounting their reactions to a woman's entry into their group. In order to understand how they and their male colleagues responded to the event, it was necessary to consider the entire interview as a unit of analysis, and to deduce the overall attitude from the signals emitted by unfinished sentences, contradictions and ambiguities.

4.3 His reaction to Her challenges

How did the men react to the challenges raised by their female colleagues? Albeit in different ways, all the male interviewees referred to a double challenge. On the one hand, they stressed the mismatch between their female colleagues and conventional expectations regarding female roles and behaviour. On the other hand, they stressed the factors that made the women's presence in the organization as non-men problematic. The emphasis was placed mainly on the former aspect: the fact that these women had chosen occupations which were not traditionally female. Many of the men also cited the disruptive elements introduced into the organization by the entry of one or more women: for example, problems to do with the use of language, the risk of emotional entanglements, a rise in litigiousness, show that the challenge was carried forward at this level as well.

The challenge was usually taken up positively by two types of men: those whom we have called 'risk-takers' and 'cadets'. The former tended to admire women entrants and to encourage them, even if somewhat paternalisti-cally. The latter had instead grown up with less traditional gender models and declared that they understood their female colleagues' problems and expressed solidarity. The other men reacted more ambiguously or contradic-torily to the advent of women in their organizations, and they often more or less explicitly disapproved of it.

The men's reactions also depended on the type of challenge represented by the women: if we consider the five kinds of challenge (as symbolic presence, struggle, adventure, affirmation, and gender denial), we can observe the dif-ferent rhetorics that expressed the male reactions.

The challenge as symbolic presence – this modality was met by a positive and accommodating attitude among the male interviewees. It was expressed in statements which acknowledged that the female presence is now a matter of fact; and the interviewees – even the most traditionalist of them – sought to avoid criticisms of women. These men were respectful and appreciative of women who worked with commitment and capability – provided that they behaved discreetly and self-effacingly – although in some cases they disapproved of their appointment to roles with especial responsibility. A paradigmatic example was the male colleague of a supermarket manageress who first fulsomely praised her professional abilities and then declared that the company should never have given her the job, and she should never have accepted it, because when she had her first child, problems would arise for both her and the company.

The challenge as struggle – the reaction to combative women was very different. This was the situation that most clearly evinced the 'double bind' (Bateson, 1969; Gherardi, 1994; Jamieson, 1995): the paradox encountered by women in male work environments, where on the one hand they are invited to imitate the behaviour of their male colleagues, but on the other are criticised for doing so. Whilst men stress that assertiveness and com-bativeness are necessary for success, they apparently dislike 'typically male' attitudes like aggressiveness and power-seeking in their female colleagues. These male accounts consequently caricatured women as cigar-smoking, foul-mouthed imitators of men, and hungry for power. Interestingly, the attitude changed when the topic turned to struggles waged in the past to obtain now recognized rights. In this case the struggle was entirely legiti-mate. The behaviour of the woman who refused to wear a black pinafore at work (see the next chapter), and who was described by a banker as a "trouble-maker" and as "one of those hard cases", is today regarded as legitimate and is part of the organization's mythology. Thus her gesture and actions have been endorsed.

The challenge as adventure – this was the type of challenge that aroused the most ambivalent response among the male interviewees. To be noted is that the vocation for work so forcefully expressed by these woman emerged from none of the interviews with their male colleagues, who at most mentioned the women's helpfulness or their abilities. In the majority of cases, the men recognized the commitment of these women, although they expressed doubts that they could be successful in occupations that make heavy demands in terms of time and responsibility and are deeply imbued with traditional male culture.

The challenge as affirmation – the male interviewees frequently expressed admiration for this type of challenge. Many of them seemed to appreciate women who sought to be independent and who invested in their work, but without adopting what were called "aggressive attitudes". These men expressed a mixture of surprise and pleasure at the professional success of their female colleagues: although these were women, they have managed to identify themselves with the organization and to achieve the professional goals set for them, sometimes better than their male colleagues. The men's initial doubts were thus confounded and transformed into pleasant surprises. This was exemplified by an interviewee's story about a female colleague who had been put in charge of a laboratory to replace a man with scant relational skills. This promotion brought about a marked change in the woman, who had previously seemed dull and unmotivated, but accepted the new job with enthusiasm. She significantly improved the laboratory's productivity and its interpersonal relations. The admiration that transpired from these interviews accentuated the exceptionality still distinctive of women's presence in certain occupational roles.

The challenge as gender denial – in general, the attitude of superiors and colleagues towards women who raised this type of challenge was positive: if they entered the organization with a certain humility and did not flaunt their educational credentials, these women were appreciated. They were also valued because they could devote a great deal of time to the company, and because they were compliant to the organization's needs, given that they knew that professional experience was essential for their careers. Rather different was the situation of the female entrants who immediately sought to assert themselves, parading their abilities and adopting exaggeratedly male postures. They were disliked by their male colleagues, who stressed their inexperience, their youth, or their poor training.

The reactions of the men to the challenges raised by the presence of women in their organizations, and in typical male roles, can be summarized as follows:

Table 4.1 *Her challenge and His reaction.*

Type of challenge	Reaction of male colleagues
Symbolic presence	Condescension
Struggle	Discredit, opposition
Adventure	Invisibility (private matter)
Affirmation	Admiration, exceptionality
Overcoming difference	Appreciation or hostility

Overall, the most salient feature of the men's reactions was their inability to question the mainstays of the sexual division of labour: the 'natural' organization of the family and the organization of work were often taken for granted, and attitudes towards the entry and presence of women in male professional settings developed as corollaries to these axioms. Women whose professional choices transgressed this order might arouse the admiration of the men, but the latter did not feel affected by the challenges brought against them. We shall now analyse the discursive strategies deployed by the men to sustain the masculinity of their world and of their work. Patricia Martin (2001) uses the expression 'mobilizing masculinity/ies' to denote the practices which men – alone or in groups, consciously or otherwise, to gain advantage or merely for their own sake – bring to bear in order to sustain masculinity/masculinities. It is to these practices that women refer when they say that men 'are behaving like men'. When this is done in the presence of women, when it interweaves with work, when it creates bonds of affiliation and exclusiveness among men, there arise practices which create and sustain the 'male' organizational culture which excludes or marginalizes those who do not belong to that culture and cannot/will not take part in those practices.

4.4 How the work of men becomes male work

What, therefore, were the discursive strategies that explained and illustrated the fact that the jobs discussed were male jobs? The distinction between male and female jobs is drawn through language, and language does not merely describe a reality that exists 'out there' independently of the person describing it. Rather, it contributes to creating that reality through the categories that it uses and the meanings that it attributes to what is being described. Reproduction is always re-presentation as well. Consequently our discourses reproduce the reality that we describe, and they produce social effects. In other words, 'saying' is 'doing', and discourses impact upon reality. To categorize occupations into male and female is to represent a world in which men and women have their specific places. This discourse generates a rhetoric which disciplines men and women by telling them what their place is in the world.

For, example by writing about 'male occupations' we perpetuate the belief that such jobs and occupations exist. It would be more correct to speak of occupations in which the female component is under-represented, even if the circumlocution blunts the language. For this reason, we shall now analyse the rhetorics used to depict occupations in which women are under-represented as male occupations.

Our male interviewees used three arguments to construct the masculinity of occupations, and to discipline women so that the privileges associated with masculinity were safeguarded: maternity, working time, and the 'toughness' of work. Of course, these arguments can be deployed in very different ways, and in this respect one organizational culture may be very different from another in its 'woman-friendliness'. For example, maternity can be regarded as an event that has a social cost and incidence, or as a problem that has to be addressed. The toughness of a job resides in its 'objective nature' or in the social and technical organization which produces it. One therefore intuits the intrinsic political significance of masculinity-promoting rhetorics in terms of the everyday micro-politics of gender relationships.

The first discursive strategy that we illustrate is the one which naturalized maternity:

"But the problem with women is always the problem of pregnancy, there's not much you can do about it. It's obviously right to protect women, but if I was an employer I'd think very carefully. In her case [the She in question] there's no problem, because she has a grown-up son and doesn't want to have any more children" (Man, 33, veterinary coordinator of a breeders' consortium).

"When you give a woman responsibility it's always likely that she'll be absent for a while on maternity leave. This causes difficulties for the company. If the woman has a job where she can be substituted straight away, the problem is easy to deal with, but if she's in a responsible position, her substitution's more traumatic. Perhaps it's this that makes the choice of a man preferable" (Man, 30, quality control manager in a wine-producing company).

"According to me, rather than a question of competence, the problem of maternity is the reason why women don't have certain positions of responsibility. We know that a career requires dedication and continuity in the job, and these are difficult to combine with having children. This creates problems for companies. Apart from this, however, I don't think there are other characteristics linked with gender" (Man, 52, branch manager of a bank).

This argument does not distinguish between pregnancy and child-rearing, and it gives responsibility for both to women. It thus endorses the practice of hiring men, or women past the child-bearing age, or occupying low-level positions. However, awareness that maternity is increasingly a pretext for employers was also apparent in the interviews:

> "I reckon that maternity has the greatest effect on a woman's career, at least as regards prejudice. Because in reality, if it's not strung out artificially, maternity leave lasts for a trivial amount of time. But when there's prejudice, it's the factor that most influences the choice between two potentially equal people. With equal abilities, between a male and a female, it's usually the male who's selected" (Man, 31, liquidator in an insurance company).

> "(Women) may have moments when they're distracted. As long as we men are unable to have children, women will have to have them, and generally when they have children their minds are at home rather than at the office. Because I believe that in a working life, if a woman is not really materially present, I mean physically present but not mentally present in the office, out of thirty-five years, yes, perhaps for two or three years she's absent, I think that's perfectly acceptable" (Man, 53, head of customer care office in a processing company).

Hence maternity is a biological fact, and therefore a fact which is natural rather than social. Women are inherently handicapped in the eyes of the organization, and the organizational culture that makes this assumption constructs women as unreliable workers who cannot be given responsibility, and who are therefore only suited to jobs where they can be easily replaced. Thus constructed is the category of the 'throwaway' woman worker, while responsibility is an honour/duty reserved for those who cannot get pregnant and therefore do not have families. This is therefore a discursive strategy which not only naturalizes maternity but takes employers' natural preferences for men for granted. A-critically reproducing this rhetoric turns it into a widely-believed commonplace.

Other discursive strategies represented motherhood as a problem to be handled within the organization, and especially within the work group. How the organizational culture dealt with the problem of maternity and discrimination was symptomatic of greater or lesser gender equality. Absence on maternity leave was obviously a problem, but it was not an individual's problem:

> "It should be borne in mind that maternity is a delicate issue. I see it as crucial because a person with a certain responsibility can't be easily substituted, so you have to find alternative solutions, you have to make plans. I have an excellent relationship with two women who work for me. They're married and we sometimes joke about it, and I say 'tell me first if you decide to have a baby', because I have to plan the work, I have to know if they're going to be absent for five months. When they come back, I have to help them because they have other problems" (Man, 42, project manager in an IT company).

"As long as work is mainly the prerogative of men, especially at high levels, I think that women should do everything to get rid of these obstacles, and the difficulties due to their being women, and therefore time constraints, language, the ability to interact with others, so you shouldn't be in a situation where certain things are not said or not done because of a woman, since if this mechanism starts up, then you're gradually excluded. So I think you pay a certain price, and then it's up to the woman to limit that price, and it's up to the company to create the conditions so that the price is low" (Man, 43, production manager in an IT company).

Constituting a value of an egalitarian gender culture is a shift of emphasis from 'maternity' (as a biological event which almost exclusively concerns the woman's body) to 'parenthood' (as a social event in adult life) which involves the social responsibility of not only people but organizations. We have illustrated two opposing rhetorics expressed at individual level but indicative of two antithetical organizational cultures embodying different modes of feeling. The social effects of the mobilization of one or the other are obvious. When maternity is represented as a biological phenomenon, women have a 'natural' responsibility for reproduction and care of the family; a responsibility which equally 'naturally' puts them in a secondary position in the labour market. This rhetoric sustains a model of 'hegemonic masculinity', the expression with which Connell (1995: 77) defines the configuration of gender practice which embodies the currently accepted answers to the problem of the legitimacy of patriarchy which garantees the dominant position of men and the subordination of women. We would add that hegemonic masculinity is such because it is sustained and reproduced by discursive practices which seek to discipline women by constructing a subordinate social and discursive position for them. By contrast, a rhetoric which constructs maternity on the basis of 'parenthood' (for individuals) and the 'problem to address' (for organizations) mobilizes a more egalitarian discourse on gender relationships and social responsibility shared by men, women, organizations and institutions.

The second rhetoric deployed in support of the masculinity of work centred on the topic of working hours, which in its turn interwove with that of maternity and care time.

Working hours were the main factor mobilised by the male discourse as responsible for the gender structuring of certain occupations:

"Working hours are reasonably civilized in the technical field. But I can't see a woman with a family and children being able to handle commercial work, where timetables don't exist, especially in the summer. There's no Saturday or Sunday, there are no evenings off" (Man, 37, general manager of an agricultural consortium).

But working time is not the real obstacle:

> "We have a series of problems with female staff … problems in the sense that these women tell us 'I can't work later than a certain time', I want to work part time, and various other things obviously to do with the family. It's easy to say 'women' but then you have to see whether or not they've actually got a family. I personally have the impression that a woman may be very similar to the typical man" (Man, 37, general manager of an agricultural consortium).

Corresponding to the rhetoric that absolutizes working time – considering it an immutable given rather than a social modality of work organization – is a pattern which can be synthesised into the woman/male stereotype. As for maternity, so for working time, alternative concrete and discursive strategies are available. These are the discursive practices that contextualize working time within both corporate and familial flexibility, and within the work life-cycle of the individual and the couple:

> "There may be problems (for women) in terms of availability when we need people for overtime. And anyway, the children can be looked after by either of the parents, as has happened in my case. Sometimes I've taken time off work when there have been problems with the children, and sometimes my wife has" (Man, 43, production manager of an IT company).

There was no lack of awareness among the male interviewees that work-time scheduling was used to discipline women. In some cases this was stated explicitly.

As we saw when discussing the women's stories, working time is not always worked time: it may be facade work designed to convey the impression of willingness and dedication.

It may also be the prerogative of those who do not need, or do not want, to share it with care time. The following excerpt is eloquent:

> "For example, last Sunday, given that the weather was bad, I went into the office for a while, but I didn't have to" (Man, 52, branch manager of a bank).

The third rhetoric legitimating a particular job or sector as 'male' was what we term the rhetoric of the 'tough job'. Jobs used to be called 'tough' because of the physical effort that they involved, or because of uncomfortable surroundings ('dirty work'); features which technology has almost entirely eliminated – besides the fact that human bodies are more or less fit for such jobs regardless of gender.

> "Newspaper work is a rather special because you have to push to create space for yourself. It's not a question of men or women, it's just hard work [...] You need character, because you have to work fifteen hours in a row, or you come

in at four in the afternoon and you don't know when you'll finish, because at eight o'clock you've just put the newspaper to bed and then at five past eight someone goes and dies, so you have to start all over again" (Man, 54, editor-in-chief of a newspaper).

However, the concept of 'tough work' persists, although it seems more to concern a social form of toughness bred by competition, conflict and aggressiveness in the workplace. These elements can be reduced or eliminated; or alternatively they may be legitimated and extolled because they render the occupation more 'heroic'. Once again, this is a matter of cultural choice rather than concrete circumstances.

To conclude, we may say that – apart from the first reply to the effect that the job in question could be done by either a woman or a man (as evinced by Her presence) – the explanations for the small number of women in an occupation centred on three arguments: maternity, working time, and the toughness of the work. These arguments were conjugated differently according to the context, and they produced – as we shall see in the next chapter – organizational cultures more or less hospitable to gender relations.

4.5 Women? They're all envious!

We have seen that the rhetorics that construct work as male are rhetorics which discursively mobilize different images of masculinity. We shall conclude this chapter by analysing a discursive construct used by the women interviewees but which the men repeated more frequently. The men described relationships among women as conflictual; yet the conflict was not between the women and the men, but among the women themselves.

> "[*When Ms *** was appointed manager*], if I'm to be really honest, but don't say I told you so, those most hostile to her appointment were the women.
> Q: Why?
> A: Ah, I don't know. I can't understand it. I don't know what was the matter with them, perhaps it was envy that she'd got a job that they couldn't have …" (Man, 53, head of customer care office of a processing company).

> "One of the problems I had when there were more women here than men was that they'd form these cliques, they'd look to see what the others were wearing, how they'd changed their clothes … So they somehow competed among themselves, but they weren't only competitive in their work, they were also competitive in their behaviour outside work, about their clothes … I mean, they'd keep watch on each other. They'd even come to me and say, 'Have you seen so-and-so? This morning she was wearing a dress, and when she came in this afternoon she'd changed'" (Man, 56, agency manager of a bank).

Women are envious harridans, therefore. How was this thesis sustained? How did this image gain such legitimacy that it was never disputed?

The relational models that characterize professional relations among women in organizations are often the subject of commonplaces that depict them as connoted by unhealthy competition, jealousy and conflict (Kanter, 1977). While Paolo De Nardis notes that the most classic examples of envy are female (De Nardis, 2000), Donatella Borghesi (2000) argues that in post-feminist society, now that the enthusiasm of gender sisterhood has waned, re-emerging from the past are archetypes of female envy which are especially manifest in professional relations.

These images, and the negative judgements associated with them, contrast with a more indulgent view of male competitiveness. This may in part be due to expectations of more solidarist and cooperative behaviour on the part of women. These expectations produce different lenses through which competitiveness among women rather than among men is viewed, giving rise to a more deprecatory attitude towards the former.

> "She's an active and energetic type. I didn't get on very well with her for reasons of personality and mentality. There was a lot of quarrelling in the group, and I noticed it as soon as I arrived. I don't know whether it's a cliché, but it often happens that there's backbiting among women, they never say things openly to each other. Even in my limited experience, I've found that men are more candid, more straightforward. I don't say this out of prejudice, they're just things that I've happened to notice" (Man, 32, environmental operator in a environmental services cooperative).

Envy and competitiveness lie along the same emotional continuum relative to feelings towards others and the perception of a gap which is not accepted (except in admiration) but for the elimination of which various strategies are devised. Two principal features distinguish envy from competitiveness: the fact that the social distance from the person envied is perceived as minimal; and the fact that the envier does not gain satisfaction from obtaining the object envied, which is instead debased for him/her (Pajardi, 1998). The competitor instead gets satisfaction from achieving what it was that previously made the other person superior. While competition is widely recognized and valued by our society, and in particular by work organizations, envy is condemned, especially because of its destructive potential. Not surprisingly, therefore, these two sentiments have specific gender connotations. The association of envy with women has ancient origins (consider popular fairytales like Snow White or Cinderella) and it has given rise to various theories (for instance, the penis envy that Freud attributed to girls), while today the socio-cultural factors which strengthen the stereotype are obvious (Vegetti Finzi, 1990). The facts that (i) for long – and still today – the opportunities open to women in organizations are limited (and depend on men)

90

and (ii) that their social distance with respect to men is more circumscribed, encourage the use of different labels for the same behaviour according to whether it is exhibited by men or women. We therefore have two rhetorics, one appreciative, the other derogatory, which contribute to the social construction of gender.

4.6 Conclusions: the reticent masculinity

The striking feature of the narratives by the men was the reluctance shown to talk about male reactions to Her entry into organizations. Storytelling presupposes reflection and the isolation of a particular episode as significant within the flow of experience. Paolo Jedlowski draws on the work of Adriana Cavarero and Luce Irigaray to suggest that men's greater reticence in talking about themselves is due to their difficulty in "descending to the particular, with regard to themselves as well" and their "propensity to abstract and generalize the notion of 'Man' and to substitute it for all the differences and singularities in which the concreteness of humanity is expressed". Jedlowski believes that this is a cultural feature more to do with modernity than with tradition: "the figure of the reticent male unwilling to talk about himself results from a process extending from the spread of Puritanism to the split between work and home in the modern West, from the organization of factory work to the separation between paternal and maternal roles in the white middle-class household since the late nineteenth century" (Jedlowski, 2000: 102–3). Whatever the contextual reasons for this reticence may be, it is curious that the under-representation of women in a work group does not raise questions, is not perceived as problematic, and does not arouse concern that the preponderance of one social group over another may be a barrier against the latter's entry. How can it be considered 'normal' that some or other occupation is predominantly male and that a woman's presence is no exception, and if it is an exception, that it requires explanation? And yet we have seen that the exception is denied and that the masculinity of the workplace is taken for granted.

Sociologists have sought to explain how the social world is constructed as such and made unproblematic, taken-for-granted, 'ordinary'. Everyday routine is the suspension of doubt that alternative possibilities exist (Schütz, 1962a; Jedlowski, 1986). It is the world that appears to us directly and about which we do not interrogate ourselves; it is the quotidian reality that we perceive as objective and as external to ourselves. But the task of sociology is to explain how this commonsense world is constructed precisely by not taking everyday life for granted. It is for this purpose that we have identified the discursive strategies which a certain social group – our male interviewees – used to construct a discourse object – Her entry – and thereby positioned themselves as the discourse subject, the narrating self.

When narrator tells a story, s/he produces social effects and provides explanations and descriptions of why and how things are as they are. We have identified three discourse figures around which explanations for the under-representation of women rotated: maternity, working time, and hard work. The topic of envy versus competitiveness is a further rhetoric employed to mobilise gender in the workplace, attributing gender connotation to conflict within a one-gender group. The way in which these categories are mobilized discursively activates diverse forms of masculinity which generate more or less women-friendly organizational behaviours and cultures.

Masculinity is therefore a social fact, a social relation which assumes different features according to the discursive and material modes in which it is sustained and reproduced. Male jobs are such because they are socially organized on the basis of a male body and a social role that attributes gender-differentiated expectations, and by the mobilization of rhetorics to support masculinity and its situated meaning within specific occupational cultures and power relations.

Chapter 5

Living in Parallel Worlds

In this chapter the narratives of men and women are merged together and compared in order to see how, from various points of view, they describe the organizations in which the respondents worked, and to obtain a composite narrative on how gender cultures are produced in particular organizations or productive sectors.

The title of this chapter encapsulates its message. There is a science fiction story in which two world differ from each other only in minor details but only occasionally come together. Only at these moments of contact is it possible to move from one world to the other. Likewise, women and men jointly construct the organizational culture and the meaning of the gender practices within it, but their respective experiences of working life are sometimes so distant that they seem to live in parallel worlds.

We shall find that gender relations are produced in a wide variety of ways and in relation to diverse factors: the nature of the work and its organizational requirements; the relational system produced by people in their everyday interactions; and the culture of the particular segment of society in which a productive sector is situated. We shall see how a particular issue – for example maternity leave or discrimination – is treated differently in traditionalist or paritarian organizational gender cultures. Also organizations, therefore, are places where a 'citizenship culture' is produced and which reflect the conception of citizenship institutionalized in a society. We shall explore how different organizational cultures give rise to different conceptions of gender citizenship by expressing diverse notions of what is 'fair' in relationships between the sexes.

'Gender citizenship' is a metaphor (Gherardi, 2003) which depicts citizenship as a social practice, or a form of action whereby people in a particular historical setting contend over the meanings of social and legal norms and struggle to define collective and individual identities. Just as society interrogates itself on how citizenship rights can be acquired through concrete civic behaviours, so organizations ask themselves how the right to express gender membership and a diversity-friendly gender culture can be achieved in everyday working life. Indeed, whether or not a social practice of gender citizenship can be constructed depends on how an organizational culture constructs the idea of justice in relationships between the sexes. It therefore relates to the legal norms that guarantee/impose equal opportunities, translating them into personnel polices on the one hand, and into organizational culture on the other.

In what follows we shall illustrate the features of various gender cultures. As far as possible we shall let the interviewees speak for themselves, thereby giving greater vividness to the local expression of cultures and the people within them.

5.1 The resistance raised by a masculinist gender culture: a construction site is no place for a woman

Construction sites symbolize the survival of 'men-only' workplaces which, although touched by the female presence, raise cultural resistance against it. And yet increasingly more girls are training to become surveyors at technical schools, and ever larger numbers of female students are attending university faculties of engineering and architecture. Women surveyors work for family firms, private businesses or public authorities as draughtswomen or as construction site accountants. But they are seldom self-employed, and they rarely work as surveyors on building sites. The explanation furnished by the interviewees was explicitly centred on the gender culture: 'a construction site', it was alleged, 'is no place for a woman'.

> "I think that lots of site engineers have women working for them as draughts-men or typists, given that the bureaucracy has increased and you've got to write letters all the time. If a woman's good at drawing and can do secretarial work, then that's ideal. [...] A construction site is tricky for women because the work's so demanding. I can't see this female presence on a construction site ... it's not easy, you see. [...] For bookkeeping, office work, if women are really determined, then I don't think there's a problem, they can easily do the work. But a construction site is a bit more difficult because there are these men ... unfortunately the men in the construction industry are not a pretty bunch ..." (Man, 37, site manager in a construction company).

The men therefore affirmed that the 'male' nature of construction sites was indisputable. But not all sites are equal, and with increased female training and professionalism, especially in restoration work, there are now sites being run by women, and even female construction firms. Yet in the restoration sector, too, there are jobs which are viewed as pertaining more to men than to women.

> "It's a field in which women have carved out a role for themselves; compared with other fields they're considered more positively by employers as well; they even have responsible jobs, like my colleague here, who's a site manager ... so women have a good position in the restoration sector ... although

in some situations certain kinds of work are assigned to the blokes [...] It depends, it depends on the type of restoration. With stonework we prefer to use boys, because of the problem with heavy loads, it's heavier work than restoring frescoes or paintings" (Man, 26, restoration technician in a construction company).

But the women's narratives about their experiences on site assumed very different overtones. These are stories of work chosen with great enthusiasm and determination, of rough initiatory practices and harassment, as well as of strategies to 'prop up' masculinity:

"They were the worst years of my life, but look, this surveyor, who's a year older than me, we've become best mates; but he told me he was sceptical about women, so for the first six months he made me sweat blood from morning to evening [...] I was terrified when I saw him in the morning and waited for the first words he'd say to me. He told me later: 'I wanted to see if you'd got the guts; I mean, if you could resist for six months, you were made to be a surveyor" (Woman, 30, site surveyor in a construction company).

"Because I give a great deal and not everyone realizes it, this has caused a lot of bad feelings: there are people who've been working here longer than me, and even if I say that I've been working for nine years, they say 'I'm not interested, you've worked two years for this firm, so there'. But it doesn't matter. I tell you, I take my work home with me, not physically but mentally; when I knock off on Friday, I'm already thinking about what to do on Monday, what materials I'll need. On Saturday I go around buying the materials, I don't think many people do that. Perhaps it's not right, but I can't work in any other way; I can't separate work from my life, because my life is my work" (Woman, 27, restoration site manager in a construction company).

There were several ways to keep women off construction sites. They ranged from organizing the work so that women had no opportunities to learn, to undermining their authority:

"I remember that I had a woman colleague in another firm where I worked, and they gave her mainly fine work to do, retouching, although she wanted to learn more advanced techniques, like glueing, mortar injections, more complex procedures. Even though, I mean, fine work requires skill as well; even more, according to me, because you need sensitivity in deciding the type of operation. Instead, the other procedures are more technical. But this girl who wanted to learn, I've known her for two years, and she still hasn't learned what she wants. They've never let her do that kind of work" (Man, 26, restoration technician in a construction company).

"It's my mentality to find out who's in command of the team, who you've got to get on the right side of, who to keep sweet, because at a certain point you can say 'Look, I'm the boss, I don't give a toss about you, I can give you a thumping and you can't do anything about it'. And they look at you and say, 'Right, what are we going to do now?' And I say, 'You dig'. 'Where shall we begin?' And then the hassle starts, because you've got two options, one right and one wrong. So I say, 'I thought I'd do it this way, for this and that reason, though there could be this solution as well...' I mix things up and then I say to him 'What would you do?', so the question's back with him. Because I've had days when things go wrong, and I say 'We'll do this way', and they say, 'Wrong, you don't know anything'. So I'm caught out, 'Okay, I've screwed up this time. Do what you want'. 'We're not going to do anything', they say, and some of them in fact will spend the whole day doing nothing. I mean, I depend on the people with me. You have to weigh them up, you need this ability to weigh them up. Anyway, I've noticed that if a man goes to the bosses to complain, that's one thing. I mean, I've seen male colleagues complaining about a workman, and that's all right; but if you complain about him, you're a whinging woman. So I look at them and I say, 'Okay, forget it; tomorrow we change places, you go and tell him, and perhaps something will happen'" (Woman, 30, site surveyor in a construction company).

"It's great being on the site ... though there's not much you can do about the tensions between men and women. As site manager I've got men under me, and they won't accept the fact that I'm the site manager. You have to use a bit of psychology, according to me: so sometimes you have to play dumb, and you have to let insults go, because you get lip from kids even younger than you are, or anyway from older men who've been in work less than you have but reckon they know how to do something better. And you have to say 'Yes, yes, you're right', otherwise they'll block the site" (Woman, 27, restoration site manager in a construction company).

The management of authority is part of both the man/woman relationship and the young/old relationship where seniority concerns both age and length of service. The women's narratives highlighted the strategies used to safeguard the gender and seniority hierarchy, while at the same time legitimating the authority connected with it.

"There's effectively a strike going on at the moment. They work and then they slow down, and they gripe about everything. This is the situation here at the moment, and you try: you change their jobs, you give them something else to do [...] Because there's this male pride that has never been overcome, according to me. I've been working for nine years, and I think I know my job, but I'll accept lessons from everyone, even if they're young. You work for some time, but perhaps you work with older people, and they won't put up with being ordered around" (Woman, 27, restoration site manager in a construction company).

"You know, something I often do is look at the family situation. I see how someone behaves with his wife or how he talks about his wife – or his mother, sister or girlfriend – and I behave accordingly. When I hear someone say 'that woman always wants to give the orders', then I know how to handle myself. I go, 'Excuse me, what would you do?' If instead he talks about his wife as a normal person and treats her decently, then you say, 'Listen, I've got this problem, I'd do it like this, what do you think?' It's another way to handle them. It's taken me years to work this out!" (Woman, 30, site surveyor in a construction company).

"There's been some turnover since we've been here, and two men have certainly left because I was put in charge of them, they'd been working some years more than me, eleven or twelve years, and they couldn't accept the situation" (Woman, 27, restoration site manager in a construction company).

Any change in a gender culture that openly seeks to exclude women seems to be unlikely but not impossible. In fact, education and training are giving women a competitive advantage in this sector, and so too is their desire to challenge established cultural models.

5.2 A traditional gender culture: agriculture

The world of agriculture is much less static and traditionalist than one might think. It too has been traversed by extremely rapid technical and organizational change, and a great deal of investment has been made in training and research. Our interviewees, both men and women, recounted very similar work histories in which careers had been chosen with strong emotional and cognitive commitment. For the women, however, a career as farm consultant or zootechnician offered few employment opportunities except in the public sector.

The gender construction attributed to the farming world can be defined 'traditional', denoting by this term the sharp division between male and female tasks that prevailed among the clients of our interviewees, and which were consequently reflected in relations with the technical professions:

"The difficulty has always been with clients, not with my colleagues, but with the people I meet on service, because the farming community tends to be very traditional and narrow-minded, where it's the men that pull the wagon because it's always been like that. It's a community that has always been particularly backward in its mentality, from all points of view" (Woman, 33, agricultural technician in an agricultural consortium).

The perception of difference was very acute.

"I've realized that you've got to win respect for yourself. But it's very difficult, because the first time that you go to a farm, when you tell them you're the consultant sent by the service, they look at you and you can read as if it's written on their forehead, 'Cripes, the first breath of wind will knock this one over, who the hell have they sent?' But if a male technician arrives, they bow and scrape, and they say, 'Ah Doctor, what a pleasure', and so on, and they offer him coffee; if they see a woman, the reaction is alarm: 'Why on earth have they sent a woman?'" (Woman, 33, agricultural technician in an agricultural consortium).

"Something I always said is that at the beginning they wouldn't have forgiven me for any mistake, but a male colleague they would" (Woman, 40, large animal veterinary surgeon in a breeders' consortium).

It is therefore apparent that the gender culture of an organization or sector is actively constructed by the active participation of its clients and the gender culture that they embrace in their respective social worlds. Gender practices in organizations and wider society are attuned to each other and there is a certain continuity between them. Organizations tend to hire personnel who embody the culture of their clients' life-world, and which they are able to communicate because they speak the same language.

Institutional isomorphism also operates through social processes of reciprocal selection between the organization's external and internal environments. Just as shops specialized in particular products tend to hire male or female staff competent in their relative social worlds, so does a particularly male sector or one with a gender culture in which male and female roles have traditionally been separate.

For the men as well, technical work in agriculture or animal husbandry was male work:

"The manager at the time didn't believe it was work suitable for a woman. I think he suggested she should become a expert on female problems ... but then I think she cut him down to size. [...] Perhaps they were afraid that a woman couldn't handle work in the field. Some years have passed, and maybe things have changed ... Anyway, women are still in the minority" (Male, 37, general manager in an agricultural consortium).

The confidence of clients therefore had to be won on the job by showing competence and professionalism. Also with male colleagues, acceptance was acquired by denying difference and by adjusting to male forms of sociality.

"Unlike that woman who was no longer recognized by her male colleagues as a woman but as a male colleague from the moment when they began to respect her. They've certainly haven't stopped seeing me as a woman; in fact, as soon as they get a chance they still make jokes behind my back, and things like that, because that's what farmers do; you know men ... put two or three of them together and they inevitably start talking about it, because of male comradeship, and we know what that's like! So these things still exist, because the farming community is still down to earth, and consequently if two or three technicians get together, these aspects are inevitable, I mean the jokes are going to get cracked" (Woman, 33, agricultural technician in an agricultural consortium).

Learning how to work as a woman in these settings means learning how to use humour to manage the forms of discipline imposed on women by language.

"So, depending on the situation, either I joke about it or I put them in their place with a nasty look, or I walk away, it depends on the situation and the people. But these are things that they'll never stop doing. I mean, you have to cope with these things at work, and I don't think that it's because of the type of work I do, in which women are under-represented, it's something that you normally see in work settings, because you can see it with the secretaries – though not the accountant, because she's woman of a certain age, although she's not married ... but with quite young women at work I've always seen it happen. [...] Working surrounded by men, I sometimes realize it's better to laugh, even through clenched teeth, and treat it like the male 'slap on the back', because otherwise relationships tend to get difficult and you can't show your professionalism. So sometimes it's best to laugh it off and say 'The next time I'll come in shorts, so you can see my legs as well', and leave it there. It's not worth getting stroppy about it, not unless things get really heavy..." (Woman, 33, agricultural technician in an agricultural consortium).

Humour as a 'tit for tat' response was one strategy used to redress the gender balance. Another strategy was withdrawing from the competition and therefore refusing to engage in the contest.

"I behave just the way I am. I'm clearly different from a man. I've never used their devices, their schemes. If there's an apparatus to use and they want to use it, I never question it ... and this can only be good for the industry, for the work climate, and in the end, the project. They don't feel threatened because I'm not competitive, I wasn't like that even when I was young" (Woman, 40, large animal veterinary surgeon in a breeders' consortium).

The female interviewees associated work relationships with giving orders and with the difficulty encountered by men in taking orders from women:

"When you're dealing with workmen, they obviously have this instinctive, deep-rooted reaction: 'What, a woman giving me orders!' A young woman giving orders upsets them. I can clearly see the male aspect affected by this mechanism, and I understand that it's very difficult to control when a man's got it so deeply-rooted inside" (Woman, 33, agricultural technician in an agricultural consortium).

The male interviewees viewed gender in work relationships in entirely different terms: although the gender division of labour was considered a convention, it entailed that administrative work should be female, while technical work could also be performed by women:

> "There are no differences, but in order to overcome this initial suspicion they have to work better than a man … because after the initial mistrust you soon see whether someone knows how to do their work, and when a farmer sees that she knows her job, that's it" (Man, 33, veterinary coordinator in a breeders' consortium).

Hence the farming community has an ideal of the quasi-male female, against whom "there are no reasons to discriminate". However, it is also a community ready to reap the advantages of substituting female for male labour:

> "We at the warehouse tend to give more work to women. We've seen that it's generally better for a female grader to learn to drive a forklift than for a male forklift driver to do the grading. And this is something you see in all fruit warehouses. Because it's easier for women to do some male jobs than the other way round, perhaps owing to some psychological or cultural factor. If the man's very young, he'll do it. But when he gets to a certain age, he finds it difficult. He tends to boss the women around. Since we realized this danger, we've always avoided having men and women work together" (Male, 37, general manager in an agricultural consortium).

These narratives evince the pragmatism of the farming world, with its readiness to grasp the efficiency advantages connected with gender socialization, and at the same time to handle gender segregation so that the symbolic gender order is not subverted and relations between men and women are stabilized.

5.3 A tendentially paritarian gender culture: the world of information technology

The world of information technology was present in our sample in the form of both a large company with strong international business relations and a small local business. It was also present in the guise of self-employment by IT personnel who had left subordinate employment to set up on their own. These three contexts displayed more similarities than differences, and all the interviews referred to an organizational culture which encompassed the IT sector in its entirety, rather than being specific to a particular organization. It should also be borne in mind that there is a very high level of job mobility in the sector. We gained the impression from the interviews that, in this field, and in a small economic system, 'everyone knows everyone' directly or indirectly.

The IT sector was described as extremely dynamic and highly demanding.

But it was also faced with a potential crisis. It is a sector that has undergone rapid formalization, and it is clearly aware of its gender structuring: hardware assistance is male, software assistance is female; the Macintosh environment is female, the PC environment is male; assistance with accounting programs is female because it deals mainly with other women; marketing is both male and female, but when sales are made by telephone, it is mainly female. Moreover,

> "the majority of recently-hired personnel have been women ... because it seems that they have greater impact in the sales area" (Man, 33, software assistant in an IT company).

This is therefore an organizational culture expressing a set of values centred on merit and the intrinsic value of performance:

> "What matters is what you're able to do and what you know how to do; the important thing is goal achievement and the ability to fulfil targets" (Woman, 43, department manager in an IT company).

> "The mentality is that you have to get results, you have to create a need in the user, which may even be a top management ... if you gradually earn your stripes in the field, you can continue to progress" (Man, 43, production manager in an IT company).

> "You always work together, and everyone knows everything about everybody; this is essential at the beginning, because you have to create a spirit of unity, so that if I need help I can ask you. It's obvious that if I only do my own thing and don't know what the others are doing, I'm in difficulties" (Woman, 41, customer relations and marketing manager in an IT company).

The firm belief in the importance of the result led to denial that whether a man or woman had achieved that result made any difference. Meritocracy is a deeply ingrained value. Indeed, not always are the examples and the rhetoric used to sustain meritocracy particularly convincing. Are a woman who drives the company's car or a man working at its call centre examples of meritocracy and non-discrimination, or do they instead reinforce occupational segregation and tokenism? Evident in this excerpt is the contradiction between the narrator's persuasive intention and the non-reflexive choice in the examples that he cites in support of his argument:

> "I don't believe that there are jobs more suited to men or women. Here all the secretaries are women. I've only ever seen one man, and he must have missed out on the selection process. But in this company there are both men and women working in the call centre, and women drive the company cars; there's a woman colleague who's entitled to use the company car. Perhaps an attractive appearance is important in other companies. Though there was a

secretary here who was placed at the reception desk, because she was pretty and had nice manners; she was average, not the best, but she was pleasant" (Man, 43, production manager in an IT company).

Nevertheless, when organizations were described as meritocratic, the rhetoric in use positioned the interviewees as democratic as well. Proof of this is provided by the presence of female executives, and by the fact that the men could cite examples of women bosses:

"No, there's no prejudice, considering that one of our directors is a woman there's no career difference here between men and women. One of the four directors is a woman. If they have the ability and the determination to get ahead, they'll do so without difficulty" (Man, 42, project manager in an IT company).

"I happened to be on the staff together with a woman manager [...], I wasn't her subordinate in the true sense, but it was certainly a subordinate relationship [...] And I got on reasonably well with her. She was a woman with a lot of drive, perhaps too much in certain situations, but I think we created an excellent relationship of parity between us, in the sense that she recognized my expertise in a certain area, and I recognized her role [...] so she wasn't just any person. We managed to work well together for a couple of years, trying to find shared values, not in terms of human values but of work priorities [...] We managed to form an outstanding team on both counts. Apart from some minor rifts [...], I'd say we established an excellent relationship based on an aspect that I think always brings success: maintaining a certain reserve, seriousness, but with transparency as well. Transparency enabled us to work well together. I must say that by the end I had formed a very firm relationship with that woman" (Man, 43, production manager in an IT company).

The narrative style was not significantly different when the woman recounted their experiences of handling authority relations:

"But the other managers that I was put in charge of were all males, and I must say that when I chaired meetings and so on, I obviously felt this, I was aware of the situation; and they certainly perceived the somewhat odd situation of a woman giving orders to smart, capable, competent people, sometimes with more technical knowledge than I had. I was in the decision-making, managerial position" (Woman, 43, department manager in an IT company).

"Perhaps my situation is a bit easier than others, because my staff are all people of a certain age. All of them have been working for at least ten years, so we're adults who work together. I mean, I'm the boss in the sense that I set targets, but it's work … it's an activity that requires the others to be independent. I believe in autonomy; that is, I think that I'd have severe problems if I treated these guys, these men, like I was their boss (by boss I mean someone who says 'There's this, this and this to be done') … I mean, the work that we do is ... it's not the sort of work where you have to do things; it involves relational work with people" (Woman, 41, customer relations and marketing manager in an IT company).

The value set on results, the nature itself of the work, a 'youthful' and paritarian work climate, as well as high educational levels, were the features cited by the interviewees when describing their organizational culture:

"It's highly individual work, so that when someone joins a group, the colleagues with more experience can't give them a great deal of support, also because the groups have heavy workloads. So the new arrival comes in at a time of rather frenetic activity. This is a persistent problem at ***, although I've seen it at other IT companies. It's the problem of never being able to identify tasks effectively, so people are thrown in at the deep end, because the managers or owners don't necessarily have technical training" (Man, 33, software assistant in an IT company).

Membership of the same generation and similar educational backgrounds, at a time when technical education is no longer a male prerogative, gave rise to friendlier relationships where gender distinctions seemingly attenuated.

"I wouldn't say that we're all the same age, but we're very close, so this is another aspect; when you're dealing with someone who's got ten years less experience than you, an age gap is certainly created, it certainly confers a kind of authority or leadership. When abilities and experience are closer in terms of age difference, people are easier to manage" (Woman, 43, department manager in an IT company).

"I don't see differences in corporate responsibilities. Because here you need a good ability to deal with problems, a certain logical capacity, but also intuition. So sometimes the male approach is more logical, the female approach is more intuitive, and the results are indubitably good on both sides. You need a certain capacity for leadership, and in today's world I don't see a difference in leadership between men and women. Probably in a less selective environment, a factory, say, or in manufacturing industry, there may still be differences, but I think a great deal depends on education. Here 75 per cent of us are graduates, and the rest have upper-secondary school certificates. So these are people with advanced training or education. I don't think differences exist at this level, and I don't see any limitations. Indeed, I can frankly say that today when they're good – a man and a woman – perhaps the women is better, and she's also more determined. They're perhaps regaining their determination after millennia, the age when they were dragged along by the hair, and after the peak of feminism" (Man, 58, chief executive in an IT company).

Both men and women in positions of authority stressed the importance of collaboration, a participative leadership style, and involvement.

"Look, I believe strongly in the team. It's obvious that someone coordinating medium-to-low levels can have a certain kind of attitude because they can simply say 'We need to do A, B, C and D', and people who are developing professionally are often unable to say 'Look, perhaps it would be better to do it this way'. So the more a person, at whatever level, is motivated and sets objectives, the more they feel involved in an activity, the greater the effort they make and therefore the better the results. I believe in the slogan 'We Win': if the two of us think in different ways, we should try to find points of agreement so that I win and you win, not you win and I lose; the 'oppositional' paradigm is wrong" (Woman, 41, customer relations and marketing manager in an IT company).

"I've never understood, and I've discouraged it in every way possible at my company, this attitude of protecting your own patch, your own turf; saying it's my information and you've got to ask for it. Unfortunately, this behaviour is quite common, and I've always detested it. So if someone has asked me to help, I've always helped. Many times in my life I've worked fourteen or fifteen hours a day, at night … and many times I've done it as a favour for someone, not just out of personal interest. And another thing, I've never tried – and this I can assure you – to trip someone up or to play dirty tricks on someone. I believe that in the end this pays off, because you can work better with your colleagues, work better with your superiors, and I think this is the most important criterion" (Man, 58, chief executive in an IT company).

Of interest is the observation by a male interviewee that female working patterns can be classified into two types:

"Quite strong personalities, determined, hard workers, willing to travel. Perhaps something changes a bit when they have children. Perhaps it's then that you begin to see the change because there's another dimension to their lives; and you see it indirectly as well, because at 5 o'clock they have to leave because the kindergarten's closing. I've noticed two categories, not in the group here but when I've been at other companies; I've seen that there are women who hire a child-minder to go and fetch the children so that they can work late and get ahead in their careers, and there are other women who give importance and priority to their families. They do their jobs very well during working hours, and then they switch off because they've got to devote their time to other things just as important as work" (Man, 42, project manager in an IT company).

In the women's stories the relationship with the partner was of crucial importance for their careers. In this culture, however, when the men talked about career and gender relationships, they stressed their involvement in caring for the children.

"There may be problems in terms of availability when we have to do overtime and it's difficult to ask someone who's on part time. And anyway, the children can be looked after by either of the parents, as has happened in my case. Sometimes I've taken time off work when there have been problems with the children, and sometimes my wife has" (Man, 43, production manager in an IT company).

"We have a female director [...] and I must say that I've got no sort of prejudice (...) this may be due to my family set-up. Apart from when I tease my wife by pretending to be anti-feminist, or my daughter, I've always maintained that the same rights, the same freedoms and the same privileges that my two sons have in the family should apply to my daughter as well..." (Man, 58, chief executive in an IT company).

Just as important as the relationship with the partner is the presence of a female role model. The literature on role modelling (Ely, 1995; Gibson, 2003; Ibarra, 1999) has highlighted that women pioneers create the perception of an opportunity. The women who follow are often unaware that they rely on a role model or of the cultural change of which their choices are part. One of these 'role models' commented on the generational change as follows:

"She [a young female colleague about to go on maternity leave] told me that she'd been struck by this thing; she'd seen that it's possible to have children and to pursue career, and so she viewed me as a positive example" (Woman, 43, department manager in an IT company).

In this culture, rather than denying the existence of discrimination against women, the male interviewees felt free to address the problem directly. But as they did so, they revealed an ambivalence:

"It would be foolish to say 'Ah, things are perfectly identical' [for men and women], no, they're not perfectly identical ... but this doesn't mean that there's any obstacle in terms of career; and at this company, I can assure you that there's no difference between the potential career paths of a male technician and a female technician" (Man, 58, chief executive in an IT company).

"I remember very well that the company had some concerns about putting women on the night shift [...] and this may have induced the company to exclude women from that sector. [...] When it was necessary to create a management post, there were probably some doubts about the fact that she was a woman. Then when it happened, it was stressed that she was a woman, so that means it had an impact, whereas nobody stressed this when it happened to me, as a man. It was emphasised because it was the first time it had happened, and it was a message that they wanted to give to everyone, that no one is excluded. And then the fact that it was stressed I believe is part of the culture, in the sense that it's not very common" (Man, 43, production manager in an IT company).

As in the farming community, the issue of language, banter and jokes arose in this culture as well. But forms of 'men-only' sociality were not taken for granted, nor were they somehow imposed. Rather, sociality was adjusted into forms respectful of gender:

> "We're talking about language, not about harassment; at least I've luckily never heard of female colleagues being harassed. But language is indubitably an element of this type. There are women who swear like troopers, but the majority of them aren't like that, and language can cause distress. Language always puts someone at a disadvantage, a woman especially. Jokes and wise-cracks are usually made by men, and I don't think they idealize women" (Man, 43, production manager in an IT company).

> "The only thing is, seeing that there's this girl, we try to act seriously… [*What do you mean?*] I mean, a joke made in some way if a girl is present, the usual things of everyday manners. It's become normal for us to behave sensibly, simply" (Man, 31, software manager in an IT company).

A mixed and paritarian work environment seemed to liberate not only women but also those men who disagreed with certain features of an aggressive masculinity at odds with their gender experiences at school or university, or men with wives or partners, or again younger men still living at home. In this more paritarian gender culture, men openly expressed their conception of how gender relationships could/should be. They drew comparisons with both traditional masculinity and what they considered to be excesses of equality or the perverse effects of a 'neutral' gender culture:

> "Today the situation's getting better and its much more balanced than the dehumanizing climate in the United States, where for fear of accusations of sexual harassment and being sacked on the spot, men can't even make a compliment like 'you're elegant today' or 'I like your hair', because if someone takes it the wrong way you're in trouble. So there's a relationship where male and female colleagues can joke together good-naturedly; a woman … is just a colleague. In Europe, thank goodness, when working women have proved their worth and ability, they still care about being women, they care about their femininity. I always notice at international meetings the difference between European and American women. The European ones make sure that they're noticed as women. They dress well but without detracting from their efficiency, their tenacity, their competence" (Man, 58, chief executive in an IT company).

> "In other companies where women have made careers for themselves … perhaps they've got ahead by masculinizing themselves rather too much. It happens. So perhaps it's difficult for a career woman not to masculinize herself too much" (Man, 43, production manager in an IT company).

"The women I've worked with have been very determined people, perhaps even more so than men. They worked hard to achieve their goals, they constantly competed against men. And this may have blurred their femininity to some extent, so that I've always seen them as male colleagues in skirts" (Man, 42, project manager in an IT company).

The representation of the female in these narratives contains a double message. On the one hand, it affirms the possibility and the desirability of a female presence in senior management; on the other, it expresses awareness of the price that women senior managers have had to pay – namely masculinization of themselves. This ambivalence connotes the emotional tone of numerous narratives, by both men and women.

5.4 The visible glass ceiling: the retailing world

The commercial sector, and food retailing in particular, has always been regarded as 'female': not only because food, its preparation, and its emotional function are associated with the woman as nourisher, but also because women are the industry's main customers. Moreover, working conditions in lower-grade retail occupations are those associated with the female component of the labour market (low schooling, high mobility, low skilling).

Work as a shop assistant was the stereotypical job for the female interviewees:

"Even as a girl my ambition was to work in a shop, a clothes or a food shop. I don't know why, but I've always had this hang-up" (Woman, 28, shop manager in a supermarket).

The shop assistant also represented the intermediary between the owners and the customers. She therefore exerted further adjunct control (Grant and Tancred, 1992) and socialized customers to sales conditions and proper behaviours.

"The ideal place for a woman in a supermarket is at the checkout. Because, like it or not, a woman is always more patient than a man [...] She understands women and most of a supermarket's customers are women [...] Men are suited to heavier jobs. But they can get on well anywhere, at the counters, in the butchery section certainly [...] I see men behind the meat counter, working in the stores, fruit and vegetables, fish, the fish counter, especially the fish counter. A women behind the fish counter looks like a cook. She gives the impression of someone who knows recipes ... who dispenses advice to customers. [...] The woman is the final halt in the shop, the last thing that the customer remembers. [...] Cleanliness and order should be the responsibility of women" (Man, 29, assistant shop manager in a supermarket).

Hence heavy jobs should be performed by men while women attend to relational work with customers. However, circumstances may change the distribution of tasks, or a man may be elderly and a woman young and strong:

> "If I can, I try not to tire the women out too much, in the sense that a woman can't unload a lorry, she can't lift heavy things like crates of beer. I mean, a woman must do what she is able to do. But then if something has to be done by two or three of them, they have to do it" (Man, 29, assistant shop manager in a supermarket).

Career structures in the sector are relatively simple, especially in medium-sized and small shops. The standard structure consists of a manager, an assistant manager and members of staff. The career path in retailing consists of a sequence of increments tied to increasing levels of responsibility. But it seems that a woman occupying that particular role in that organizational culture was an exception, given that we encountered only one other similar case.

For the manageress, however, her situation was not so much exceptional as humorous:

> "When someone new arrives, for example a representative who's used to seeing a man in the office, he says 'What? Her?'. In fact they always go to my male colleague, who's almost fifty, and they ask him if he's the manager. Because it's not that we're distinct, we wear the same shirt, so there's no difference. They always go to him, the oldest person in the shop, and a man, so they always go to him. Being manager hasn't caused me major problems, because you run your shop as you want, and we don't have many outside dealings" (Woman, 28, shop manager in a supermarket).

Although, outside the shop and in the management hierarchy:

> "There have been meetings and I've felt uncomfortable because I was the only woman present. It's not that I consider myself inferior, but I feel a bit out of place. They treat me like one of them, though" (Woman, 28, shop manager in a supermarket).

Work to assert one's capabilities was once again necessary when a working woman functioned as a 'token' or a symbol for her sex:

> "I don't know whether it's a female characteristic, but in some jobs where women are discriminated against, they make an even greater effort in order to show that what the others think is not true" (Woman, 28, shop manager in a supermarket).

This woman's choice of career, and the fact that she had broken through the invisible ceiling the separates women from male managerial jobs, were unacceptable to both her husband (who worked in the same sector) and to her male colleagues with the same job grade. The reasons adduced to explain why women should not undertake managerial careers concerned motherhood and the irreconcilability of work and family because of working hours:

"It's pointless, because like it or not, some day a woman is going to have a child, and then ... Already a woman can't work the hours that we do, because we have a ten-hour daily schedule, eight hours at any rate, eleven, nine. I mean we have a strange schedule which a woman couldn't work because, as I said, one day a woman is going to have a child and then everything changes, and what are we supposed to do? We haven't got a manageress at the moment, but we've got someone with the right qualifications. I told this to the inspectors. It's not that she shouldn't become manageress but I find it ridiculous, because ... I mean, it's not an office job" (Man, 29, assistant shop manager in a supermarket).

"When he [the husband] heard that I'd been promoted to manager, although I hadn't been asked whether I was interested, he was furious, he wouldn't speak to me for almost a week. I really didn't want to accept [...] He was absolutely against it, and I said to him, 'Sorry, but as long as there are no problems, why can't I do it?. If I can't handle it, I'll just say goodbye and thanks, no hard feelings'" (Woman, 28, shop manager in a supermarket).

However, the organization of work was not in question, and starting a family was a personal choice whose consequences impacted on the woman:

"Because I want to have children, working as manageress is going to be a problem. I might try to move to purchasing or sales, but the two big bosses are there, the secretaries are girls, and I don't want to go and be a secretary. Even if the working hours are more decent and I might be better off, as a woman with a family, at least [...] Because the job keeps you busy from Monday to Saturday, eight hours a day, and as manageress you have to be present. You can stay at home for a week or take half a day off once a week, but working half days across the week would be impossible! So, I don't know ... I may quit and do something else, or I don't know, I could get a job somewhere else, in a bigger shop perhaps, but that would amount to the same thing in the end" (Woman, 28, shop manager in a supermarket).

Hence the kind of organization described by the two interviewees, and which from their accounts seem typical of the retail industry, configures a two-tier system: subordinate work is characterized by marked occupational segregation between female and male jobs; managerial work is culturally constructed as male work on the basis of different roles in the family. Long working hours are cited in justification of female exclusion. Not even, it seems, does the presence of two-career couples – such as the one described above in regard to the IT sector – counteract the implicit rules dictating the division of labour within the family. The work schedule is an 'objective constraint' or a 'problem to be dealt with' according to the organizational culture defining the employment relationship.

5.5 The small family firm grows and discovers women

In Italy, the porphyry (ornamental stone) industry is characterized by the presence of numerous small family-run firms. One would therefore expect to find a predominantly traditional organizational culture and a paternalistic managerial style, as well as the forceful presence of an entrepreneur running all aspects of the business. This expectation probably still corresponds to the reality of numerous small firms, but at a time when the market is rapidly expanding and globalizing, even small businesses are increasing their high-skilled personnel. Our research has shown that these small firms display lower levels of prejudice compared with longer-established industrial cultures, and considerable expertise in personnel recruitment. They express gender consistency by hiring women with advanced professional abilities but who do not represent a threat to the entrepreneur's authority and status.

There is no doubt that porphyry is of male gender:

> "My employer is young, and I believe that this counts for a great deal, because otherwise I would never have joined a firm like this one, with such masculine work to do" (Woman, 33, exports manager in a construction company).

> "So even if the material isn't female, let's say, neither is the environment female, because all the supervisors in the quarry are men" (Man, 23, administrative manager of a construction company).

The selection of a skilled employee was represented as being unconnected with gender, although the organizational logic behind it was obvious:

> "It's easier to find women who know languages than men. They're more inclined towards the commercial market, let's say, to commercial work. But we've also got a man in the commercial department, for example. It's not that ... it depends on requirements ... We'd probably select a man as a commercial representative, because he has to travel more, he has to put in more hours. Instead, for office work and so on, the women do everything that needs doing, although they go to trade fairs as well" (Man, 23, administrative manager of a construction company).

The women therefore had to earn credibility. But alongside these individual experiences one discerns a change in the market, as well as in the gender of this kind of work:

"In the ornamental stone and marble market, they find it odd to be dealing with a woman, no doubt about it. When I have an appointment at a trade fair, making the initial contact, they see me and they say 'Oi, what's this all about!', and I say 'Look, you can just as easily talk to me' – it's something I often say. It's because the industry is still largely in the hands of men. There's more flexibility abroad because women have moved into this field as they have into others; but in Italy there's still some difference as far as trade fairs are concerned. It's a relatively minor thing, but I often meet other firms at fairs, it's always the same people, and at the beginning it was a bit difficult, although I believe that on the whole they're beginning to accept women – both the customers, who feel more pampered if they're handled by a woman, and the representatives from other firms. So overall there's a good relationship" (Woman, 33, exports manager in a construction company).

The current expansionary and innovative phase for the firm and its market has created opportunities for both men and women equipped with new skills:

"I know the industry and the firms in it quite well, and he – my boss, the commercial manager – is a rarity. His firm was one of the first to have a computer program designed specially for us, who deal with just about everything. And we're continuing to evolve. We were the first firm to have a website. In fact, we may be going a bit too fast for the others involved, the quarry, the workshop, the work itself. The two owners, the two brothers – the commercial manager is the son of one of them – are some distance away from the ideas of this son and nephew. They realize that the firm's growing, and they're pleased about that, of course, but they also realize that the workload is increasing, and they see this as a problem. They say, 'Good grief, we were so much better off when we were small...'" (Woman, 33, exports manager in a construction company).

"The two owners sometimes feel somewhat excluded, and so they by-pass us, both me and my colleague; they did so especially at the beginning, now a bit less because they've got used to it, but it's still rather difficult to persuade them that women can easily do this work and get to know the material and the product as well as they do. But it's not a question of men and women. It's actually more a question of mentality. This is an industry that's going to expand enormously; it's an industry made up of very small firms, and few of them have the courage to promote themselves, to invest in advertising, in image" (Woman, 33, exports manager in a construction company).

The gender culture of a firm of this kind is substantially ambivalent. It resembles a meeting where the speakers still have to position themselves reciprocally. Needing skilled personnel and finding a woman who meets the criterion means that she is given space to fulfil herself. On the other hand, the fact that she is a woman is reassuring because respective power positions can be maintained. Various work-related 'talents' are attributed to femaleness but, strangely for an organization undergoing rapid change, no mention is made of the woman's family role as either an obstacle or a typically female characteristic.

5.6 Industry innovates and takes on graduates: the dual-regime gender culture

Italian industry is split between tradition and innovation, although it seems able to reconcile the two dimensions without excessive strain. In this section we examine two firms, both of which had appointed young women to positions of responsibility but which differed in size and longevity. The first was a medium-to-large sized company with a consolidated position in the market; the second was a very young firm undergoing rapid expansion. We shall keep them distinct in order to show the specificity of their internal situations when the decision was taken to hire the young female graduates.

In the case of the first company – the 'consolidated' one – innovation of its business strategy had entailed organizational specialization. The management had concentrated on marketing and on creation of a brand image, while also boosting technical capacity by developing in-house research and obtaining quality certification. To do so it had recruited graduate personnel – a novelty for the company – and among them two young female graduates, who were immediately assigned to posts with responsibility and autonomy. The search for highly-trained personnel therefore established a satisfactory match between the company's needs and the career expectations of young women who had made large investments in their educations and initial career paths.

The traditional dimension was instead represented by the persistence of a traditional gender-based structuring of jobs in the company:

> "There were at least fifty percent more men than women working in the offices. We've never had many women on the shop floor because of the type of work. The majority do clerical jobs. There are various secretarial sections: general management, the Italian commercial division, the foreign commercial division, the customer department. These are roles better suited to female staff, while others are better suited to men. I'm thinking about the area heads, for example, who have to travel around specific geographical areas. They go out on Monday and return on Friday.
>
> In production, we use female personnel mainly in the packaging department. This is because women are much more careful and precise in doing certain jobs. They're also more reliable. If you use men in a department where they perform dull but important work, they want to change, to find another job, which causes difficulties for the company. Female remain longer with the company, so they're more reliable. We've also got two women in the

warehouse, where they set up the loads. An area connected with production is the analysis laboratory: there, too, women analysts are more careful and meticulous than men, who want to change for something better after one or two years. I think men have greater mobility because it is easier for them to find work. When a woman's got a job, she has to manage her family and her work, so I'm not saying that they give up, but they have less desire to get ahead. They have this desire initially, when they don't have a family. But then it fades because there are other needs, the children, the family" (Man, 40, administrative services manager in a wine-producing company).

"Automation has reduced our female staff. But this isn't the only reason: some women have retired, some of them have got married. There were certainly more women previously than there are now" (Man, 39, quality control manager in a wine-producing company).

Not only was the distinction between male and female work taken largely for granted, but the form and duration of female employment in administrative positions was seen as subordinate to family exigencies:

"We find in the administrative area that if a woman has a second child after some years of marriage, she normally either asks to go on part-time or she quits. Recently, a number of women have left because their family responsibilities took priority. They had to make a choice: devote themselves to the family or find a less demanding job" (Man, 40, administrative services manager in a wine-producing company).

However, this largely traditional organization had seen marked innovations, which were described as follows:

"The fact that we've hired a woman as head of marketing, or I think of a woman like *** who's been appointed to an important post, shows that there's no exclusion here" (Man, 37, public relations manager in a wine-producing company).

"Because this company is expanding it gives people a chance to develop professionally, so I think there are still broad margins for collaboration. Then we'll see" (Woman, 29, quality manager in a wine-producing company).

"We don't have a significant hierarchy here. No, there are three directors, four middle managers, and some first-level office staff … But this has little influence, it has little effect on the responsibility that someone has, or the job that they do. And it also has little effect on how the company is presented, in the sense that the company is now establishing very important relations with foreign customers, so we're looking for people with good presence, who speak foreign languages, and who've had experience abroad" (Woman, 29, quality manager in a wine-producing company).

"The fact that they came looking for me, that they selected someone who had just graduated, without experience, as I hear happens in other companies as well, is mainly because they wanted someone new, creative, full of enthusiasm, who didn't have preconceptions or prejudices perhaps acquired from working for other companies. Perhaps this didn't use to happen because they preferred people with experience. But I think this is why they chose me, also because there was this climate of renewal, so that they wanted someone they could develop" (Woman, 28, marketing manager in a wine-producing company).

Three factors were cited in explanation of this openness to young female graduates: culture, market requirements, and training policies targeted on women. For example, a male interviewee interpreted the field of quality certification as follows:

"In a company that's beginning to develop this mentality, the head of quality is seen as a busybody, with all that paperwork. Then if the job is given to a woman, some people in the company are certainly going to regard her as a pain in the neck. But she's had the management's support. And she has a pleasant personality, as well as incredible will and determination. So she's achieved excellent results and the management is pleased with her [...] Compared with other sectors, quality isn't male, although men may be in the majority. I don't know whether female personnel have adjusted more rapidly to quality issues, whether they were the first to get wind of this new opportunity. I know that the provincial administration has commissioned agencies to run training courses on quality management for women, and this induced the company to hire someone who had attended a specific course. It's a great help to companies, because they can take on people who've already been trained. This has contributed greatly to the choice of female personnel" (Man, 40, administrative services manager in a wine-producing company).

The female interviewee's account instead stressed her initiative and her ability to be propositive:

"During my research I began to get interested in quality systems, and so I made some preliminary proposals on what a quality system might be like. In some way I volunteered to go into the question, and there was immediate interest on the part of management. And this went ahead together with the ideas of a consultant, with the suggestions that I made and requests by customers, especially abroad. And so *** [the company] decided to obtain certification. And I was practically the right woman at the right time, because I had to establish my place in the company, and luckily I had enough time to show that I could get things done, organize quality activities, also abroad, and so I was given this task. *** also helped me to complete my training. I attended a specialist course on quality systems, and in parallel with the course I developed a prototype program for a quality system at ***. I finished the

114

course and presented the program to the board" (Woman, 29, quality manager in a wine-producing company).

A striking feature of the interview extracts that follow is the match between a company seeking to innovate and the experiences of two female graduates and a chemical technician. These young women described a careful process of career planning which enabled them to find the jobs that they wanted and which would bring them satisfaction.

The young graduates told similar stories about their first entry into work, emphasising their ability to take the initiative and to innovate. The stories of both women began with choice of topic for their degree theses, and with finding a field of empirical analysis that brought them into contact with the company where they subsequently obtained jobs.

The chemical technician was recruited by the company via an agency. She told a similar story. She decided to study chemistry because she was intensely interested in the subject and then attended a specialist course financed by the European Social Fund. She chose between the two companies which offered her a job on the basis of their laboratory facilities, and therefore of the quality of work in them. She finally recounted how she had been able to change previous work practices in the laboratory.

All three women exhibited an intense commitment to their work and described how they had planned their careers according to the satisfaction that they would gain from them.

> "As long as I find the work so interesting and pleasant, I reckon I'll stay with this company. But I don't rule anything out. I might find something more interesting and decide to change if it suits me, so there's nothing to say that I'll stay here forever. As long as it's stimulating and I enjoy it, all right, but if the job becomes more routine, I may consider other possibilities" (Woman, 23, chemical surveyor in a wine-producing company).

> "I've been lucky enough to bring new ideas into a place which already had a high cultural level and a great deal of experience, so that it was difficult to get myself established. So I found two areas new to the company – microbiology and quality – and then everything was easy" (Woman, 29, quality manager in a wine-producing company).

> "Finding a job that you like is essential. I mean, for me at the age of twenty-eight the most important thing is my work, not a career, ambition, but my work. Also because if you study until you're twenty-five, then quite rightly you want a job that gives you satisfaction" (Woman, 28, marketing manager in a wine-producing company).

The work environment did not dampen the determination with which these women pursued their careers. These young interviewees, with their advanced educational credentials and specialized skills, narrated how they planned their careers and entered employment in terms not dissimilar from those used by their male counterparts. A new generation of women and a new order of intra-couple relations seem to be emerging. If firms are able to offer opportunities for self-fulfilment through work, a change in the gender culture is bound to arise even where occupational segregation still persists. Confirmation of this was provided by a man of a different generation from his colleagues:

> "This is something which I've noticed and have been pointing out for some time. Today it's easier to find motivated women to fill responsible positions than it is to find men. *** [*the female colleague*] is highly motivated like many of the women entering the world of work at a certain level" (Man, 39, quality control manager in a wine-producing company).

The internal environment at the second company – the 'young' one – was that typical of an expanding business:

> "[The company] was founded in 1989 and its personnel is very young. The management sets great store on recruiting young people, which is probably one of the reasons why it's stimulating to work here, in the sense that enthusiasm counts for a great deal. Experience certainly helps, but sometimes enthusiasm or the desire to do things well produces unexpected results" (Woman, 30, production manager in a wine-producing company).

> "The company has grown tenfold in personnel, sales volume, market and turnover. It's going through a growth phase. Moreover, making a profit is much more difficult today than it was some years ago" (Man, 33, commercial manager in a wine-producing company).

The hiring of a young female graduate in engineering and her appointment as head of production – after six months of flanking the director prior to his retirement – had produced changes and immediate results:

> "Previously, the work used to be much more pragmatic. [*The new head of production*] has replaced members of staff without formal engineering qualifications who'd worked their way up, and who had a much more practical approach based on experience rather than theory. From this point of view things have changed a great deal. Some people have left" (Man, 33, commercial manager in a wine-producing company).

> "Perhaps there was this suspicion at the beginning: 'What, she's head of production?' Also because I look young for my age. However, to be sincere I didn't really care [...] I've had spanners put in the works for reasons other than being a woman. Perhaps also because the results have backed me up, not because I've done something or other. If the figures add up, they mean that you're doing okay" (Woman, 30, production manager in a wine-producing company).

Setting value on performance and its attendant culture of calculus were reminiscent of the information technology sector. But in this case the firm's gender structuring was of the traditional kind.

> "Almost all the office workers are women, but in production the only woman is me, with forty-four men, so there are no women among the foremen, shift leaders and technicians in my department. But ninety-nine percent of the office staff is made up of women" (Woman, 30, production manager in a wine-producing company).

Ten people had been interviewed for the job:

> "There were two women, and all the others, eight of them, were men, and the final choice was between two women [*laughs*] ..." (Woman, 30, production manager in a wine-producing company).

This woman's investment in her current and future career resembled that of the other two young graduates working at the 'traditional' company discussed above: fieldwork for the degree thesis, followed by a job application, and then:

> "Then I got a job interview with this company because my name was in the university graduate database. They'd used this resource [...] So I was introduced to the company, so to speak, via the university database. There was a job interview, three interviews in fact, three meetings, and so we got to know each other" (Woman, 39, production manager in a textiles company).

Her motivation and attitude to work were also similar to those of the two previous interviews, and also those of her young male colleagues:

> "I enjoy doing what I do; I repeat, I want professional gratification from my work" (Woman, 30, production manager in a wine-producing company).

The trajectories of these young graduates were characterized to a lesser extent by gender. Their firms accepted the change that they represented; indeed they helped produce it.

5.7 Multinational companies and local cultures

Our initial research hypothesis was that the local subsidiaries of multinational or European companies are 'frontier' localities where the influence of a large-group culture, inclusion in an international network, and the long shadow of the parent company isolate the subsidiary from its surroundings and therefore nurture a distinctive organizational gender culture. But this hypothesis, we discovered, was entirely unfounded.

The organizational culture of the parent company was reflected in its local affiliates in various forms: strategic choices, corporate image, and the values of a mixed nationality management, whether actually present or vicariously represented by the local management. But the mismatch between the parent company's culture and its local-level variant was openly acknowledged and explicitly thematized.

One feature shared by all three organizations studied (American, Japanese, and English) was that they enhanced human resources by offering internal career opportunities to personnel who had previously given good account of themselves. The companies' investment in training indirectly evidenced this value in operation. Moreover, the larger size of these companies, compared with the average in the sector, entailed more elaborate personnel policies and more specialized human resources management.

These various factors suggested to us that opportunities would be equally distributed between men and women. Yet we found that a traditional gender culture still segregated the distribution of opportunities horizontally and vertically. There were exceptions to this rule, but they were precisely that: exceptions.

We shall now examine the interweaving among a blue-collar culture in a traditional manufacturing industry, values imported from abroad, and the experiences of women in occupations where they were under-represented.

For example, diversity enhancement was translated into local terms and incorporated into personnel policies. But when the results were presented, they concerned only a handful of women performing token roles:

> "One of the main values of American management is what they call 'diversity'. But diversity assumes different values and meanings in different countries. Diversity in the United States essentially means hiring ethnic minorities, multi-racial recruitment. But look at Europe, at Italy. Given that our company is strongly committed to creating a common culture, diversity is a value that we pursue in it itself, but here it has different connotations. Real diversity in Italy, as the term is understood at all our plants and because of the way it is defined at headquarters, is the hiring of female personnel. [...] Now, there are fifteen managerial posts here, eight of them for service heads, and there are no women at that level. But recently, and this I would stress, we've promoted a woman who previously performed functions, let's say, of an important nature, responsible for millions in reject checking, we promoted her, a big step forward I'd say, to department head [...] And another step forward, which is mainly my doing, we've managed to include a number of women in our year-on-year recruitment for the factory. I'm thinking of one woman in particular, who's already earmarked for a job as line superintendent, which is step towards department head" (Man, 36, personnel manager in a metalworking company).

Attempts had been made to increase the number of women in 'male' blue-collar jobs. Their failure is significant.

> "In 1996, something that had never happened before, we organized courses for trolley drivers, and we included some women. I must say it caused some surprise, because there's never been a female trolley driver here. But I don't think it was a great success. I mean, the women did this course together with the men, but I don't think it had any significant results in operational terms. Frankly, I can't call to mind a single occasion when I've seen a woman driving a trolley. There are probably some girls who know how to do it, but operationally the course hasn't been a success. Probably people were a bit bewildered" (Man, 36, personnel manager in a metalworking company).

The was a woman occupying a high-level post in this organization. Her difficulties are now recounted from her point of view and from that of a man:

> "Ms *** was given a great deal of space in which she could obviously find ample opportunities to express herself. But I don't know how many, certainly some, members of the management, all of them I wouldn't know, were unwilling to grant her this space" (Man, 36, personnel manager in a metalworking company).

> "There's no hostility against me, but sometimes, how can I put it, there's a certain closure against proposals that might seem too innovative" (Woman, 36, personnel manager in a metalworking company).

When the cultural environment is traditional in its conception of gender, even the most open policies clash with self-selection by women:

> "We've got what you could call a 'masculinist' mentality in the factory, in the sense that all the managers are men, and so they prefer to use men, also because, they say, women are going to have problems, they'll get married, have children, and so ... the senior jobs in the factory are all filled by men. Last year, we organized some training courses jointly with the provincial government. We also included some women, but it was difficult, and not just because the managers prefer men; the women are affected by this climate, they say that they're not suited to certain jobs traditionally done by men. So, for example, forklift driver, which is a specific job, it's not difficult to drive a forklift truck, but there are only men doing it; then the plant operators are all men; the welders are all men. There are some women inspectors, but only a few of them" (Woman, 36, personnel manager in a metalworking company).

The accounts by blue-collar workers of the same events assumed a different connotation of predominant respect for older age (but the more elderly workers were men) with the expectation that the younger generation would bring a change of mentality. It is interesting to note that the introduction of self-managed lines supervised by a team leader was cited as resolving the problem of a woman exercising authority over a group of older men, forgetting that social hierarchies were then re-established in the groups on the basis of gender and generation:

> "So the 'woman problem' doesn't exist, because in a group like this each member knows whether his job is more or less heavy than the others, because there's no longer a boss who says 'You go there and work'. In a group you can say, 'Okay, you do this', and if someone has to crack the whip, it's me, to put it more plainly, right?" (Man, 44, skilled worker, metalworking company).

> "I like ***, I like it as a company. Except that, I don't want to be a snob, but the assembly lines are culturally very simple. It's the women themselves: rather than unite and say 'Let's make an effort, let's go for it', they back off, because they have this idea that they can't compete with men" (Woman, 30, leak detector, metalworking company).

This self-selection by women, their meek submission to their male colleagues, seemed to be less marked among the younger generation. Indeed, we found evidence of the reverse phenomenon at another plant, where women put themselves forward for more highly skilled jobs and had their requests granted:

> "Women are therefore given quality control tasks in production, and they have spontaneously applied to become machine tool operators. The change of roles has come about without detriment to production, and on their request. Some women have changed jobs, although some of them found the work too physically demanding" (Man, 57, building manager, metalworking company).

> "Management had some doubts at the beginning, but then we started with the best of the applicants. The smartest girl went on the thickness measuring machine and got the workman to show her how to use it, and then she tuned the machine for him. The English engineer arrived, and this girl – I don't whether she studied languages at school or something like that – but she talked to him and showed him how it worked. And once she'd got in, the others followed ..." (Man, 57, building manager, metalworking company).

This plant was more accommodating to woman, although it too had its 'token' female:

> "There are no women in the technical sections. I'm the only woman among all these men. By profession I'm a mechanical engineer, and I think that too makes me a rarity" (Woman, 34, designer, metalworking company).

Unlike in the previous situation, this woman was not accepted out of choice, but in order to 'make a virtue out of necessity':

> "[The chief engineer] had left; and automatically – because someone had to do the work – I did it ... and I carried it through successfully. This probably influenced their decision to give me the job on a permanent basis" (Woman, 34, designer, metalworking company).

In the following excerpt the woman explicitly narrates her difficulties when she joined the company, and the strategy that she used to gain acceptance as an 'alien' presence:

> "This barrier of being a woman is not at all easy to overcome [...] I think that if you have to do a job where all the others are men, you have to be better prepared than they are. Because they ask so much of you, because they're all males, and doing jobs which they believe only they can do, managing, giving orders, and suchlike. A woman in this situation must always make sure she's got the right answers ready. Though they're not acknowledged, and you may even have a good idea but ... you almost never get any recognition" (Woman, 34, designer, metalworking company).

This theme of better preparedness, of greater effort, of being constantly put to the test, of having to prove one's worth, and of having to earn respect on the job, traversed all the narratives and was confirmed by both men and women interviewees. It was absent – or better, less present – in the stories of younger women graduates, and in tendentially more paritarian gender cultures.

Conversely, two contrasting values coexisted at the plant owned by the Japanese multinational: on the one hand, recognition of proven abilities; on the other, the invisible ceiling represented by ascribed characteristics (being Japanese) or acquired ones (educational credentials).

> "They called me specifically for this job. I said to them, 'But I haven't any experience, I haven't got anything.' – 'That's all right, neither have we, we'll have to work it out together. You'll go to France'. So I went to France, to learn, to understand what experience they had, and we gradually gained experience together, we grew together. When I had the interview, all the other candidates on the short list were males. They selected a woman and not an engineer, because all the others were engineers, and I can flatter myself by saying that I must have made a good impression, because they couldn't evaluate me on my technical knowledge since I hadn't got any, so it must have been my language skills" (Woman, 28, special coordinator packaging, metalworking company).

> "I was already at ***, and this post came up later. I know that they advertised for someone and interviews were held with men, only men as far as I

know, but they couldn't agree. But I don't know whether it was the type of production that didn't interest the others, it wasn't clear what was involved, whether it was finance or something else … There's another point: this function is usually performed by a Japanese. But in Italy we've got a woman, who's not Japanese, and not even a graduate either!" (Woman, 49, production-sales clerk, metalworking company).

But the woman's function was not acknowledged, and apart from her pride in doing a demanding job, there remained the suspicion of discrimination and the fact – not new in the interviewees' stories – that the content of the work was superior to the job grade allocated to it. Schooling was said to penalize women because personnel management choices hinged on educational qualifications:

"Another distinction is that women usually don't have all the educational qualifications, perhaps they only have a middle-school certificate, while the men who get hired have normally been to technical school. So there's a difference in schooling levels. A second thing is that if men are given repetitive work like women do, they'll do it, but they get bored more quickly. So rather than lose these workers, we look for alternatives if we've got them" (Man, 35, production manager, metalworking company).

To conclude, we may say that the local culture prevailed over the multinationals' policies, and that the gender culture of long-established industries with mature products reflected the gender structuring of the society in which the plant was embedded. The situation will probably change with the younger generation and its higher schooling levels, but it will need the support of company personnel policies and government labour policies.

5.8 Licence to compete: journalism

The gender culture that transpired from the stories of interviewees working for newspapers or television closely interwove with the nature and culture of work. Strongly individualist work, undertaken with a strong sense of vocation predicated on personal uniqueness, pushed gender competition into second place, replacing it with competition *per se*. Hence this was an organizational culture which by legitimating competition also legitimated open competition between men and women.

Confirmation of this somewhat bold assertion seems to be provided by the fact that the formation of workplace couples – and therefore of alliances – was condemned to an equal extent in both the organizations studied:

"From the company's point of view, if a woman is capable there's no ostracism against her. No one goes, 'God, women no, because they cause havoc in the newsroom'. It's true, though, that the worst thing which can happen is for two people to fall in love and get together, because this has a disruptive effect on the others" (Man, 54, editor in chief, newspaper).

"They may cause problems in the newsroom, and not only in the newsroom but elsewhere, because they get married to colleagues, as has happened, and this obviously causes tensions, and if she has a row with her husband she goes into a sulk, and so does the husband. This is a problem. We've had some couples here at ***, journalists but not only journalists, who've married office workers or other journalists, and this has created problems" (Man, 45, assistant editor at a television centre).

The newspaper was depicted as a demanding work environment which had apparently welcomed the advent of women, but where the latter still formed a tiny minority:

"Newspaper work is a rather special because you have to push to create space for yourself. It's not a question of men or women, but character is important, as well as curiosity and good training" (Man, 54, editor in chief, newspaper).

"Women journalists are usually more capable than men because they've had to struggle to get into this strictly male profession. Numerous women journalists have entered the profession in recent years, but I started twenty-five years ago and there was only one of us. I see that they still find it difficult, but not because they're women" (Man, 45, assistant news editor at a television station).

"Women first started working for the newspaper in the early 1980s [...] The first ones were the daughters of journalists and correspondents who'd seen what the work involved, liked it, and felt they had a talent for it. It wasn't just that women came to be noticed; there were more and better-trained women around, and I think that their attitude to work had changed as well. Today if women decide to work, they do so, even sacrificing their families, and this has created an entirely different situation" (Man, 54, editor in chief, newspaper).

These narratives exhibit a feature which we have already encountered and which explains the female presence in terms of the more rigorous selection process that women must undergo. Consequently, those women who present themselves for selection, and who pass, are on average better qualified than their male competitors. This feature seems to be shared by all 'pioneer' women. The argument adduced is therefore that 'they passed because they were better qualified', or put otherwise 'qualifications remaining equal they would not have passed'.

Work was described as an all-embracing and individual endeavour involving the relation between the writer and the keyboard in one case, and as a craft in another.

"You don't become a journalist, you're born one; either you're a journalist or you're not. I personally began to think about being a journalist when I was ten years old" (Man, 45, assistant news? editor at a television station).

"Ours isn't intellectual work, it's a craft. Making a newspaper is like making a chair" (Man, 54, editor in chief, newspaper).

"There's now this pressure by women because they feel that they're well-prepared, they're more curious, and they're more strong-minded. You need character, because you have to work fifteen hours in a row, or you come in at four in the afternoon and you don't know when you'll finish, because at eight o'clock you've just put the newspaper to bed and then at five past eight someone goes and dies, so you have to start all over again. We have a day off, but we work on Saturdays and Sundays, there are lots who quit. But I've seen that these women today are determined to succeed, to achieve something" (Woman, 48, newspaper editor).

"You need a good cultural background, but you also have to work with your hands. It's also a craft where you have to coordinate your face, voice and hands. Either you've got it or you haven't, because at school you can copy, in life you can bluff, but you can't bluff yourself, when you're sitting at the computer and you have to write a story; either you can do it or you can't" (Man, 45, assistant news editor at a television station).

"Journalism is not filing sensational copy. In reality, it's work you do day in day out, it's handling trivia, and you can only be a good journalist by dealing with the nitty-gritty. But this close link in the job between living and writing produces competitiveness in the newsroom" (Man, 54, editor in chief, newspaper).

The social dimension of power relations only became evident when the interviewees talked about how they had got their jobs and about co-option – a pervasive mechanism even though it was denied – or about how the medium influenced interpersonal relationships:

"There's always been a certain amount of co-option because we work together, so it's not easy. Also because it's work that's difficult to quantify, and nobody has ever been hired by a newspaper against the wishes of the editorial staff, because if your colleagues are against you, after a couple of days you're screwed, it doesn't matter how good an editor you are" (Man, 54, editor in chief, newspaper).

"Radio and television are nasty devils because they heighten this craving that we all have for the spotlight. Not only women but both males and females; we're all rather vain, and television and radio, especially television, amplify our vanity, distorting the personality and interpersonal relationships" (Man, 45, assistant news editor at a television station).

When the male and female interviewees talked openly about how gender was constructed in this organizational culture, they sought to convey an image of parity between the sexes. Yet segregation was nevertheless apparent.

"Women have now won a generic type of formal respect. But there are completely different attitudes towards them: I've always found this among my male colleagues. But I brought a baggage of experience with me, and a certain amount of 'fame' in inverted commas, and you can't mess with me. So I've been saved from annoying situations at work. *De facto* discrimination exists because there are only a few women in print journalism. There are a lot more in television, where physical appearance and so on are more important ..." (Woman, 48, newspaper editor).

"So women journalists complain that they're largely excluded from the corridors of power, so to speak. But it is strange that here only one of the senior editors is a woman. Not many women have got to the top, but I don't believe it's their fault, it's due to the fact that they are few" (Man, 45, assistant news editor at a television station).

"I'm in a rather paradoxical situation because I'm senior editor with a male editorial staff. Which is rather curious from a statistical point of view. The fact that I'm an woman has never caused problems for me; nor am I aware that it's caused problems for my female colleagues. However, this is not say that this is the general reality; no one would ever admit it, though, even if discrimination did exist" (Woman, 48, newspaper editor).

"They complain about some sort of discrimination. But I don't see it. In fact, I'd say that as far as work is concerned, or the workload, my female colleagues get off rather lightly, in the sense that they're given special treatment. Dangerous assignments, unless a female colleague specifically asks for one – I'm talking about this paper but it applies to other newsrooms as well – are never given to women. I mean, if there's any discrimination it's not deliberate but imposed by the situation. So I don't think that we men have any particular problems with our female colleagues. They may complain, but I don't think they're always justified in doing so. [...] It's not because someone's pretty or pleasant or available that they climb the career ladder, a woman gets ahead because she's clever and has balls" (Man, 45, assistant news editor at a television station).

In this organizational culture, too, acceptance of women passed through homologation which, in this case, also justified competition:

"I think that many of the men here consider me to be a colleague. This both pleases and displeases me, because I'd like women to be granted a specific status in this profession. Women make an extra contribution, and the majority of men don't realize it. Too bad for them, I believe the readers realize it more" (Woman, 48, newspaper editor).

"I'd say that we men treat her as if she was a male colleague, even if we're aware that women have special problems" (Man, 45, assistant news editor at a television station).

The ambiguity and ambivalence between equality and parity becomes evident when on the one hand equality legitimates competition and on the other gender is labelled 'a woman's problem'.

5.9 When jobs are feminized, they are taken by women: the insurance world

The insurance company that we studied represented an interesting case of generational change and a new form of gender structuring.

Only a minority of insurance adjusters in Italy are women, and this company was described as exceptional because it had two of them. In the years between 1989 and 1991 the company had hired a large number of new personnel, while also restructuring and making large investments in training. It was at that time that several woman were hired, together with a considerable number of young people. This gave rise to a marked age difference between senior management and the new entrants, many of whom were graduates. Previously, the women who worked for the organization had secretarial jobs.

The culture of service quality, as well as the relative managerial techniques, seem to have produced a different conception of the insurance adjuster's work:

> "In the past an adjuster was seen as a nasty piece of work who halved claims or even divided them by four, who shouted all the time and sent people away empty-handed. It was seen as 'risky' work for men, and you had to be tough to do it" (Man, 31, liquidator in an insurance company).

Customer orientation has produced a change in the image of the adjuster:

> "They've tried to change the image of adjustment by introducing women, perhaps also to convey a image of the service different from previously. It was perhaps for this reason that there were no women doing the job" (Man, 31, liquidator in an insurance company).

In his or her new guise:

> "The adjuster must seek to give a more efficient service, because he's the person who deals with the customer when he finds out exactly what he has bought with the insurance policy. Because at the time when the customer took out the policy he bought air and when the policy is liquidated he realizes what he's done" (Man, 31, liquidator in an insurance company).

The relational aspect of the work has increased because its service component and image have been enhanced so that it no longer involves merely economic assessment. This strategic reorientation has led to the 'discovery' of women, both because they are regarded as possessing better relational skills, and because female work in positions of authority brings with it what Grant and Tancred (1992) call 'adjunct control'. This concept denotes the fact that the number of women in intermediate managerial posts have increased because, by representing an authority delegated to them, they socialize 'difficult' customers or users to the dictates of the authority which they represent but do not exercise. In other words, they serve to inhibit aggressiveness towards a superior or someone exercising powers of discretion. Put more colloquially:

> "[Being a woman] may be a help in the sense that if someone comes in who's angry with me, they may calm down if they find themselves faced by an attractive woman …" (Man, 31, liquidator in an insurance company).

We may therefore conclude that the service culture has led to rediscovery of the so-called 'female resource', and that the organizational position of adjuster is female because it constitutes the classic closed-ended career.

> "Adjustment is rather particular because there comes a point when your career possibilities shut down. For us working outside, and therefore at a distance from company headquarters, we can either agree to transfer back to central office or our career is blocked, and this applies to women as well. So there are no major differences in career, at least potentially. I can't tell you what happens in reality, because there have been women adjusters for too few years to know whether they reach the 'maximum achievable' outside" (Man, 31, liquidator in an insurance company).

It is therefore because the job of adjuster has become feminilized that women are now able to enter the profession.

The narrative by a woman describes training in parallel with that of her male colleague, who joined the company at the same time. It portrays a strictly individual work situation, although this is supported by comparison with the experiences of colleagues of the same age, in a climate where the challenge of learning and youthfulness boosts motivation:

> "I was talking in the office the other day, and [the boss] said 'I did really well to take on two women in the office', because he could see that things are done very precisely, while men are often less meticulous. And then men customers are a bit more submissive when they find a woman, because they come in intending to bang their fists on the table. I have a lot of dealings with lawyers and prosecutors here and I've always got on very well with them because they have this tendency to pamper us, especially the men, because

we're known throughout the area as rarities" (Woman, 31, loss adjuster in an insurance company).

Career advancement was out of the question:

"When you speak to the bosses they say 'Work hard and you'll get ahead!'. But I don't think there's much chance now, given that the post of senior claims adjuster is disappearing. I mean, when they retire, they won't be replaced" (Woman, 31, loss adjuster in an insurance company).

For the time being, the woman's perception was one of parity, although she knew about the 'invisible hand' governing what she called the "decisive leap":

"There's no rivalry [with the male colleague], absolutely not, if there's some promotion going, or if they give me a bonus, they say 'You deserve it, you've been working like a maniac', I mean, it's not like that … not so far. But perhaps, if the decisive leap has to be made, I reckon it's more likely they'll choose the man, thinking that when I get married and have children they could have major technical problems. But so far we've moved forward in parallel" (Woman, 31, loss adjuster in an insurance company).

In insurance companies, and as we shall shortly see, in banks, the nature of the work is changing, and its greater service content, together with general deskilling, makes access by women easier.

5.10 Bureaucracy as the guarantor of parallel paths: the world of banking

Here the expression 'world of banking' denotes three organizations very different in terms of their operations but which display surprising similarities in terms of the organizational construction of gender. The narratives of the eight interviewees often referred to the banking sector as a life-world and stressed the differences within it, describing situations about which they had either direct or indirect knowledge.

All the accounts stressed that the Italian banking sector has changed very rapidly over the past fifteen years, and that femalization has been an important feature of such change. Yet it is not the only nor the most important one, because it has been accompanied by a silent organizational revolution: customer orientation, marketing, product differentiation, as well as the globalization of the economy and financial markets.

The change was also narrated as a change in mentality. In this respect, the gender culture afforded insight into how change has been accompanied by the persistence of the more traditional culture envisaging a rigid division between male and female roles. For this reason we use the metaphor of 'modernization' to define the gender culture. Modernization has engendered the bureaucratic model as the everyday exercise of legal-rational power which comes about without superseding the legacy of traditional power. Thus the banking world expresses emergent femalization and the expectation that it will soon affect even the highest levels of the organization. At the same time, it comprises considerable ambivalence of behaviour and attitudes, as well as laying down parallel paths not so much for men and women – as a traditional gender culture would have them – but for males and females according to their attitude to work.

Indeed, the second feature of the Italian banking sector is its marked occupational segregation of women (both female clerical and managerial staff are few and far between). Bank workers wishing to rise to senior positions must emit clear signals of their interest in pursuing a career. The male interviewees not only confirmed the existence of this behavioural requirement but extended it to women as well. Three career paths were described:

- the path pursued by personnel who had taken the high road of career advancement and actively constructed their paths;
- that of personnel who could not or did not want to take the high road but instead valued extrinsic features of their work (working hours, job security, etc.);
- the traditionally female path of women with families and scant investment in their work, the so-called 'mommy track' (Benshop and Dooreward, 1998).

While the first and the last path used traditionally to be male and female, a third one has now appeared. It is 'neutral' in the sense that it differs from the two previous ones and is followed by both men and women working for 'flat' or 'lean' organizations.

The following excerpts illustrate how the interviewees described the modernization of the banking sector:

"I remember the first case, which caused a sensation at the time because when you got married, you were automatically dismissed, you had to leave the bank, and the first woman who sued the C*** to keep her job won her case. I remember it must have been '64 or '65" (Man, 56, agency manager in a bank).

"The first woman to be appointed a branch manager caused a stir, also at the bank, though everyone knew that she was competent and knew the service perfectly. She wasn't married so she was able to devote herself body and soul to her job. But perhaps it caused a greater stir among the customers, because when people came into the bank and said 'I want to speak to the director', and a woman came, at the beginning the customers were suspicious. Women against women even!" (Man, 56, agency manager in a bank).

The diffidence of customers towards women was an argument frequently used to legitimize the maleness of managerial positions. It was related in particular to outlying bank branches and to a traditional mentality:

"You have to select clients of a certain type [poorly educated] with whom you communicate with the back-slapping routine ... I think a male functionary is better able to deal with customers like this" (Man, 34, bank official).

"In some cases there have been customers who say 'I don't talk about money with women" (Woman, 36, bank official).

Banks have changed their attitude, however, as again symbolized by the figure of the customer:

"The way customers approach the bank has changed, because they used to come into the bank cap in hand ... Now you have to go out and get your customers."

But the true symbol of this change in gender relationships is the 'black pinafore', which banks once required women employees to wear to conceal a still alien femaleness. A female and a male interviewee recounted the practice as follows:

"At the beginning there was a quite ridiculous episode: they asked me (after I'd been there a month) to take my measurements for a pinafore to be made ... this was fifteen years ago ('85 or '86) and the women still wore pinafores ... I told them that I'd never wear one ... and anyway my female colleagues didn't wear them ... in the end the pinafore wasn't made and the practice fell into disuse" (Woman, 36, bank official).

"A colleague told me that she was working at the time in the bookkeeping section, where they still used perforated cards. So there were these women who did the perforating, around fifteen or twenty of them. There were no customers at all, but these women had to wear black pinafores, because if the director passed by and you weren't wearing a black pinafore, he'd send you home because you had to wear a black pinafore: that was the fashion, ha ha ha! [...] Another one came, and she was a bit of a rebel. At first she wore the black pinafore, and then she dumped it and came to work in jeans and a t-shirt, infuriating the director, because he was of the sort who like men to wear ties. This woman who refused to wear a pinafore created some problems ..." (Man, 56, agency manager in a bank).

While the pinafore – a symbol of a mentality that existed until quite recently – was superseded with relative tranquillity, the progressive femalization of banks was described in different terms by the male and female interviewees:

"The bank has adjusted to these changes, probably because there are rather fewer male employees than previously, so that the number of women has increased. But at the same it was found that there was this somewhat old-fashioned mentality that customers liked being served by women, that perhaps female staff are better suited to doing repetitive, routine work because they are interested in other things. This – or better this belief that women behave differently – has contributed to the change. So woman have been appointed directors, not to make 'a virtue out of necessity' but as part of a non-traumatic change process. Giving deserved recognition to people who work with dedication, who make an effectively useful contribution, who set themselves really significant goals ... hasn't been imposed on us, it's a matter of evolution and adjustment" (Man, 47, final products manager in a bank).

"It may be a coincidence, but we appoint more women than men. The banking sector has been abandoned by men to some extent, because they look for opportunities elsewhere, with the same professional status but better pay. So [banking] has been somewhat deserted by men [...] You can see this in all sectors, and not just banking. Perhaps banks have been affected more rapidly, because male employment has decreased, this is a matter of fact and I can tell you it with confidence because I've got the figures. Men are more likely to prefer other jobs, perhaps with private companies offering opportunities to work abroad" (Woman, 36, branch manager in a bank).

The bureaucratic model has therefore enabled more women to enter the banking sector after apparently performing better in entrance examinations. But the expected results in terms of career advancement are still not apparent. Besides this confidence in more or less automatic progress is the symptomatic fact that the few women today in executive posts stress that it is necessary to signal an interest in pursuing a career. This was confirmed by the male interviewees:

"My aim was to become an executive ... I wanted to know what I had to do and how long it would take [...] After some time I told my superiors about my intentions. I put my cards on the table and asked for a suitable course" (Woman, 36, bank official).

"I believe we create our own opportunities; I mean, we often confuse the opportunities that we want to create with those that we want others to create for us. I've always known that I wanted to achieve something extra, so I've always fought to obtain this something extra. Expectations are practically the goals that we must set ourselves" (Woman, 36, branch manager in a bank).

The parallel paths followed by men and women who expressed an interest in pursuing a career, or who conversely did not, were described as follows:

"Work entry depends on women, on the fact that they want to take on these male jobs (I'm single, I don't have children) ... when a woman wants to have a child, I won't say she's finished but she's certainly strongly penalized" (Woman, 36, bank official).

"I'm talking about a certain kind of woman who wants to achieve something in the world of work, because for example I have loads of colleagues who don't want to follow a schedule from morning to evening, they finish at four o'clock and think no more about it. But I think that a woman who wants to carve out a space for herself or wants to achieve a more important position in the company is more determined, she's more intuitive, less rigid, she knows how to handle herself in any situation" (Woman, 44, brand manager in a bank).

"They're happy they've got good jobs and that's all … They don't have careers because they don't want them" (Woman, 59, inspector in a bank).

But this plurality of career paths concerned both female and male choices:

"It's a question of how the work is perceived, everything depends on the initial motivation. I work in a bank because I can't do anything else. It's not that they haven't offered me opportunities, but I took this job in the same way as I'd have taken any other job, because it suited me to have a couple of quid in my pocket at the end of the month … If I instead wanted to do a job that gave me something extra, there's training available for both men and women, to the same extent and without exceptions" (Man, 47, final products manager in a bank).

The dictum 'where there's a will there's a way' therefore seemed to be generally accepted in this organizational culture. However, it was equally well-known and frequently reported that when women returned from maternity leave, they did not get their jobs back: as in the game of snakes and ladders, they had to start again from the beginning:

"[When I returned from maternity leave] they moved me to another job. Before I'd worked in *** […] They asked my if I minded not returning to my old job. I said 'No, no, I understand completely, I'll do whatever you want'. I knew that I couldn't take anything for granted. Anyway, they didn't downgrade me" (Woman, 59, inspector in a bank).

"Then there's this problem that when you've been six or seven years at the bank, been on training courses and got experience, you get married, have a child, and everything falls apart. There's nothing you can do about, even if they tell you otherwise, there's absolutely nothing you can do! I seen my female colleagues when they come back from maternity leave, and none of them has returned to the job she had before; unless they'd been at the cash till, so they went back to the till" (Woman, 44, brand manager in a bank).

Some female interviewees also perceived discrimination in the fact that young men were offered more training opportunities than young women.

We may conclude by saying that the principles of transparency and universalism regulating the banks' internal labour markets have led to the femalization of the sector and modernization of the gender culture. Although this may have reduced vertical segregation, traditional cultural factors still confine women to female jobs. Alongside these factors are new ones to do with the femalization of organizational positions which give rise to more service work and therefore more 'female' work.

5.11 A paritarian gender culture: desk work

Not all white-collar jobs are the same. The main differences among them stem from the relation with the organization in which they are undertaken, and in particular from the system of contractual guarantees that regulate the employment relationship. We have seen that recruitment procedures and career allocations in the banking sector produced several employment paths which proceeded in parallel. In the case now examined, employees of two recently-privatized state enterprises narrate how the gender of these organizations was constructed by the system regulating entry, and which related the organizations with the external environment and the political system in particular.

The gender of these organizations was described in terms of two broad categories of work and career path: secretaries and switchboard operators did traditionally and culturally female work; the men did 'gender-neutral' deskwork and managerial work:

"I see the female environment in this company as represented by secretarial work. It's also a question of numbers: the majority of women here do clerical jobs. Which is simple, tranquil work without responsibilities … apart from some rare cases where a woman stands out from the crowd, someone who effectively has responsibilities. When I think of male work I think of people who … have some responsibility, initiative, choice" (Woman, 37, head of the commercial office in a processing company).

"The first selection examinations brought the first women into the company, and they were given equal status and treatment with men. I don't think that since I've been here there've been preferences for either men or women […] I can say this with confidence because ours is deskwork […] it's not work that discriminates between being done by a man or a woman, it's work that can be done by both: it's office work, right?" (Man, 53, head of the customer care office in a processing company).

"Unfortunately, recommendations and political contacts still count for a great deal. Things are changing a bit now ... but I get the impression that there's no direct and proportional relationship between a person's work and his or her career" (Woman, 37, head of the commercial office in a processing company).

"Training remaining equal, a man gets further ahead than a woman. This happens in ninety percent of cases. Even at this company, with its large number of women employees, the senior posts are almost always filled by men" (Man, 38, shift foreman, telecommunications company).

The system of competitive entrance examinations was regarded as a guarantee for women entrants, who were apparently more successful. This better performance was explained in terms of relational skills:

"I say 'Let's take an admission exam'. There are ten candidates, five women and five men. The first five are women. I don't know, they've got an extra gear, they're able to express themselves better, they're better able to exploit what little they have [...] So you say, 'They've probably got a different way of presenting themselves', they know how to handle people. I don't know why, we men have this difficulty in presenting ourselves" (Man, 53, head of the customer care office in a processing company).

Consequently, there was substantial parity between men and women in office work. Those women interviewees who had moved up to more responsible positions said that it was by virtue of a meritocratic and transparent system:

"I'd say that what has been given me has always come easily, I've never had to ask, or put myself forward, in the sense that I've always done my work, and my work has been appreciated, I think that it's been fair recognition. Perhaps it's because I moved up when the struggle for parity between men and women, for equal wages, was going on. This was between '63 and '68 when things changed. I've never felt that I've been passed over merely because I'm a woman" (Woman, 52, section head in a telecommunications company).

"I think it's better for the coordinator to be chosen from the group, rather than have someone come in from outside and upset everything. She was the most suitable person in the group, and there were men in it as well" (Man, 38, shift foreman, telecommunications company).

The first level of responsibility therefore required a certain amount of commitment, but the gender culture had by now taken the presence of female office heads for granted. However, a female engineer was accepted differently by her older male colleagues:

134

"There've recently been a lot of women in *** levels, which incidentally are quite low. Compared with other women they have to show greater dedication to the company, in the sense that they must do more than women who perhaps have the home and the family on their minds. Besides knowing the work, which obviously matters, it's important to be willing to take on these roles" (Man, 38, shift foreman in a telecommunications company).

"There was no such thing as a woman engineer. Around a year ago my boss told me he didn't know what to call me ... so I told him to call me whatever he liked, but I wouldn't put up with discrimination. Since then he's called me 'Engineer ***', but he often forgets and begins a sentence with Miss ... then he corrects himself" (Woman, 37, head of the commercial office in a processing company).

The interviewees described a form of cultural friction at executive levels or in typically male professions:

"There are other roles at our company filled by women, and they've got on just as well as the men, if not better. A woman with responsibility gets results more rapidly than men. This is because of the characteristic I talked about earlier, their dedication to work. But here, as in other companies, there's this belief from the past that certain positions should be filled by men. I don't know what the explanation is. I'd say it's a hangover from masculinism. Things here have changed since fifteen years ago: certain roles are filled by women. The percentage is not what it should be, but there's a tendency to assign responsibility to women" (Man, 48, plant and maintenance manager in a telecommunications company).

The explanation was the co-option mechanism:

"Promotions are decided by senior management, although the rank and file can boost someone's image and help them in their career. But normally it's senior management that decides, and seeing that it consists mainly of men, the situation I've described arises. Except in cases where a woman has proved her worth much more than her male colleagues. According to me, it depends much more on this than on a clinical assessment of potential. There's this masculinism at work, said without negative connotations, which leads to men being preferred to women" (Man, 48, plant and maintenance manager, telecommunications company).

Gaining promotion was described as an unremitting battle, but when it was won, the fruits of victory turned sour:

"I immediately clashed with the technicians, with the chief technicians and the engineers. They felt awkward with this woman who they thought had pinched the job from someone else, because there was someone else who wanted the job they gave to me. So I was the newcomer, I was the woman" (Woman, 35, production unit manager in a telecommunications company).

135

"So my relations with the men – who form the majority – are difficult. The fact that I'm practically the only woman with a certain level of responsibility here at the branch has piddling advantages, I mean the everyday ones of being a woman, they buy you a coffee, they try to be nice, they moderate their language, they act like gentleman, or they try to be funny, which is annoying, but it doesn't give you any more substantial advantages, because in the end you never stop battling against these people. They feel rather threatened by these professional women, who are indubitably becoming more common. They're not technicians or accountants but work in management and human resources. These women are beginning to make their presence felt, and in certain jobs they are certainly much better than men. And they probably realize this, and the crisis that men generally have in their relationships with women can also be seen in the workplace" (Woman, 35, production unit manager in a telecommunications company).

5.12 Being a couple in an organization

Among the narratives collected there were several stories about couples who worked together in the same organization – a phenomenon which concerned considerably more female than male interviewees. This was a topic of particular interest because it enabled us to explore one of the principal taboos of many organizations, which – as we shall see later when we analyse the symbolic gender order – disapprove of the mingling between affective and professional relations.

The stories of the women who shared both family and work with their husbands highlighted several aspects. Various female interviewees described working in the same organization as their husbands as a positive experience where greater confidence and a closer relationship enabled the members of the couple to work together more effectively. In these cases, couplehood was a resource for the organization as well. In the following excerpt, for example, the fact that the two members of the couple were responsible for two different sections was advantageous to the company, because it could count on smooth communication between two departments sometimes in conflict:

"The fact that we work for the same company hasn't created problems, for the moment it hasn't caused us problems, also because he has a specific post, though to a certain extent it overlaps with [my section]. He's also attended courses, so he too supports this idea of working together with colleagues and is a source of strength for me. So I'd say we work in substantially different areas although they obviously come into contact […] but we work together well as a team. It's easier for me to yell at him if something goes wrong, while with a colleague you're more restrained, with a husband you can raise your voice […] We had some American customers here yesterday and my husband made a presentation […], then they called me to present the quality control system, the documentation on what we can guarantee. So I went and did my presentation and then we started talking to these clients, and in the end it came out that we're husband and wife. The business conversation inevitably turned into a friendly conversation, so in my opinion it's almost an advantage. So far, it certainly hasn't caused problems; we'll have to see what happens in the future" (Woman, 29, quality manager in a wine-producing company).

Despite the positive effects of couplehood in the workplace, the organization and its members was often hostile to the formation of couples. Although in the above two cases the fact that the couples had formed outside the organization made their situation less 'grave', and they therefore enjoyed greater legitimacy, numerous interviewees stressed that it was inadvisable to form affective relationships with work colleagues. The organizations seemed to be afraid that such relationships might respond to external dynamics (as a female interviewee put it, "there's a complicity that extends beyond"). A couple was perceived as a free-standing entity within the organization less manageable than a single individual, and therefore influenced more by emotional factors than by the instrumental rationality on which organizations are usually based.

"I mean, if you row with a work colleague you don't have an emotional relationship with, you treat her as you'd normally treat a colleague, this creates superstructures or tensions. Because then everything gets blown up out of proportion. I mean, if I have a row with a female colleague, it's obvious that her husband's going to be angry with me [...] It's inevitable. And vice versa!" (Man, 45, assistant news editor at a television station).

It is for this reason that the symbolic gender order of organizations has various methods with which to discourage and sanction affective relations among organizational members. From comments and teasing by colleagues to career obstacles, there are numerous devices with which organizations demonstrate their disapproval of working couples.

"It may complicate things: my partner has certainly suffered because he's with me, it hasn't helped him professionally more than me, in the sense that he's probably been penalized more than I have. There have been several situations where he could have had benefits but he didn't because I was in the way. Things get complicated when there are affective relations or friendship between people, because they try not to put the wife in the husband's section or the husband in the wife's. Also because no matter how discreet you try to be, the gossip soon starts and everybody knows all about it" (Woman, 35, production unit manager, telecommunications company).

"I think that having a wife with this job has always been a bit difficult for him, because the others point it out whenever they can ... it's the others who make you feel awkward by constantly mentioning it" (Woman, 43, editor at a television station).

For some women there was the added difficulty of having a partner reluctant to accept their position, or the embarrassment of having a more prestigious job than their partner – which was inevitably pointed out in the organization or the wider social context.

> "My biggest problems have been with my husband, because he didn't want me to take the job as manager. He was already a manager. We both started out as assistant manager. Then we got married, and somehow or other we both got appointed managers. Even when I was made assistant manager he didn't like it, because he said the job was too difficult, because your mind's too taken up by the organization, you're stressed, it's work for men. He's a male chauvinist, 'they're not things for women, then they go on maternity leave' ... all that nonsense. When he heard that I'd been promoted to manager, although I hadn't been asked whether I was interested, he was furious, he wouldn't speak to me for almost a week. I really didn't want to accept. I don't know whether he was afraid of some sort of challenge between us or whether it was a man's thing" (Woman, 28, shop manager in a supermarket).

> "[The fact that I've achieved a higher position than he has] has been the subject of endless joking [...] First there were the jokes of my colleagues, which may have been funny but irritated him all the same, right? Then also friends, relatives, parents, the family ... there was probably some resentment on the part of my husband's family as well" (Woman, 43, department manager in an IT company).

For the female interviewees, therefore, working in the same organization as the partner only became a problem when it transgressed the symbolic gender order. When there was no sanctioning behaviour by the organization and work colleagues, the only problem was the family, not the work setting. The risk, in fact, was that of "taking your work home with you", of talking about work in the private sphere as well:

> "My husband does the same job as me, he works at *** and he's a manager like me. We have the same work problems, the same working hours, and sometimes we discuss work at home, which is bad" (Woman, 28, shop manager in a supermarket).

> "[We talk about work at home] a great deal, endlessly. I must say that our children censor us, they've made the rule that we can't talk about work when they're present" (Woman, 43, department manager in an IT company).

However, doing the same job as one's partner meant sharing a common enthusiasm and therefore finding greater understanding within the couple by participating in the partner's problems and receiving greater sympathy for one's own. And the interviewees felt more supported in their work: not co-incidentally, they talked frequently of 'teamwork'. Their testimonies seemingly depicted a more satisfactory balance of personal identity within the couple and at work:

> "I must say, the fact that my husband does the same work as me has been important, because there's been complete understanding between us about aspects of our jobs. If he'd been a doctor, a teacher or a factory worker, etcetera, we'd have found it very difficult to understand each other" (Woman, 43, department manager in an IT company).

> "It's certainly teamwork, because he knows what I'm thinking and I know what he's thinking. It sometimes happens that I say one thing and he says another to the same person, and this person looks at us and says 'make your minds up', and it's true, I have one way of working and he has another; but that's okay as well" (Woman, 27, restoration site manager in a construction company).

Hence, as on other issues, maternity leave for example, in the case of working couples we find a 'socially constructed' problem: couplehood in organizations is perceived as a threat to the dominant organizational culture based on opposition between the genders, not their integration. It therefore incurred symbolic sanctions – in the form of jokes, criticisms or career impediments – imposed by the organization's members.

Once again, the norms defining the boundaries of what is acceptable and legitimate organizational behaviour as regards gender relationships were functional to the maintenance of the organizational system, while they appeared immune to pressures for change, especially in terms of people's needs and respect for gender citizenship.

5.13 Conclusions: cultural regimes and gender citizenship

This broad narrative on the ways in which the gender culture is produced and reproduced in various organizational domains has highlighted the existence of multiple cultural regimes. These regimes can be located along a continuum ranging from a sharp distinction between gender competences and attributes at one end, to greater interchangeability and parity of professional roles and tasks at the other. These regimes not only relate to the sector of activity (and to its culture), they also traverse organizations – as we saw in the case of different branches of the same organization (centre/periphery) – or different roles within the same organization (subordinate/managerial roles).

Awareness that these are 'situated' experiences and therefore determined by the organization's features, the relational context in which interactions among its members take place, and the symbolic culture of the reference society, mean that it is necessary to analyse the context in which gender is 'done'. The superseding of cultural regimes which produce gender-based occupational segregation can only be possible if the 'situated' nature of such segregation is recognized.

Such recognition would stress that organizations carry moral responsibility for the way in which gender is constructed and enacted, and therefore also for the social relations that ensue. The construction of new models of gender citizenship therefore necessarily entails increased awareness and an endeavour to change organizations themselves.

The interpretative task of a civic discourse on gender citizenship is to overthrow the tyranny of gender based on the male/female dichotomy and hierarchization so that both men and women are freed from their biological destinies. It consequently entails multiple in-differentiations, where gender is only one of the criteria for the formation of identity and difference.

Gender citizenship is the metaphor used here to position gender narratives within an organizational culture and to illustrate a variety of conceptions of citizenship:

a) an organizational culture which claims to be neutral, denies any relationship between the organization and the gender of the people who work for it, and establishes a gender regime based on universality as denial of gender differences;

b) an organizational culture which holds that women are practically the same as men, promises equal treatment for equal performance, and establishes a gender regime based on cultural integration;

c) an organizational culture which considers the female to be a specific resource for the organization and establishes a gender regime based on the stereotypical dichotomy between what is specifically female and what is specifically male;

d) an organizational culture which declares itself committed to effective equality, implements an equal opportunities policy, and recognizes that men and women are not equal but should be. This culture's core value is emancipation, although rarely to be found is a gender culture systematically predicated on substantial equality;

e) an organizational culture which expresses a traditional conception of gender roles and establishes a gender regime where – recognition of both genders notwithstanding – male work is primary and female work is auxiliary to it;

f) a postmodern organizational culture which is aware of the gender trap and seeks to establish a gender regime which incorporates the constant

140

change in the meaning of gender and the practices which support that change.

Different gender cultures respond differently to the following two questions:

- Why are women today entering terrain from which they were previously excluded?
- How are they still kept out of allegedly male jobs?

One can answer the first question by pointing out that that historical change in gender as an institution has been co-produced also in (and through) organizational processes which have 'discovered' the female resource as a response to the crisis of *hegemonic masculinity* (Connell, 1995). The authority and the authoritativeness of a form of masculinity that has historically claimed to represent universality – because the category 'man' comprised persons of different gender and therefore erased gender as a dimension of power and difference – has been progressively delegitimated in numerous spheres of society. Within companies, the man/agerial model (Collinson and Hearn, 1996) based on the hierarchy, control, authority and rationalization that sustained one form alone of masculinity has been called into question by 'lean' organizational forms and supportive leadership styles. In the world of work, the gradual supplanting of manual labour (and its more 'male' connotations of fatigue, risk and general unpleasantness) by 'knowledge' work has undermined the social categories of male and female work. The destabilization of gender categories and gender relations is a pervasive social phenomenon that traverses the boundaries between spheres – public/private, family/work or inside/outside the firm – where they were previously kept separate. But, alongside the destabilization of gender categories, there still persist resistance and the defence of traditional conceptions, as well as the use made by men and women of rhetorics which explain, justify and legitimate the 'male' character of the territory. We have seen, and will see again, that the territory is defended by mobilizing rhetorics on the naturalness of care, on working time, and on settings that 'are not suitable for women'. But the defence of male territory is not based on discursive strategies alone, for numerous material practices are used to marginalize women in workplaces:

- not offering them opportunities to train for more specialized occupations,
- delegitimating their professional authority,
- using coarse language and making sexual comments,
- manipulating working time schedules,
- using meritocracy as a universal yardstick so that evaluation criteria do not consider difference.

Chapter 6

In a World of (Gendered) Rules

Exceptional situations are useful for understanding what is normal. By creating dis-order, such situations make it possible to consider taken-for-granted aspects of reality from a new and unusual standpoint, thereby bringing out features of everyday life which are difficult to perceive. Erving Goffman (1964) and Harold Garfinkel (1967) have shown that the breach of everyday rules highlights their operation and meaning. An event or an action that cannot be labelled according to social expectations is always a challenge to the constituted normative order, and they give salience to the nature of sense-making mechanisms (Garfinkel, 1963; 1964). One may likewise say this of social actors who are outsiders in a particular social group or – as Garfinkel puts it – who are 'fish out of water' or cultural 'troublemakers' (Garfinkel, 1967): they enable us to problematize taken-for-granted aspects of social action and to highlight their social construction and performativity.

Conceptualizing the entry of women into traditional male settings as raising a symbolic challenge against a static gender order is thus also a way to shed light on the rules and values system of the order being challenged. Analysing violations of the symbolic gender order, in fact, requires us to determine what is being challenged so that we can understand the meanings and contents of its underpinning norms.

The interpretation conducted in this chapter dwells in particular on the profound ambivalences and contradictions that seemingly characterize organizational rules. Within every organization there are rules, implicit and explicit, which regulate the behaviour and interactions of its members: they define who must do what, and how. When a person enters an organization s/he seeks to understand its rules, while being socialized at the same time (March and Olsen, 1989). These rules also define gender positionings and relations, expressing the normative order immanent to the organization's gender culture (Davies and Harré, 1990). Thus, women who enter traditionally male organizational cultures and positions are confronted by an array of consolidated rules which define the explicit and implicit gender contents of their role and of the organizational setting. These rules are transmitted through the details of quotidian experience that Martin and Meyerson

(1997), citing Foucault, term 'normalizing micro-processes'. These are practices, values and norms which reflect the socially constructed images of maleness and femaleness, define specific power relations among the organization's members according to their sexual membership, and discipline deviant behaviour.

The attitudes of women to the organization's implicit and explicit rules may assume different forms and nuances, ranging from acceptance to negotiation to rejection. Whatever the case may be, as soon as women enter a male role or setting, they produce a rupture in the existing order to which the women themselves and the organization's other members give sense. In fact, every system of norms comprises interpretative procedures for sense-attribution to situations in which those norms are breached. Hence, while rules are often taken for granted and are therefore not explained or made explicit, when people witness or commit transgressions, they seek to give meanings to them, to make them comprehensible. We have analysed how the narratives of women 'pioneers' in male-dominated environments are stories of challenges against the social order and consequently strewn with assertions and descriptions concerning the rules which define gender relations and attributions within the organization.

Our following analysis highlights in particular how accounts produce and reproduce three different kinds of organizational rules, which we distinguish according to the subjects asserting them and their ambit of application:

- the first are universally applied rules defining the necessary conditions with which all the organization's members must comply, regardless of gender;
- the second are specific forms of advice which have a gender connotation in that they are prescriptions specifically directed at women;
- the third group of rules concern strategic behaviour: they reflect the tactics that our women respondents said that they deployed to 'get by'.

Before analysing these three groups of rules in detail, we must stress that we will reason in processual terms, not synchronic ones. That is to say, these rules interest us insofar as that they are constructed, disseminated, modified and transgressed through organizational practices and individual behaviours. Narrative is particularly suited to this purpose because it helps reveal not only acceptance or rejection of the rules but also the process by which they are consolidated or undermined (Personal Narratives Group, 1989). Narrative is in fact a prime locus for the construction of pragmatic rules of behaviour because it is a relational activity which, through the use of examples and accounts, produces and offers situated strategies of action. When individuals narrate, they enact practices which reproduce or dismantle the norms consolidated in the social and organizational context concerned. Through the rhetorics utilized in recounting their stories and those of their male and female colleagues, the narrators emphasise or neglect, legitimate or sanction, and define what is normal and what is exceptional, thus contributing to collective sense-making and to the social negotiation and construction of the organization's rules.

Table 6.1 *The rules for getting ahead in male-dominated environments.*

The necessary condtions	*Genderless ambit of application*	*What men and women believe to be binding for both genders*	• show willingness and dedication • work long hours: 'face time' • give priority to work over your family • identify yourself with the organization
The pre-scriptions	*Gendered ambit of application*	*How women are advised to behave to become competent members*	• be determined and assertive • value aggressiveness and competitiveness • take risks
The tactics	*Ambit of strategic behaviour*	*What women say they must do to cope*	• prove your worth and pass 'tests' • adopt 'one down' strategies – deliberately but critically assume a female posture • establish co-equal relationships and adopt a 'warm' relational style

In what follows we examine these various groups of rules by analysing extracts from male and female narratives. We show how individuals – through accounts of their professional or organizational experience – produce and reproduce the normative models defining what is appropriate or inappropriate behaviour for those who wish to get ahead in organizations.

6.1 Necessary conditions

This first group of rules define conditions with which all organizational members must comply: we may call them the 'rules of the game'. They are largely implicit and taken-for-granted, and if they are not obeyed – according to our interviewees – it is impossible to construct a career. They refer to attitudes and behaviours widely considered to be constitutive of the profession and from which there are no exemptions.

Analysis of the accounts, by both males and females, yields a representation of the rules of the game where:

- companies require proof of willingness and dedication;
- this proof takes mainly the form of putting in longer hours than actually required to get the work done; and
- putting work before the family. The organization considers acceptance of this rule as indicative of loyalty and commitment, and therefore as signalling organizational membership.

We now analyse these rules in detail, our intention being to bring into focus the subtle ambivalence which on the one hand maintains that they are principles that apply equally to men and women, and on the other is a rhetoric which disciplines those who do not abide, in word or deed, with them.

Showing willingness and dedication

Many narratives stressed that one of the main conditions for getting ahead in an organization was to show more willingness than formally necessary. Some respondents described how colleagues would go into work even on their days off to see if they were needed. Willingness concerned both schedules and workload, but in general it implied unconditional acceptance of the organization's superordinate needs. Several interviewees set willingness in relation to the level of responsibility: as responsibility increased, so did the type of demand considered legitimate by the organization.

> "I reckon that if you take on a managerial job you have to give much more to the company in terms of hours, commitment, availability, participation. We often have meetings, and it's not every evening that you can go home when you've put in your hours" (Woman, 59, inspector in a bank).

However, willingness is not a passive attitude; it has to be enacted. The accounts stressed, in fact, that organizations above all rewarded self-promotion, or the ability to make one's willingness visible.

> "She was pushy, she'd ask 'Why do you do this, why do you that', she was always around, she immersed herself in her work. But you've got to push, put yourself forward, be very active, curious, extrovert. She wanted to make it, and if someone gets themselves seen and knows how to do it …" (Male, 37, site manager in a construction company).

A type of willingness that was especially valued was 'geographical mobility' or readiness to accept temporary transfers. In large companies with branches around the country or multinationals, a willingness to accept transfers (which must be explicitly declared) was an attitude to be rewarded, and it was an explicit indicator of career investment.

"I've always been ready to learn something different, something more, everything in fact, also because afterwards it works to your advantage, being open to everything new (...) They asked me if I'd be upset if they transferred me, and I said 'no, no, I'd entirely understand'" (Woman, 59, inspector in a bank).

"Apart from some grades, they ask you what your goals are in the company, and also if you'd agree to being transferred, and where (in Italy, Europe, the world), and I had no difficulty in saying that I'd accept any kind of transfer" (Male, 36, personnel manager in a metalworking company).

This type of willingness belongs within the discretionality associated with the social image of specific professional roles. It concerns definition of the boundaries of the job with respect to exceptional demands made by the organization. Willingness is therefore represented as the person's area of choice and also as a signal emitted to the organization.

It emerged from some accounts that more important than actual willingness was its 'virtual' aspect: sometimes, in fact, even the mere perception of a person's diminished commitment was sufficient to trigger organizational dynamics of dis-investment in him or her.

"One of the hold-ups in my career certainly came when I let slip to the company that, seeing that I'd been married for some time and I wasn't a youngster any more, I might be planning to have a child (...) When I pointed out that I had desires on the family front which I couldn't ignore was probably when my boss changed his mind about me. He needed someone he could count on one hundred percent, and he realized that I couldn't (...) But then my life went in a different direction. I left my husband, so at the moment I haven't got any children. The fact that I separated and then got divorced, and I haven't remarried, has probably set his mind at rest. They perceive these things and take account of them" (Woman, 48, production unit manager in a telecommunications company).

We can treat this as a case of 'virtual' maternity and stress the ambivalence whereby many organizational cultures consider motherhood to be a 'private fact' but then intrude into this private sphere to discuss the woman's intentions and her diminished availability. The choice between family and work is in the air even when it is not expressed in words.

In many testimonies the notion of willingness was expressed through the concepts of dedication and sacrifice. The theme of virtual willingness was thus further emphasised in an almost religious sense. It was not tied to specific organizational contents or exigencies but was instead an indicator of organizational loyalty, a demonstration of faithfulness and dedication intended to obtain recognition from the company.

"A spirit of sacrifice. People should be willing to make sacrifices, first giving and then receiving" (Male, 39, quality control manager in a wine-producing company).

This is an organizational rule whose range of application extends beyond the company into the public domain, and thence into the private sphere and family life. Interestingly, some men described it in terms of a 'common sacrifice' (required not only of the person concerned but also of his/her family).

"When I decided to join the company I already knew my wife, and it was very clear to us that if I wanted a career, I'd have to accept transfers, and therefore lead the life that I do now (commuting, absence from home)" (Male, 36, personnel manager in a metaworking company).

"My wife worked until we had our first child. Then we made a choice. We both worked outside town. Either we could leave the boy with his grandparents or at play school and then each of us would go off to work and we'd see each other in the evening, or we could opt for something else. The choice was made, and my wife quit work" (Male, 48, plant and maintenance manager in a telecommunications company).

The sacrifice demanded of women was different from that required of men: it was a pervasive, all-encompassing sacrifice which almost entirely excluded the option of professional employment.

"She's a lady of a certain age, she hasn't got young children, she hasn't got a husband, so she can do her job with great flexibility and commitment, and even sacrifice I'd say" (Male, 37, general manager in a IT company).

This mutual exclusion between work and family appeared to be taken for granted. This emerges very clearly from the next account, in which the dichotomy is introduced with an impersonal verb to emphasise its normative nature.

"One knows that a career requires dedication and uninterrupted service which cannot always be easily combined with motherhood" (Male, 52, branch manager in a bank).

The importance and normativity of the different social expectations towards men and women is also evident in remarks made by the interviewees concerning 'geographical mobility', another important indicator of willingness for organizations. For women – unlike men – missions and transfers are irreconcilable with the presence of a family.

"When a woman is married she must … it's difficult, it's more … I don't say normal, more traditional, it's regarded as better if a woman stays at home. Perhaps she has a job, and the husband goes off to Milan during the week, or to Germany ... my colleague's been working in England for two years, and his wife teaches here and she stays here. He comes home once a month and then during the holidays she joins him in England ... they organize it that way. Male commuting is more common. I don't know: a woman who has to catch the train, go off to work, come home; and then if she has children there's the problem of looking after them. She can get a baby-sitter, use the cleaning woman, but the child ... you have to spend time together in the evening, don't you? I mean, it's not as if you can leave the child with his grandmother and say: 'Right, I'm in Catania and she's in Munich and we'll see each other at the weekends'" (Male, 57, building manager in a metalworking company).

This is therefore a rule that applies to all members of the organization. It sanctions membership and celebrates the priority of the organization over the individual, but its consequences impact differently on the professional paths and opportunities of men and women.

Face time as competent performance

The narratives collected evince that one of the main conditions for obtaining a responsible job concerns working hours, which are usually very long, indeed often much longer than stipulated by contract. That this is a condition not sufficient but indubitably necessary was expressed (and justified) by numerous testimonies.

> "You're required to commit a great deal of time, and above all be very flexible: sometimes, you have to work twelve hours a day because you have to be there in the evening and then the next morning, so you work practically non-stop" (Woman, 40, general manager in an environmental services company).

However, some interviewees pointed out that the time requirement was related less to a heavy workload than to the need to 'be there', to be present and visible in the organization as much as possible.

> "Our managers stay late at the office ... they're sometimes there even on Saturdays. I don't know how far it is necessary ... I think they also do it out of habit: a career man has to stay late at the office, and anyway there's his wife at home who thinks of everything" (Woman, 37, head of commercial office in a processing company).

This is therefore a symbolic obligation which concerns what Goffman called 'face work': the set of actions which construct a person's social image in terms of approved social attributes (Goffman, 1963). In this case, the willingness to be present in the organization for longer than contractually necessary is an indicator of professional success. These are not necessarily hours of actual work; rather, they serve to be visible in the company for longer than is formally required: for which reason they can be termed 'face time' (Boyett and Boyett, 1996, Fuchs Epstein *et al.*, 1998).

The dimension of dedication exhibited by long working hours is further consolidated by their gratuitous nature. Not only did male interviews stay longer than was usual in their workplaces, but there was a tacit agreement that the extra hours were offered in sacrifice to the organization in exchange for a reward in terms of career and/or prestige.

> "There are more delicate roles where the institute risks more, for example those where you're in direct contact with valued customers. Taking on one of those roles necessarily means that you have to work in a certain way. If the customer wants a reply within a month, you have to get it to him. Those who put in extra work should be rewarded. But as far as I know, none of my colleagues has ever claimed overtime, because it wouldn't make sense. This is work by objectives very similar to that of self-employed professionals, and it doesn't fit with fixed working hours" (Male, 34, bank executive).

Working time was a recurrent topic in the male accounts. Almost all the male interviewees described working hours that extended well beyond the norm (very often reaching fifty hours a week). They adduced a wide variety of reasons for this – the annual general meeting, difficult customers, late deliveries, a computer program to complete – which can be summed up by saying that the contracted working hours were not enough for these individuals to meet their workloads and responsibilities. They very often worked in the evenings and at weekends and consequently described their jobs as the most important components of their lives.

> "You work as much as you want in this company. Few of us have fixed schedules. We're not like public-sector workers who clear off at five o'clock. You have to adjust to the working hours, which aren't 8–12 and 13–17. I'm often here outside those times. My job requires me to get together with people at dinner, even four or five dinners a week, also in Rome and Milan. The events take place on Saturdays and Sundays. I devote eighty per cent of my time to the company" (Male, 37, public relations manager in a wine-producing company).

> "When you work in the IT sector, you realize that you can't stop after eight hours just because the bell rings and you have to leave, because you're thinking about something and if you go home, the next day it takes you two hours to get back to the point" (Male, 42, project manager in a IT company).

This rule was reported by almost all the male interviewees, but their attitudes towards it differed. Some described it as an unavoidable obligation, others as a habit. But there were also those who described it as a strategy to cause difficulties for their female colleagues.

"In the company (...) you can make things difficult for a woman by obliging her to work unsocial hours. I went around all these companies in Rome ... they could start a meeting at ten in the evening, and I sometimes suspected that they would arrange a meeting at eight in the evening to cut out a woman they didn't like" (Male, 43, production manager in an IT company).

Time therefore acts as an indicator of investment and cooperation, and therefore as a criterion for classification and recognition (Baylin, 1993). It can be used to discriminate between those willing to dedicate most of their time to the company and those who instead have other concerns and/or priorities. It is consequently not a gender-neutral criterion, given the organization culture and the social division of family labour.

"Having working time problems makes you vulnerable (...) Almost all my male colleagues have wives at home, so they don't have problems, and they all so love being away from home that they enjoy work more than being at home, so for them putting in extra hours is not a problem" (Woman, 43, editor in a television).

While the majority of male interviewees were supported by wives who had abandoned their careers, matters were indubitably more complex for the women. In the majority of cases, they either had to rely on the support of their families of origin or – more often – they had to renounce or postpone motherhood. Some of the female interviewees, indeed, saw their futures as determined by the choice between the mutually-exclusive alternatives of work and child-rearing.

"I find that instead of having steady hours, we watch to see who'll be last to leave the office in the evening (...) The point is that this is a small firm, you can't just work your hours and then clock off. I realize that I've taken on a job without fixed working hours. If I get married and have a child, I'll have to quit this job" (Woman, 30, site surveyor in a construction company).

"I haven't got ambitions. Also because I intend to have children, so being a manager as well will be difficult (...) The hours I work now are already soul-destroying" (Woman, 28, shop manager in a supermarket).

The resignation apparent in these women's remarks evidences the extent to which the culture whereby work is an all-exclusive option, and the organization is all-encompassing, is profoundly rooted in the organizational imagination.

Face time is therefore the social division of labour taken to its extreme. This apparently neutral organizational rule consolidates the societal gender attributions which emphasise the complementarity between men committed to their work and women willing to abandon their careers (or alternatively their families). By complying with and justifying an organizational model that requires temporal overexposure in work settings, these interviewees therefore contributed to the reproduction of social gender asymmetries.

Giving priority to the job over the family

The demand by organizations that those aspiring to senior roles should show absolute dedication is, in fact, an empirical means to ascertain loyalty. Rosabeth Moss Kanter has demonstrated that companies want to be sure that the loyalty of managers to them will override other kinds of loyalty, and they endeavour to prevent any feelings that conflict with loyalty (Kanter, 1977).

Many of our interviewees stressed that full participation in the organizational game required putting their job before private and family life, and emitting clear signals that this choice had been made. This obligation also applied to men, but in their case it was not problematic insofar as the traditional division of familial roles persists. The model of the two-person career family (Papanek, 1973) had enabled the men to devote themselves to their careers while relying on the support of their wives. But the situation of the women was more complex, in that the choice between investing in a career or a family – especially in the case of the older women, for whom the allocation of domestic care tasks was more rigid – often had dramatic implications.

> "Every so often we talk [my husband and I] about the problem of a family and having children, but what can we do? Because the job keeps you busy from Monday to Saturday, eight hours a day, and as a manager you have to be there, you can stay at home for a week or take a half-day off once a week, but you can't be at work for only a half-day a week, that would be impossible!" (Woman, 28, shop manager in a supermarket).

> "I've realized that having children, probably ... or having small children ... matters. For a company deciding to hire a person, it matters if a woman has small children ... perhaps for me, yes, the fact that I haven't got children was influential" (Woman, 34, designer in a metalworking company).

As evinced by these testimonials as well, this is one of the rules that contributes most to the segregation of women because it maintains the traditional asymmetrical division of roles. Above all, though, it makes much greater demands on women than on men.

> "I don't have a personal life, I don't have a boyfriend, there wouldn't be the space for it. I've completely given up that kind of life (...) I've chosen work ... if you make the right choice, you'll make it somehow, although you have to make enormous sacrifices ... but you have to have priorities. Yes, I believe a man can have a family, but a woman has to make choices if she wants to do a certain kind of job (...) I'm not a woman who says 'I want to work

eight hours a day because I've got a child'. I mean, I don't think they'd have hired a woman who started off by saying something like that. Choices are inevitable, and I chose work" (Woman, 40, large animal veterinary surgeon in a breeders' consortium).

There is often no appeal for those who breach the rule by not respecting priorities. Choosing to have a child may mean having to abandon one's career, or at least interrupt it.

> "When a women wants a child I wouldn't say she's finished, but she's certainly heavily penalized" (Woman, 36, bank executive).

> "A woman who wants this kind of success, if you can call it that, certainly can't afford to have a child" (Male, 33, commercial manager in a textiles company).

These extracts express the extreme conviction that motherhood and a career are irreconcilable, and that this is an alternative which exclusively concerns women.

This first group of rules therefore defines the regulatory framework applying to anyone who intends to pursue a career within an organization. Presenting them as norms which constitute organizational action gives them a connotation of gender neutrality. The rhetoric sustaining these rules serves less to ensure the organization's smooth operation than to mark out roles within it. It performs a symbolic role, in fact, by sanctioning membership and celebrating the collective identity of the organization's members. The 'sanctification' of these rules and their alleged universality conceal a coerced standardization, however, because they reproduce a traditional conception of gender and thereby justify discrimination.

6.2 Prescriptions

The second group of rules comprises a set of recommendations which advise women how to become 'competent members' of an organization. We have called them 'prescriptions' because they prescribe the procedures that should be followed to acquire space and recognition in the organization. Beneath these prescriptions (which are issued by both men and women) lie male-connoted models of gender identity. In fact, they emphasise features – assertiveness, grit, identification with the profession – which have traditionally been considered male attributes. We now analyse the prescriptions that advise women to be determined and assertive, pugnacious and competitive, and also to take risks.

Being determined and assertive

Some of the women interviewees said that the most important factors for success at work were self-knowledge and understanding of one's aspirations. Being clear about goals and aware of the choices to be made were described as crucial for creating personal space in an organization.

> "Work isn't something that you can take or leave like a sweater you don't like any more. I mean, when you start work, you have to be aware of what lies ahead. So I suppose that some kind of self-assessment is important; then we all make our choices, and when you've made your choice you have to see it through" (Woman, 52, section head in a telecommunications company).

The most important qualities seem to be determination and assertiveness. The interviewees' accounts stressed the importance of pursuing goals with tenacity and determination. This required what Judy Marshall has called 'agentic planning', or forward-directed and goals-focused planning (Marshall, 1995).

> "I must say that if you believe in yourself and want things, then they'll come, though perhaps not exactly as you intended; but if your work is completely focused on them, these things will come" (Woman, 41, customer relations and marketing manager in an IT company).

> "I believe that if you're decisive and know your life, everything will conspire to let you succeed" (Woman, 40, large animal veterinary surgeon in a breeders' consortium).

Some of the male interviewees argued that these characteristics were more common in women because their role as a 'token' minority made them more vulnerable in organizations.

> "I've known clever women who put a great deal into their work. I've seen a determination which made them tougher, and so I'd say, on average with only a few exceptions, I've thought them, creating not controversy but anyway bad feelings, more reliable than men when they put everything into their work, because men have the attitude that they have little to lose, but not women" (Male, 43, production manager in an IT company).

Whilst successful women are "on average" more determined and reliable, the others, as said in the next extract, "on average don't think they can handle" their work. Several men, in fact, cited a lack of determination and self-confidence as responsible for women's lesser success at work.

> "Women have problems because they think they're going to fail in certain jobs. They have less self-confidence than men. A man says 'Yes, I can do it' and then maybe he can't. Women ... apart from some with stronger person-

alities, the others on average don't think they can handle the work, you have to explain things to them twice. A man tends to have more character than a woman. So that's why I say that women can succeed, but they have to have rather strong personalities" (Male, 35, production manager in a metalworking company).

This discourse stresses the exceptional nature of certain female workers and emphasises their difference from the female stereotype (which is thereby reinforced):

"The women I've worked with were very determined, perhaps more so than men. They worked hard to get what they wanted, they constantly challenged men, and this perhaps blurred their female character somewhat, so that I've always seen them as male colleagues in skirts. And I'm not talking about secretaries" (Male, 42, project manager in an IT company).

"I don't deny that there are tough women around. For example the owners here are all women, the owners of our company are people with a certain strength, a certain determination. But my female colleague doesn't have this grit" (Male, 37, site manager in a construction company).

In some accounts the male interviewees used metaphors based on body parts to indicate the determination of their colleagues. In some cases, the image concerned a parallelism between fingernails and claws (which in other excerpts instead denote weakness[1]).

"I got on well with her, she was very competent, a person with claws, in the sense that she knew how to do things, she didn't say 'But that's something, well all right, I'll do it'; she was decisive" (Male, 37, site manager in a construction company).

Claws are associated in the imagination with feline predators – animals which in the last century were often used to describe women who rebelled against their subordination to men. Today, argues Ada Neiger (1995: 164), women are required "to abandon certain female qualities and to assume male attitudes". It is no coincidence, in fact, that in the narratives of other men, features like decisiveness and determination are conveyed by a metaphor referring to male sexual attributes, and therefore to virility.

"Better a woman with balls than a man without. What is important is being able to do what's got to be done" (Male, 38, shift foreman in a telecommunications company).

---

[1] "If she has to move something, she tells me it'll ruin her nails" (Woman, 21, programmer in an IT company); "When she answers the phone she picks it up with a pencil so she won't ruin her nails" (Woman, 30, production manager in a textiles company).

"You can get ahead if you're good and have balls" (Male, 45, assistant news editor at a television station).

To get ahead in male professions, therefore, both men and women said that it was necessary to be decisive and assertive. When a woman was aggressive, the fact that she was a woman was overlooked. Because determination is a male feature, and is indeed likened to virility, a woman was accepted when she revealed her masculine side, when she became "a woman with balls" or a "man in a skirt". The rhetoric that sustains this prescription is evinced by the last excerpt cited: "a women will have a career if she's good and if she's a man".

Valuing belligerence and competitiveness

Some of the female interviewees reported that they sometimes had to activate typically male dynamics of aggressiveness and competitiveness in order to resist and succeed in their work. Grit, toughness, stubbornness and competitiveness were of help in these situations. "Be gutsy", "be pushy", "be hard-nosed" "attack instead of giving in" were some of the slogans used.

"A woman should learn to be a bit more competitive; which a woman is normally not thought to be; in fact, I've been told that sometimes being pushy doesn't do any harm" (Woman, 36, personnel manager in a metalworking company).

"If you go to a farmer and tell him politely, timidly 'Look, you should use this treatment', and you write it down for him on a piece of paper and give it to him with the smile of ... the good little woman, he'll do what he wants, and he'll do it one, two, three times, and when you realize you're not tough enough to go and deal with him, and that he's doing what he wants instead of what you told him, you're finished (...) You have to get tough, you've got to have guts in a situation like that (...) They expect a woman to be submissive, all sweet and smiling ... and these aren't bad characteristics, but behind them there must be aggressiveness, determination, obstinacy if you like, and also toughness" (Woman, 33, agricultural technician in an agricultural consortium).

"So instead of submitting I went on the offensive, and I must say I've always been aggressive (...) And then when push comes to shove (...) and I go at it hammer and tongs" (Woman, 43, editor in a television).

This type of prescription appeared in very few of the male interviews. Indeed, aggressive behaviour by women was not always viewed favourably. This has already emerged when we considered the reaction by men to challenge as struggle, and it has been well illustrated by Kanter when discussing the stereotype of the domineering and disagreeable woman with reference to female managers (Kanter, 1977). However, in some cases it was justified by the difficulties encountered by women who worked in predominantly male work settings.

Being able to take risks

Another important ingredient of career recipes was risk. Several interviewees maintained that taking risks, rather than passively let things take their course, was important for success.

> "You could say to me 'Maybe your decision was too hasty, a bit thoughtless', and I would say that, according to me, I see it now and I've seen it in all my career, that it's essential to take risks and obviously be aware that the risk you're taking should then be compared with your choices" (Woman, 36, branch manager in a bank).

> "I accepted for one reason above all, to take risks in first person (...) This was the choice I made, because I needed to test myself, because first, as they say around here, being an assistant is the easiest thing in the world, you do what you do, but the others sign, so it's those above you who obviously carry the risk. Here it's me who signs" (Male, 36, personnel manager in a metalworking company).

Risk-taking was described as the assumption of responsibility, as showing a spirit of initiative, but also as testing oneself. In no case, however, was it a gender-neutral feature; rather, it was presented as a typically male characteristic, with the relative lack of success of women in work being blamed on their lesser propensity to take risks.

> "Men have an attitude towards risk that women don't have: men take risks. Without a spirit of initiative you can't do anything even if you're really good (...) You have to try to stand out. When a woman joins the firm, she settles down, does her job, and that's it. It's difficult to find a woman who wants to get on, be promoted, take responsibility. My female colleague thinks she's good enough to get ahead, I see that she really works hard to stand out, while the others don't bother" (Male, 33, commercial manager in a textiles company).

We have stressed elsewhere that risk is perceived and described as a symbolic feature distinctive of managerial and entrepreneurial activity, and that it assumes a specific gender connotation in organizational discourses (Bruni, Gherardi and Poggio, 2000). Here we would emphasise in particular that also this type of prescription, like the previous ones, urges women to assume attitudes traditionally regarded as male. Both our male and female interviewees said that if a woman wants to succeed, she must seek to resemble a man: she must value determination, assertiveness and competitiveness like a

156

man, and she must take risks like a man. What this group of rules proposes, therefore, is that women should close the gap with men; and it therefore consolidates an image of the 'handicapped' woman with a long historical and cultural tradition behind it.

Whilst the prescriptions for success convey an image of the career woman which is entirely similar to that of her male counterpart, analysis of the tactics used by women to achieve success – which we now consider – yields a partly different picture.

6.3 Tactics

The rules just considered mobilize and reproduce the official rhetoric on gender in organizations; in other words, they state what women ought to do to get ahead in organizations, rather than what they actually do. To use a metaphor, this is what every 'recipe book' for career women would suggest (White, 1995). On moving to the third group of rules – concerning what women actually do – we enter the terrain of tactics.

Tactics, as defined by Michel de Certeau (1984: xi–xxiv), pertain to the territory of the Other. While strategy assumes a place that is circumscribed as proper and thus serves as the basis for generating relations with an exterior, "a tactic insinuates itself into the Other's place, fragmentarily, without taking it over entirely, without being able to keep it at a distance (...). A tactic depends on time, it is always on the watch for opportunities that must be seized 'on the wing'. Whatever it wins, it does not keep. It must constantly manipulate events in order to turn them into opportunities." An example provided by de Certeau is a housewife in a supermarket, where she confronts heterogeneous and mobile data (what she has in the refrigerator, the tastes, appetites and mood of her guests, the best buys and their possible combinations with what she already has at home) and she takes a decision according to how the opportunity is seized. The intelligence of tactics is what the Greeks called 'metis', i.e clever tricks, knowing how to get away with things, 'hunter's cunning', manoeuvres, polymorphic situations, joyful discoveries, poetic as well as warlike. Many everyday practices are tactical in character, and de Certeau defines them as victories of the 'weak' over the 'strong', whether the strength is that of powerful people or the violence of things or of an imposed order.

Tactics emit a message that apparently contradicts the previous normative prescriptions. While the 'recipe book' for success prescribes the use of male ingredients, and therefore urges women to imitate typically male behaviours and attitudes, the 'tactics manual' instead describes an array of actions with which to soften the impact of entry by women in male roles and positions and to restore harmony. These rules, in fact, prescribe that women should assume gender-appropriate postures in organizations. They should mobilize their femininity and avoid conflict, using non-authoritarian relational modes and learning how to cope with the ambivalence of gender models which at the same time require them to command respect and be authoritative.

These recipes therefore reflect a behaviour typically attributed to token women (those forming the minority in an organization: Kanter and Stein, 1980): their tendency to assume the dominant rhetoric and thus distinguish themselves from their group of membership and be assimilated into the dominant group. But by deploying their tactics, women enact different patterns of action. The most common tactics narrated by our interviewees concerned (i) the methods used by women at work to demonstrate their worth and to pass the tests set for them, and (ii) the opportunities afforded by assuming 'typically female' behaviours such as placing oneself in a 'one down' position and (iii) adopting a warm relational style. We now analyse these three types of tactics.

Proving your worth and passing 'tests'

Some of the most interesting stories recounted by the female interviewees concerned the tests set for them by male colleagues when they entered the organization. Similar to 'rites of initiation', these tests exposed the newcomers to snares and pitfalls in order to gauge their resistance and to mark their difference.

The 'proof' was narrated as an inevitable requirement for entry to the kingdom of men. The women often had to demonstrate not only that they could handle situations but also that they were 'better' at doing so.

> "You have to be much smarter than a man, much more competent, better trained, you have to be much more resilient, because you have to work much harder than a man to gain the confidence of your clients over the years" (Woman, 33, agricultural technician in an agricultural consortium).

> "If a woman has a responsible job she must be twice as good, showing more ability and determination than a man in the same position" (Woman, 23, chemical surveyor in a wine-producing company).

Hence, given the disruption that they cause, these women had to prove they had excellent credentials if they were to gain respect. Their accounts describe the importance, in order to survive in their organizations, of devising tactics to evade traps, learning how to respond correctly, avoid making mistakes, and to resist.

> "I don't know whether it's a female characteristic, but in some jobs where they discriminate against women, you work even harder, to show what they think is wrong" (Woman, 43, department manager in an IT company).

"You mustn't make mistakes, it's difficult for a woman's failings to be over-looked, a woman is not forgiven (…) A woman must be worth more than a man to have the same job grade and the same respect" (Woman, 40, general manager in an environmental services cooperative).

In the end, if the tests have been passed and the woman has proved herself capable and competent, she is accepted and finds her place in the organization:

"When the technicians realize that I know how to shift a tube clamp, that I know how to do that as well, I reckon they'll respect me" (Woman, 29, quality manager in a wine-producing company).

In many cases, the women interviewees stressed that they had to be worth more than their male colleagues if they were to occupy a traditionally male role, or at least they had to show that they were more capable. This was pointed out by some of the male interviewees as well:

"A woman must prove her worth more than a male colleague if she's going to get ahead" (Male, 48, plant and maintenance manager in a telecommunications company).

By means of this greater effort, argue Ivonne Benshop and Hans Dooreward (1998), women try to break down the gender boundary by personifying the ideal worker, or the 'disembodied worker' described by Acker (1990). Some men, however, are critical of this behaviour by women, considering it excessive and unnecessary.

"I've had female assistants who really overdid things to show that they were capable, and so I said to them: 'Look, this isn't necessary, all you have to do is get this and that done" (Male, 36, branch manager in a bank).

In this case, therefore, the greater activism of women was interpreted as due to their (erroneous) perception of the organizational context. When women form the minority, argues Kanter (1977), they tend to consider themselves symbols of their gender, and therefore seek to compensate by proving that they are capable through their work and their success.

Adopting 'one down' strategies – deliberately and critically assuming a female posture

A camouflaging tactic of 'non-visibility' was expressed by the remarks of some female interviewees concerning the expediency of a gradual career pursued 'off the beaten track'. In fact whilst it is important for a woman to demonstrate her ability and competence, she should not seem to be better or more competent than men. They would thus avoid the risk of being perceived as a threat to male security. Male colleagues, these female interviewees maintained, tended to be suspicious of women who had progressed too rapidly, especially if they were in jobs considered strategic and therefore 'dangerous'.

> "I immediately felt that I was being watched, because they were very suspicious of this newcomer who had had a more rapid career than usual" (Woman, 48, newspaper editor).

> "The male majority did not consider this job to be dangerous. It was a newly-created post and was not regarded as dangerous and therefore to be impeded" (Woman, 36, personnel manager in a metalworking company).

The tactic was therefore to gain greater acceptance by proceeding marginally to central roles. In the next extract, for example, a man praises his female colleague for entering the organization in the right way by adopting an unassuming demeanour.

> "She came in very timidly, without stuck-up attitudes like 'I've got a degree, I've been to Bocconi University[2]' (...) She entered in the right way, so she settled down very well" (Male, 37, public relations manager in a wine-producing company).

Another risk to avoid was competing against male colleagues. In this case the likelihood of failure was high because the men might feel threatened. The tactic suggested was therefore to put oneself on a different 'wavelength', thereby avoiding confrontation on masculine terrain:

> "I behave the way that I am, and I'm obviously different from a man. I've never used their mechanisms, their mind-set. So they see that I'm not competitive, if there's an apparatus to use and they want to use it, I'd never ... and this can only be good for the company, for the work environment and, in the end, for the project. They don't feel threatened, because I'm not competitive (...) Men are different, it's pointless to confront them on the same wavelength, because we're not ... it's only an enormous waste of energy" (Woman, 40, large animal veterinary surgeon in a breeders' consortium).

> "I try to keep to my part as a woman and beat them with my professionalism. If you adopt male behaviour, try to compete with men, you're going to lose. I respond with facts, with my work" (Woman, 44, brand manager in a bank).

The female interviewees also said that it was advisable not to be too innovative. Certain novelties were welcomed, but you should not push things too

---

[2] One of the most prestigious Italian universities.

far. Organizations were described as resistant to innovations, all the more so if they were proposed by women.

> "It's true that here they don't want people who think too much; or better, they say that they want people with ideas, who are creative, but in fact you have to be very careful about being creative, because if you're not creative in the way they want, you become a threat" (Woman, 35, production unit manager in a telecommunications company).

> "The head of internal communications – a woman – was disliked because she suggested changes, and without her knowing it, certain tasks were taken away from her and given to the male head" (Woman, 36, personnel manager in a metalworking company).

One of the tactics employed was therefore to act with caution, without giving offence to male colleagues and provoking hostility.

> "It's obvious that they've got much more experience, they've been here for years; I arrived six months ago … and they say 'What do you want? You've just arrived and you think you can change everything?'" (Woman, 21, programmer in an IT company).

Concealing one's successes and visibility in the organization was therefore the way ahead for women when they perceived themselves as more symbols than individuals in the organizations for which they worked (Kanter, 1977).

> "I've never allowed myself to take liberties with my superior, because someone might say: 'Ah, she can do it because she's a woman'" (Woman, 30, production manager in a textiles company).

One form of behaviour both useful and appreciated in predominantly male organizations was activating relational strategies which valorized male colleagues and extolled their competence while adopting the posture of the attentive learner.

Asking questions, seeming curious, seeking opinions, were often actions performed by the female interviewees not only to learn but also to gratify male colleagues and gain their acceptance.

> "Feign ignorance, ask questions, try to make the other person feel somehow superior to you, so that you can be treated better, because if you enter a male work environment as a woman, and you're a surveyor, and you start to make comments, they cut you out. After which, after some time, when you've gained their confidence, then you can make suggestions and they'll listen to you" (Woman, 30, leak detector in a metalworking company).

"Curiosity has helped me: I used to go down to the shop floor and ask the workmen what they were doing. They were pleased if you said 'Explain it to me, I don't understand ...' You just have to know what to do and you can get all the information you want" (Woman, 28, special coordinator packaging in a metalworking company).

The women therefore recounted that they adopted a conciliatory attitude in order to carve out space for themselves in their organizations. They made sure not to be assertive towards their male colleagues, and instead to seek compromises.

"You have to pretend to be thick sometimes, you've got to ignore humiliations, because kids even younger than you are, or older men who haven't worked as long as you have, say they know how to do something better, and you have to say 'Yes, yes, you're right', otherwise they'll block the site" (Woman, 27, restoration site manager in a construction company).

Narratives of this kind help maintain a culture of obedience by communicating the futility of protest. Marsha Witten explains this phenomenon by referring to the rule of anticipated reactions: that is, the conviction that people with less power in a group are bound to fail if they challenge the *status quo*. They realise that they are in conflict with the dominant values system but construct a self-fulfilling prophecy of failure (Witten, 1992: 112) and thus perpetuate their position of relative disadvantage.

Establishing co-equal relationships and adopting a 'warm' relational style

An aspect emphasised by many female interviewees was the importance of maintaining good interpersonal relations and establishing co-equal relationships which reduced formal distances. Some of the women, for example, said that they proposed to new colleagues, even ones in subordinate positions, to switch from formal 'lei' to informal 'tu'. Obtaining the consensus of the work group (and not only its male members but also its female ones) was regarded as vital for achieving good results.

"I'll say that relationships with my predecessor here were rather formal, in the sense that he used 'lei' with colleagues, and not just with the director. I also addressed him with 'lei' because he was older than me, but I always used 'tu' with the secretary here and other colleagues. At first, when I said to the secretary 'If you like, we can use 'tu' with each other', she said no. But when she saw that I used 'tu' with the others and they did the same with me, she said 'You can use 'tu' with me as well if you like'. So we began this more informal relationship. I cultivated this much more informal, let's say friendly, relationship with my work colleagues right from the start, and also with the shop-floor workers, because there are older workers who say to me 'Ciao, how's it going', and I say 'Ciao' back. So it's not the relationship between a manager and a subordinate … that wasn't the relationship that I wanted to have, the one they had with my predecessor, given what I'm really like" (Woman, 36, personnel manager in a metalworking company).

This excerpt clearly evinces the way in which the interviewee sought to establish a 'friendly' and 'informal' relationship with her colleagues. Her description stresses the difference with respect to the person (a man) who previously occupied her post. Also of interest is the relational asymmetry whereby age was a factor that maintained distance only with male superiors (the director) but not with subordinates (the production workers).

A tactic used by some of the older interviewees was not to impose their hierarchical superiority on colleagues, instead emphasising that they were at their service.

"People went to my colleague, I let them talk to him and then I quietly took the decision myself, but I never imposed my authority to humiliate him, or threw my weight around" (Woman, 59, inspector in a bank).

"I don't feel like their boss, more than anything I feel that I support them, they see me as a reference figure, more than as a boss. Obviously, they come to me with all their needs, from outside work as well. I mean, they call me 'the boss', but it's more of a joke, because I don't act as their boss, instead I'm their support. I'm their point of reference more than their boss" (Woman, 52, section head in a telecommunications company).

In this way, the women contributed to constructing an identity in line with gender expectations and sought to remedy the disruption caused by their entry or their advancement in male roles. They thus agreed to follow a dance routine where the lead (him) and the follower (her) together reproduced the rules.

6.4 The double bind: how to manage the ambivalence of models

There follows a folk tale from Liguria recounted by Italo Calvino in his *Fiabe Italiane* as a metaphor for what happens to women when they enter organizations or roles hitherto reserved for males.

> **Fanta-Ghiro**
>
> A king had three daughters but no sons. The king was of a sickly disposition. One day a Turkish king declared war against his land, but the king was too ill to take command of his army. So his three daughters offered to take his place. The father at first refused, because commanding an army was not the work of a woman. But then, given the seriousness of the situation, he agreed to send his eldest daughter, but on condition that she dressed and behaved like a man. He warned her that if she started talking about women's things, his trusted squire would immediately bring her home. The daughter left for the war, but during the sea voyage she saw a gaily coloured fish and remarked that she wanted a ball gown in the same colours. So the squire took her straight back home. The same thing happened to the second daughter. During the voyage, when she saw the colourful sails of the fishing boats, she began talking about the fabrics she wanted to decorate her bed chamber. So the third daughter, Fanta-Ghiro, then set off to fight the war, even though she was still so small that her armour had to be padded before she could put it on. The sea voyage passed without incident, and the young princess went to parlay with the enemy king. The king was intrigued by the 'iron general' and set traps to see whether he was not really a woman. He took Fanta-Ghiro into the armoury and then into the garden, asking questions to catch her out. Fanta-Ghiro passed all the tests until the king invited her to go for a swim. This forced her to find an immediate excuse to return home. But she left behind a letter explaining who she really was. The king, by now in love, followed Fanta-Ghiro and asked her to marry him. Peace was made, of course, and when Fanta-Ghiro's father died he left his kingdom to his son-in-law.

Both the heroine of the story and her sisters assumed that most masculine of guises: a suit of armour. They did so, like several of our female interviewees, because they had no other choice. There were no men who could don the armour, and the sisters were determined to do their duty. But to qualify for warfare, they had to pass a test set by one man (the father) and verified by another (the squire). The test consisted in concealing their femaleness. Our female interviewees had similarly been obliged to renounce their gender membership on entering male organizations, and they had to be constantly alert not to commit fatal errors. Fanta-Ghiro passed the test, she reached the enemy king and obtained peace; but in order to do so she had to remove her disguise and become a princess again. The moment likewise comes for women entering male organizations to drop the pretence and assume the female role again, renouncing war and removing their armour.

As the prescriptions required, women entering male organizational cultures must learn how to gain respect and impose their ideas, and not to yield excessively to the authority of their male colleagues. They must consequently be well-prepared, have strong personalities, and show that they have 'backbone'. For some women this awareness emerges after some time, when they realize that the use of typical female traits (being conciliatory and submissive) is not always the best tactic. Learning to speak your mind, protesting against discrimination, asserting yourself, are some of the actions that help women create space for themselves in organizations.

> "Perhaps a woman should learn how to be assertive and speak her mind ... A woman should be able to say 'I see it this way', like a man" (Woman, 36, personnel manager in a metalworking company).

> "Personality: more than anything else, showing you've got the sort of personality that men don't usually expect in a woman. Personality counts a great deal in getting what you want" (Woman, 36, branch manager in a bank).

Also some of the male interviewees stressed that women should be able to assert themselves, especially in male work settings – like a factory or a construction site – where they have to work with male subordinates who on the other hand have lower educations and are perhaps scornful of women, and on the other, are older and with longer experience, so that they are resentful of a female superior.

> "A girl in charge of line operators is not something that you find every day, also because, if you think for a moment, here we've got someone who's little more than a kid, twenty-six years old, who inevitably has hassles with these old lags who know the score, who are 40 to 45 years old, with 20 to 25 years of experience, who find themselves being ordered around by someone who's only twenty-six" (Male, 36, personnel manager in a metalworking company).

> "You've got to have quite a strong personality. You've got to have character to handle positions of responsibility and deal with males" (Male, 35, production manager in a metalworking company).

The dissonance between these recommendations and the tactics used by women show that ambivalence is a constant feature of female experience in traditionally male-dominated organizations. Women entering organizations in which the dominant gender order is male find themselves caught in the 'double bind dilemma' (Gherardi, 1994; Jamieson, 1995). They can behave like women, accentuating their 'otherness' with respect to the male organizational culture; or they can seek to comply with masculine norms, thereby provoking disapproval by the organization, which regards them as women trying to act like men (Martin and Meyerson, 1997). This phenomenon was apparent in many of the accounts of our female interviewees, who stressed the need on the one hand to adjust to predominant models, and on the other to depart from them. In the former case – of conforming with female models and therefore being conciliatory and submissive – the risk is surrender. In the latter – that of assuming more typically male forms of behaviour – the risk is censure by colleagues.

With reference to feminist autobiography, Carla Locatelli defines a double-bind situation as one in which "speaking out means being silenced, being party to a biographical contract which precludes the possibility of self-representation in one's own and/or appropriate terms" (Locatelli, 2000: 178).

> "When you dig your heels in over something, if you're a woman they say you're being hysterical" (Woman, 49, production-sales clerk in a metalworking company).

> "An assertive woman is disliked here. You realize that kind of behaviour is not going to work and you try another. So women probably say that they get much more with behaviour, I don't know ... perhaps because the man doesn't see them and doesn't appreciate them in that way, and squashes them; but with a different attitude, perhaps conciliatory at first and then ... you get much more out of it. But I think it's wrong" (Woman, 36, personnel manager in a metalworking company).

> "I'm conciliatory by nature, because I'm always amenable to everyone; I mean, it's difficult for me to say I won't do something. But I've come to realize that if I don't show a bit of grit, they'll wipe their feet on me, so I'm determined more than anything, I sometimes force myself to keep calm in certain situations, because they'd say 'But she's hysterical, than one'" (Woman, 44, brand manager in a bank).

The double bind was also apparent in the male accounts. The men said that women should acquire certain characteristics regarded as male, but at the same time they should not lose their femininity.

> "There are some women who swear worse than dockers, but most of them aren't like that (...) The women I've known in senior managerial positions had very male attitudes ... there was one woman who smoked cigars, not cigarillos, just like John Wayne. She was a bit off-putting, but I realised it was all a pose ... it was just a stereotype, apart from her appearance – which was elegant – her behaviour, her attitudes were those of the worst kind of chauvinist male. She'd probably had to pay that price to rise to her level in the organization. Really crude language, coarse behaviour. Everything that you find in offices run by men, even of a certain age I'd say. A woman certainly has to pay that price; she was able to salvage a bit of pride paying as little as possible" (Male, 43, production manger in an IT company).

Women in male organizations are therefore subject to two demands: on the one hand, they are expected to adjust to behavioural styles typical of the roles and positions that they have entered, and which have hitherto been a male preserve; on the other, they are required to restore the gender relationships disrupted by their entrance, undertaking repair work, deploying mediation strategies, and mobilizing their femaleness.

Analysis of the accounts displaying the regulatory, prescriptive and descriptive features of the procedures adopted in organizations has enabled us to show the existence of a gender sub-text (Benshop and Dooreward, 1998) which systematically reproduces gender distinctions and maintains power asymmetries. When discussing rules we sought to show that women under-represented in male organizations are required to privilege features considered typically masculine, like determination and aggressiveness. But at the same time they must devise strategies of action and relation which safeguard the social order organized around difference.

To gain acceptance in organizations, women must sometimes espouse the rules even to the extent of affirming the myth that work and family are irreconcilable, and therefore accepting the sacrifice that this entails. This is the most demanding of a series of tests that organizations set for women in the various rounds of the career tournament (Rosenbaum, 1989; Luciano, 1993). When a woman fails the test and loses the challenge, she is excluded and rejoins the group of the 'others'.

The rules that we have identified, and the symbolic order that characterizes them, are functional to the organization, not to its members, be they men or women. An organization which requires its members to give up their private lives and devote themselves entirely to their work (even if by symbolic means and not those of material exploitation) will not maintain the commitment of those members for long – especially if this requirement is based on a sharp distinction of roles now largely obsolete. The narratives of the young women interviewees were more similar to those of the men, and less similar to those of the *other* women: those, that is, who represented the *sin qua non* for the existence of men dedicated only to their work. These women did not regard motherhood and work as mutually exclusive options. They were aware of the difficulties but had decided to confront them, without feeling obliged to surrender.

"If all women had decided to have careers, by now humanity would no longer exist" was the apocalyptic threat of the symbolic gender order expressed by an interviewee. In fact, however, motherhood and a career are incompatible only to the extent that organizations and men want them to be. Where organizational models are more flexible and/or the division of domestic labour is less asymmetrical, there are women who have been able to balance a professional career with a family. The more active involvement of men in family duties required by the greater professional commitment of women also entails more responsible fatherhood. The stories of fathers so often absent from home that their children no longer recognize them depict a scenario certainly more realistic and worrying than that of a childless world of career women. If all women pursued careers, humanity would probably continue to exist, provided that men spent a little less time at the office.

The challenges raised by women against prescriptive organizational discourses – whether these refer to the necessary conditions, tactics, or prescriptions for success – are forms of resistance against the organizational culture of obedience, and for this reason they provoke suspicion and fear. However, they may also generate changes that are also to the advantage of men still entrenched in obstinate defence of rituals to support masculinity. Today, there are far fewer 'naturally' male occupations – those which involve manual labour, for example, or which require work in dirty, noisy, or dangerous conditions. The real stronghold of male specificity in work now seems to be a willingness to show total temporal and mental commitment. Hence challenging the dominant rules may liberate men as well, especially those – the younger generation – who do not regard work as the defining dimension of their identities.

Conclusions

"In the space of a language (as in that of games),
a society makes more explicit the formal rules of action
and the operations that differentiate them."

(de Certeau, 1984)

If one abides by the vocabulary of narrative, on reaching the end of a book one should ask oneself what the moral of the story has been. Of course, stories are open texts which not only permit, but indeed encourage, the reader to participate in their interpretation, and to share the emotions, meanings, and fragments of life portrayed. We therefore hope that the reader of this book will draw his or her own conclusions, but this does not exonerate us from our responsibility as authors. Consequently, in order to reflect on what have learnt from the stories recounted to us, we shall reprise the questions from which we began: (i) why focus on pioneer women and the reproduction of the masculinity of male jobs when studying gender as a social practice and institution?; (ii) why focus on women who work in male-dominated settings and work groups?

An intuitive answer might be that, when masculinity represents the culture of a homogeneous or quasi-homogeneous group, it is a barrier against entry by persons dissimilar to it. The same obviously applies to female-dominated work groups. The psycho-social dynamics connected with similarity and difference (of gender, race, class, age, or other parameters) operate wherever there exists a minority. But these dynamics were not the specific object of our interest. Instead, we were interested in the presence of a minority as an arena in which gendered social processes unfold. In other words, women who do not work in traditionally female occupations and jobs provoke a breach in the symbolic order which reveals the social processes enacted to repair the 'anomaly' and to restore the situation in a manner acceptable to the predominant social culture of gender. Every social culture, and within it every organizational culture, creates a symbolic order of gender which assigns the female and the male with meanings, expectations, and social representations of what is proper and improper to femaleness and maleness. This order appears to be fixed and immutable because its pervasiveness in everyday life makes it invisible: it is removed from awareness and included in the domain of the obvious, among the things taken for granted by commonplace thought. But this immutability is only apparent, because commonplace thought is the social and historical product of a community whose discursive and material practices reproduce it in quotidian life.

We may therefore consider the symbolic gender order to be a discursive formation which is situatedly mobilized in order to produce and reproduce gender relations. Organizational scholars, inspired by Foucault, have looked at broad discursive formations like the development of expertise in human resources management (Townley, 1993), the discourse of strategic planning (Knights and Morgan, 1991), or surveillance in organizational and managerial studies (Sewell and Barker, 2006), but few have shown how they are enacted in specific organizational contexts (Deetz, 1998; Hassard and Rowlinson, 2002; Clegg and Courpasson, 2004). This analysis has shown that the gender discourse mobilized in male-dominated environments is an element of organizational surveillance which is based upon, and supports, a form of masculinity, and disciplines the organization's members, both male and female. Practising gender can be seen as a delicate form of worker engagement which "constructs the subject through the fixing of his/her identity" (Hodgson, 2003: 14). And both gendering practices and practising gender can be done intentionally or unintentionally (Martin, P.Y., 2005). It is therefore important to expose the micro-physics of power intrinsic to gender relations in order to show how surveillance and power act in everyday practices, whether or not the subjects are aware of it.

Narratives on the presence of women in male jobs have highlighted the presence of a plurality of discursive communities (groups of people who share common knowledge, beliefs and values) within and across several organizational settings. The rivalry that exists among these communities is played out in various forms that link statements about how the world is with normative statements about how it ought to be. The masculinity of male work is asserted, practised and theorized in order to discipline all those engaged in that work, both to defend the territory and to exclude discursive formations alternative to it. However, whilst the rhetorics that sustain the masculinity of male work can be represented as discursive forms of surveillance and discipline matched by forms of compliance and/or resistance, also to be borne in mind are the forms that observance may take. Iedema et al. (2006: 1126–7) stress the concept of 'observance' in order to underscore that the view of workers as being caught between being determined by surveillance or forced into resistance misses some central facets of contemporary workplace dynamics. According to Iedema and colleagues, analysis of observance in practice enables one to capture the varied, multiple and unpredictable aspects of how people respond to the dynamic character of workplace interactions. This concerns people's engagement with the unfolding of the interaction to which they are party. And people's enactments manifest their ability to extend the normative and affective scope of self and the relational span with others.

Given a set of organizational rules, discursive practices position people and their modes of 'doing gender' within practices of observance of that normative and cultural set. Analysis of these discursive practices has given us insight into the practical ways in which people negotiate the differences between self and others, and also their reflexive capacity to enact gender at work.

Paradoxically, therefore, the symbolic gender order is constantly changing in its apparent immobilism. The diversity of organizational cultures in their conceptions of the female and male roles in work and organizational practices expresses diverse senses of gender citizenship within an organizational culture.

We have therefore defined, and seen in operation, gender as a social practice which anchors a set of other practices (Bruni, Gherardi and Poggio, 2000). In other words, the conventional attribution of male or female features to beliefs, behaviours and expectations does indeed generate social processes external to workplaces, but these workplaces in their turn reproduce and change gender-based social practices. In so doing, they contribute greatly to redefining the historical and situated meaning of gender. The social division of labour is its sexual division, and the categorization of work into female and male is an example. Likewise, change in this categorization is an evident example of how gender relationships change across historical periods lasting for decades, not centuries. This is why study of how organizational cultures act and react in actively constructing the symbolic gender order violated by an 'alien' presence brings to light the often invisible operation of practices that repair the symbolic order, reaffirming its assumptions when unexpected events or dis-order impact upon them.

Amid surveillance, resistance and observance, this book has illustrated the implicit rules of the symbolic gender order in organizations: what men and women are equally obliged to do as 'citizens of organizations'; what women are advised to do to make their presence discreet; and what women say they do to cope in jobs and occupations at odds with the symbolic gender order.

To draw together the many threads of our argument, a second answer to the above question concerns our reasons for choosing the narrative approach. The recent rediscovery and appreciation of narrative as well as analytical knowledge also comprises the rediscovery of the 'discreet charm' of Cinderella. However, just as the appeal of folk tales consists in their repetition, which transmits their messages of popular wisdom across generations, so narrative of others' experiences is a 'hot' communication medium able to convey often implicit knowledge, which thus finds expression, also emotionally. Giving 'voice' to the ordinary members of equally ordinary organizations has methodological value in that it makes it possible to illustrate –

through situations that the reader may have encountered in his/her everyday life – of the action in organizations not only of Logos but also of Pathos. Our choice of the narrative approach has given us access to the discursive practices that construct gender. In particular, it has enabled us to describe the following processes:

- the way in which narratives contribute to the social construction of organizational selves. The third and fourth chapters on the narratives by women and men interpreted, in fact, the positioning of the narrating Self and the implicit construction of the Other.
- the way in which narratives give sense to people's experience. The 'challenge' as the elementary construct of Her experience and the 'no problem' as the core of His experience in reaction to a breakdown in the symbolic order of gender synthesise two diametrically opposed phenomena expressing 'normality' of the everyday for the dominant gender and its 'extraordinariness' for the minority one. For Him, gender and work are coherently inscribed within the same symbolic universe, so that gender becomes invisible and taken for granted; for Her, gender and work are inscribed in different symbolic systems, and must therefore be related to a symbolic universe which legitimates their presence and restores signification.
- the way in which narratives favour cultural transmission. The chapter in which He and She describe a third subject common to the experience of both is entitled 'In Parallel Worlds' precisely to convey how a theoretically shared experience may give rise to very different life-outcomes. The voices of both Her and Him reconstruct the organizational culture and its assumptions concerning the gender citizenship that a certain job and a certain organization permit. We have described very traditional cultures in which, despite the evidence to the contrary provided by the presence of women, it is openly asserted that 'this is not the place for women'; largely egalitarian cultures; and a wide range of intermediate situations.

To conclude we must itemize the findings of our research. The most important of them concerns the mechanisms that reproduce gender relations, and in particular how gender discourse mobilizes a set of discursive practices that men and women deploy to discipline the female as the subordinate gender. Speaking is doing, and it is doing gender in contexts of situated interaction.

The discursive practices which construct gender, and in so doing create a hierarchical relation in which one gender is dominant and the other is subordinate, have been described in terms of the following processes:

- removing one of the terms of the gender relation, or silencing the masculine. Making gender synonymous with 'of women' creates the discursive illusion that only women have a gender, and that 'gender' is the most up-to-date and correct term for sexual membership. This rhetoric renders the male invisible. It thus operates as a disciplining practice, in that the male becomes the sole benchmark with which to assess human behaviour. A vocabulary for denoting gender as a relation and as reciprocal definition is still largely undeveloped. However, a critique of the 'old' vocabulary is already an act of insubordination because it lays bare the purpose of that vocabulary to dominate and reproduce gender inequality.

- naturalizing gender. The rhetoric depicting motherhood as the social destiny that gives women prime responsibility for the family on biological grounds consigns them to the natural kingdom rather than to that of culture and society. This discursive practice should be considered illegitimate in the gender game because it involves the naked use of power. We have noted its diffusion, but we have also noted a shift to the rhetoric of parenthood and to an organization of work which flexibly allocates the domestic workload between both partners in particular periods of their working lives.

- desocializing work time. The rhetoric that mobilizes work time and the practices associated with it in terms of immutable schedules and places of work comprises a gender sub-text which implicitly affirms that such work is not for women. It also implicitly affirms forms of masculinity that exclude women. Ignoring the fact that the organization of work is a human artifact and as such can assume a variety of alternative forms is to bolster the exercise of power.

- using disqualification heuristics if the same behaviour is enacted by a man or a woman. The disqualification of women as the second sex comes about in discourse and through discourse, and in discursive practices involving both men and women. Everyday conflict among men is described in terms of power, negotiation and combat, while that among women is described in terms of envy and similar traits.

It is undeniable that there is an everyday micro-politics of power between men and women, and that the asymmetry of power in gender relations gives men an ascribed rent position. But these inequalities are sustained by social practices and enacted through them. One understands that there may be a certain reluctance to openly discuss the conflict and competition that tie men and women together in the 'war of the sexes'. Yet recognition of the conflictual relation is apparent in both the challenge and the negation of gender as a barrier.

In order to forestall the idea that gender is reproduced by social practices alone, we now list the material practices most frequently used to marginalize women in workplaces:

- not offering them opportunities for training and specialization;
- delegitimating their professional authority in the presence of third parties;
- using coarse language and tolerating sexual comments;
- manipulating work schedules;
- regarding merit to be the universal yardstick of quality regardless of gender differences.

However, the image of the gender relation based metaphorically on conflict and zero sum games is victim to the selfsame vocabulary that it uses and which conceals the other side of the coin: complicity or the bond of intimacy and solidarity deployed in gender relations. In other words, what is excluded by the discourse of gender as power is the image of the 'gender trap' which closes on the inseparability of One from the Other. Not only are male and female discursively inseparable because one acquires meaning only by difference from the other, and because each supplements the other in that the term suppressed to reinforce the definition of the other inevitably resurfaces, but men and women are equally caught in the gender trap in their material relations.

Work is terrain on which it is easy illustrate the ambivalence of the gender trap. The marginalization of women from the sphere of prestige and power may sustain a form of hegemonic masculinity just as the marginalization of men from the sphere of care and service may hamper the development of more complete humanity. We have shown that men and women equally acknowledge the imperative of the organizational logic that absolutizes the value of efficiency and consequently requires people to demonstrate absolute dedication both material and emotional. In the name of equality, this organizational logic declares itself blind to gender; and in fact it often is, especially if it can rely on a tactical alliance with women to reduce the privileges of a hegemonic masculinity often no longer compatible with the new forms of work flexibility.

Contrary to this organizational logic, which is less taken for granted by women because their socialization is more recent, arises the doubt that we have represented with the dialogue between Don Quixote and his faithful squire. Don Quixote personifies the enigma of reality and its meaning, and we may say that this concerns as much gender relationships as work relationships. In fact individual strategies cannot challenge a system of discrimination.

At the end of this book we leave two questions still requiring an answer. Are present gender relationships the best that we can construct? Are present organizations the best that we can conceive?

Appendix

List of organizations and employees' profiles

Organization	Profile woman	Profile man
Agricultural consortium	agricultural technician	general manager
Bank A	executive	executive
Bank A	branch manager	agency manager
Bank B	brand manager	financial products manager
Bank B	inspector	branch manager
Breeders' consortium	large animal veterinary surgeon	veterinary coordinator
Construction company A	site surveyor	site manager
Construction company B	restoration site manager	restoration technician
Environmental services cooperative A	environmental operator	environmental operator
Environmental services cooperative B	general manager	economic manager
Environmental services cooperative B	chemical section manager	environmental survey manager
Insurance	loss adjuster	liquidator
IT company A	department manager	production manager
IT company A	customer relations and marketing manager	project manager
IT company A	department manager	chief executive
IT company B	programmer	software manager
IT company C	IT consultant	software assistant
Metalworking company A	designer	building manager
Metalworking company B	production-sales clerk	personnel manager
Metalworking company B	special coordinator packaging	production manager
Metalworking company C	production plan manager	production manager
Metalworking company C	leak detector	skilled worker
Metalworking company C	personnel manager	personnel manager
Newspaper	department head	manager
Processing company	head of commercial office	head of customer care office

Organization	Profile woman	Profile man
Quarrying and export company	exports manager	administrative manager
Supermarket	shop manager	assistant shop manager
Telecommunications company	production unit manager	plant and maintenance manager
Telecommunications company	section head	shift foreman
Television	editor	assistant editor
Textiles company	production manager	commercial manager
Wine-producing company	quality manager	administrative services manager
Wine-producing company	chemical surveyor	quality control manager
Wine-producing company	marketing manager	public relations manager

References

Acker, Joan (1990) Hierarchies, Jobs, Bodies: A Theory of Gendered Organizations. *Gender & Society*, 4(2):139–58.

Alvesson, Mats, and Billing, Yvonne (1997) *Understanding Gender and Organizations*. London: Sage.

Ashcraft, Karen, and Mumby, Denis (2004) *Reworking Gender*. London: Sage.

Baylin, Lotte (1993) *Breaking The Mold: Women, Men, and Time in the New Corporate World*, New York: The Free Press.

Benshop, Yvonne, and Dooreward, Hans (1998) Covered by Equality: The Gender Subtext of Organizations. *Organization Studies*, 19(5):787–805.

Bergvall, Victoria L. (1999) Toward a comprehensive theory of language and gender. *Language in Society*, 28(2):273–293.

Bertaux-Wiame, Isabelle (1982) "The Life History Approach to the Study of Internal Migration: How Women and Men Came to Paris Between the Wars," in *Our Common History: The Transformation of Europe*. London: Pluto Press.

Bing, Janet M., and Bergvall, Victoria L. (1996) The question of questions: beyond binary thinking. In: V. L. Bergvall, J. M. Bing, and A. F. Freed (eds.) *Rethinking Language and Gender Research. Theory and Practice*, New York: Longman.

Bird, Sharon R. (1996) Welcome to the men's club: Homosociality and the maintenance of hegemonic masculinity. *Gender & Society*, 10:120–132.

Blixen, Karen (1937) *Den afrikanske Farm*. Copenhagen: Gyldendal (Engl. Transl. Dinesen, Isak. *Out of Africa*. New York: Random House, 1970).

Boje, David M. (1995) Stories of the storytelling organization. A postmodern analysis of Disney as "Tamara-Land". *Academy of Management Journal*, 38(4):997–1035.

Boje, David M. (2001) *Narrative Methods for Organizational and Communication Research*. London: Sage.

Borghesi, Donatella (2000) *Specchio, specchio delle mie brame. Luci ed ombre dell'invidia tra donne*. Milano: La Tartaruga.

Bourdieu, Pierre (1994) *Raisons pratiques. Sur la théorie de l'action*, Edition du Seuil, Paris (Engl. Transl. *Practical Reasons*. Cambridge: Polity, 1998).

Boyett, Joseph H., and Boyett, Jimmie T. (1996) *Beyond Workplace 2000: Essential Stategies for the New American Corporation*. New York: Penguin.

Britton, Dana (1999) Cat fights and gang fights: Preference for work in a male-dominated organization. *The Sociological Quarterly*, 40(3):455–74.

Brooks, Peter (1984) *Reading for the plot. Design and Intention in Narrative*. New York: Routledge.

Brown, Andrew D. (2006) A narrative approach to collective identities. *Journal of Management Studies*, 43(4):731–753.

Bruner, Jerome S. (1986) *Actual minds, possible worlds*. Cambridge Mass: Harvard University Press.

Bruner, Jerome S. (1987) Life as Narrative. *Social Research*, 54(1):11–32.

Bruner, Jerome S. (1990) *Acts of meaning*. Cambridge Mass:Harvard University Press.

Bruni, Attila, and Gherardi, Silvia (2001), Omega's story: the heterogeneous engineering of a gendered professional self. In: M. Dent, and S. Whitehead (eds.) *Knowledge, Identity and the New Professional*, Routledge, London: 174–198.

Bruni, Attila, Gherardi, Silvia, and Poggio, Barbara (2005) *Gender and Entre-preneurship. An ethnographic approach.* London: Routledge.

Butler, Judith (1990) *Gender trouble: feminism and the subversion of identity.* New York: Routledge.

Butler, Judith (1993) *Bodies that matter: On the discursive limits of 'sex.'* New York & London: Routledge.

Calás, Marta, and Smircich, Linda (2006) From the 'Woman's point of View' ten Years Later. In: S. R.Clegg, C. Hardy, W. Nord, and T. Lawrence (ed.) *Handbook of Organization Studies.* London: Sage, 248–346.

Calás, Marta, and Smircich, Linda (1991) Voicing seduction to silence leadership. *Organization Studies,* 12(4):567–602.

Calvino, Italo (1956) *Fiabe italiane.* Torino: Einaudi (Engl. transl. *Italian Folktales,* Penguin, Harmondsworth, 1982).

Cameron, Deborah (1992) *Feminism and linguistic theory,* London: Macmillan.

Campbell, Hugh (2000) The glass phallus: Pub(lic) masculinity and drinking in rural New Zealand. *Rural Sociology,* 65(4):562–581.

Cavarero, Adriana (1997) *Tu che mi guardi, tu che mi racconti.* Milano: Feltrinelli.

Chodorow, Nancy (1978) *The Reproduction of Mothering.* Berkeley: University of California Press.

Clegg, Stewart, and Courpasson, David (2004) Political hybrids: Tocquevillean views on Project organizations. *Journal of management studies,* 41:525–47.

Collinson, David, and Hearn, Jeff (1996) *Men as Managers, Managers as Men: Critical Perspectives on Men, Masculinities, and Management.* London: Sage.

Collinson, Margaret, and Collinson, David (1996) 'It's only Dick': The sexual harass-ment of women managers in insurance sales. *Work, Employment, and Society,* 10:29–56.

Connell, Robert (1995) *Masculinities.* Cambridge: Polity Press.

Cooper, Robert, and Burrell, Gibson (1988) Modernism, Postmodernism, and Orga-nizational Analysis: An Introduction. *Organization Studies,* 9(1):91–112.

Cunliffe, Ann (2002) Social Poetics as Management Inquiry: A Dialogical approach. *Journal of Management Inquiry,* 11(2):128–146.

Czarniawska-Joerges, Barbara (1997a) *Narrating the Organization.* Chicago: The University of Chicago Press.

Czarniawska-Joerges, Barbara (1997b) *Narrative Approach in Organization Stu-dies.* London: Sage.

Czarniawska, Barbara (2000) Identity lost or Identity Found? Celebration and Lamentation over the Postmodern view of Identity in Social Science and Fiction. In: M. Schultz, M. J. Hatch, and M. Larsen (ed.) *The Expressive Orga-nization,*Oxford: Oxford University Press, 271–283.

Czarniawska, Barbara (2004) The Uses of Narrative in Social Science Research. In: M. Hardy, and A. Bryman (ed.) *Handbook of Data Analysis,* London: Sage.

Czarniawska, Barbara, and Gagliardi, Pasquale (2003) *Narratives We Organize.* Amsterdam: *By* John Benjamins.

Czarniawska, Barbara, and Höpfl, Heather (2002) Casting the Other: Introduction. In: B. Czarniawska and H. Höpfl (ed.) *Casting the Other: The Production and Maintenance of Inequalities in Work Organizations,* London: Routledge 2002.

Davies, Bronwyn (1989) *Frogs and Snails and Feminist Tales.* North Sidney: Unwin Hyman.

Davies, Bronwyn, and Rom, Harré (1990) Positioning: The Discoursive Production of Selves. *Journal of the Theory of Social Behaviour*, 1:43–63.

Davies, Julia (1992) Careers of trainers: biography in action, the narrative dimension. *Management Education and Development*, 23,(3):207–214.

De Beauvoir, Simone (1949) *Le deuxième sex*. Paris: Gallimard (Engl. Transl. *The Second Sex*. New York: Vintage, 1989).

De Certeau, Michel (1984) *The Practice of Everyday Life*. Berkeley: University of California Press.

Dellinger, Kirsten, and Williams, Christine L. (2002) The locker room and the dorm room: Workplace norms and the boundaries of sexual harassment in magazine editing. *Social Problems*, 49(2):242–257.

De Nardis, Paolo (2000) *L'invidia*. Roma: Meltemi.

Dent, Mark, and Whitehead, Stephen (2001) *Managing Professional Identities: Knowledge, Performativity and the 'New' Professional*. London: Routledge.

Denzin, Norman (1989) *Interpretive Biography*. Newbury Park: Sage.

Derrida, Jacques (1967) *De la grammatologie*. Paris: Minuit (Engl. Transl. *Of grammatology*, Johns Hopkins University Press, Baltimore, 1976).

Derrida, Jacques (1972) *La dissémination*, du Seuil, Paris: (Engl. Transl. *Dissemination*, Chicago: Chicago University Press, 1981).

Deutsch, Francine (2007) Undoing Gender. *Gender & Society*, vol. 21(1):106–127.

Eckert, Penelope, and McConnell-Ginnet, Sally (1992) Think Practically and Look Locally: Language and Gender as Community-Based Practice. *Annual Review of Anthropology*, 21:461–90.

Edmunson, Mark (1995) *Literature Against Philosophy, Plato to Derrida*. Cambridge: Cambridge University Press.

Elder, Glen H. Jr (1974) *Children of the Great Depression: Social Change in Life Experience*. Chicago: University of Chicago Press. Modificare nel file 1964.

Ely, Robin J. (1995) The power of Democracy: Women's social construction of gender identity at work. *Academy of Management Journal*, 38(3):589–634.

Ely, Robin J., and Meyerson, Debra E. (2000) Theories of gender in organizations: A new approach to organizational analysis and change. *Research in Organizational Behavior*, 27:105–153.

Fletcher, Joyce (1999) *Disappearing acts: Gender, power, and relational practice at work*. Cambridge MA: MIT Press.

Freccero, John (1986) Autobiography and Narrative. In: T. C. Heller, M. Sosna, and D. A. Wellbery (ed.) *Reconstructing Individualism: Autonomy, Individuality, in Western Thought*, Stanford: Stanford University Press, CA, 16–29.

Freed, Alice F. (1992) We understand perfectly: a critique of Tannen's view of cross-sex communication. In: K. Hall, M. Bucholtz, and B. Moonwomon (eds.) *Locating power: proceedings of the second Berkeley women and language conference*, Berkeley: Berkeley Women and Language Group: 144–52.

Fuchs Epstein, Seron, Cynthia Carroll, Oglensky, Bonnie, and Saut, Robert (1998) *The Part-Time Paradox: Time Norms, Professional Life, Family and Gender*. New York: Routledge.

Gabriel, Yiannis (2000) *Storytelling in Organizations*. Oxford: Oxford University Press.

Garfinkel, Harold (1964) Studies of the routine grounds of everyday activities. *Social Problems*, 11: 225–250.

179

Garfinkel, Harold (1967) *Studies in Ethnomethodology*. Englewood Cliffs N.J. Prentice-Hall.

Gergen, Kenneth J. (1991) *The Saturated Self. Dilemmas of Identity in Contemporary Life*. New York: Basic Books.

Gherardi, Silvia (1994) The Gender We Think, The Gender We Do in Everyday Organizational Lives. *Human Relations*, 47:591–609.

Gherardi, Silvia (1995) *Gender, Symbolism and Organizational Cultures*. London: Sage.

Gherardi, Silvia (1996) Gendered Organizational Cultures: Narratives of Women Travellers in a Male World. *Gender, Work and Organization*, 3:187–201.

Gherardi, Silvia (2003a) 'Feminist Theory and Organizational Theory: A Dialogue on New Bases'. In: H. Tsoukas, and C. Knudsen (ed.) *The Oxford Handbook of Organization Theory: Meta-theoretical Perspectives*, Oxford: University Press Oxford.

Gherardi, Silvia (2003b) Gender Citizenship in Organizations. In: P. Jeffcut (ed.) *The Foundations of Management Knowledge*, London: Routledge.

Gherardi, Silvia, and Poggio, Barbara (2001) Creating and recreating gender in organizations. *Journal of world business*, 36(3):245–259.

Gherardi, Silvia, and Poggio, Barbara (2007) 'You, Who Narrates, We, Who Listen: Narratives, Experiences and Gendered Leadership'. In: M. Reynolds, and R. Vince (a cura di) *Experiential Learning and Management Education*. Oxford: University Press (forthcoming).

Gherardi, Silvia, and Strati, Antonio (1990) 'The 'Texture' of organizing in an Italian University department'. *Journal of Management Studies*, 27(6):605–618.

Gibson, D. E. (2003) Developing a professional self-concept: role model construct in early, middle and late career stages. *Organization Science*, 14(5):591–610.

Giddens, Anthony (1991) *Modernity and Self-Identity*. Cambridge: Polity Press.

Giddens, Anthony (1994) *The Trasformation of Intimacy*. Cambridge: Polity Press.

Gilligan, Caren (1982) *In a Different Voice: Psychological Theory and Women's Development*. Cambridge:Harvard University Press.

Goffman, Erving (1963) On Face-Work in *Interaction Ritual*. New York: Anchor Books.

Goffman, Erving (1976) Gender Display. *Studies in the Anthropology of Visual Communication*, 3:301–31.

Good, Byron (1994) *Medicine, Rationality, and Experience: An Anthropological Perspective*. London: Cambridge University Press.

Grant, Judith, and Tancred, Peta (1992) A Feminist Perspective on State Bureaucracy. In: A. Mills, and P. Tancred (ed.) *Gendering Organizational Analysis*, Newbury Park CA: Sage.

Hanappi-Egger, Edeltraud, and Hofmann, Roswitha (2005) Narratives, Gender and Organizations. In: G. Schreyögg, and J. Koch, *Knowledge Management and Narratives*, Berlin: Erich Schmidt Verlag, 215–228.

Hassard, John, and Rowlinson, Michael (2002) Researching Foucault's research: Organization and Control in Joseph Lancaster's monitorial schools'. *Organization*, 9:615–39.

Haug, Frigga (1987) *Female Sexualization. A Collective Work of Memory*. London: Verso.

Hodgson, Damian (2003) 'Taking it like a man'. Masculinity, subjection and resistence in the selling of life insurance. *Gender, work and organization*, 10:1–21.

Hogan, Dennis P. (1978) 'The variable order of events in the life course'. *American Sociological Review,* 43:573–586.

Höpfl, Heather (1994) 'Learning by Heart: The Rules of Rethoric and the Poetics of Experience'. *Management Learning,* 25(3):463–474.

Ibarra, Herminia (1999) Provisional selves: experimenting with image and identity in professional adaptation. *Administrative Science Quarterly,* 44(4):764–791.

Iedema, Rick, Rhodes, Carl, and Scheeres, Hermine. Surveillance, Resistance, Observance: Exploring the Teleo-affective Volatility of Workplace Interaction. *Organization Studies,* 27(8): 1111–30.

Jamieson, Kathleen Hall (1995) *Beyond the Double Bind: Women and leadership.* New York: Oxford University Press.

Jedlowski, Paolo (1986) *Il tempo dell'esperienza: Studi sul concetto di vita quotidiana.* Milano: Angeli.

Jedlowski, Paolo (1995) *Introduzione* a Alfred Schütz, *Don Chisciotte e il problema della realtà.* Roma: Armando.

Jedlowski, Paolo (2000) *Storie comuni.* Milano: Mondadori.

Kanter, Rosabeth Moss (1977) *Men e Women of the Corporation.* New York: Basic Books.

Kanter, Rosabeth Moss, and Stein, Barry (1980) Building the Parallel Organization: Toward Mechanisms for Permanent Quality of Work Life. *Journal of Applied Behavioral Science,* 16:371–388.

Kerfoot, Deborah (1999) 'The organization of Intimacy: Managerialism, Masculinity, and The masculine Subject'. In: S. Whitehead, and R. Moodley (ed.) *Transforming Managers: gendering change in the Public Sector,* London: Taylor and Francis.

Kerfoot, Deborah, and Knights, David (1996) 'The best is yet to come?': The quest for embodiment in managerial work. In: D. L. Collinson, and J. Hearn (ed.) *Men as Managers, Managers as Men: Critical Perspectives on Men, Masculinities, and Managements,* London: Sage 78–98.

Kerfoot, Deborah, and Knights David (1998) Managing masculinity in contemporary organizational life: A 'man'agerial project. *Organization,* 5:7–26.

Klein, Melanie (1957) *Envy and gratitude: A study of unconscious forces.* London: Hogarth Press.

Knights, David, and Morgan, Glenn (1991) Corporatte Strategy, Organizations, and subjectivity: A Critique. *Organization Studies,* 12:251–273.

Kondo, Dorrine (1990) *Crafting selves: Power, gender, and discourses of identity in a Japanese factory.* Berkeley: University of California Press.

Kvande, Elin, and Rasmussen, Bente (1994) Men in Male-Dominated Organizations and Their Encounter With Women Intruders. *Scandinavia Journal of Management,* 10(2):163–173.

Lave, Jean, and Wenger, Etienne (1991) *Situated Learning: Legitimate Periperal Participation.* Cambridge: Cambridge University Press.

Laws, Judith Long (1975) The Psychology of Tokenism: An Analysis. *Sex Roles,* 1:51–67.

Locatelli, Carla (2000) Passaggi obbligati: la differenza (auto)biografica come politica co(n)testuale. In: C. Locatelli (ed.) *Co(n)texts: Implicazioni testuali,* Trento: Università degli Studi di Trento, 151–196.

Lorber, Judith, and Farrell, Susan (1991) *The Social Construction of Gender.* London: Sage.

Louis, Meryl R. (1980) Surprise and sensemaking: What newcomers experience in entering unfamiliar organizational settings. *Administrative Science Quarterly.* 25(2): 226–251.

Luciano, Adriana (1993) *Tornei. Donne e uomini in carriera.* Milano: Etas.

Lyotard, Jean François (1979) *La condition postmoderne*, Minuit, Paris (Engl. Transl. *The Postmodern Condition: A Report on Knowledge.* Manchester: Manchester University Press, 1985).

March, James, and Olsen, Johan P. (1989) *Rediscovering Institutions.* New York: Free Press.

Marshall, Judi (1984) *Women Managers: Travellers in a Male World.* Chichester: Wiley.

Marshall, Judi (1995) *Moving on.* London: Routledge.

Martin, Joan (1990) Deconstructing Organizational Taboos: the Suppression of Gender Conflict in Organizations. *Organization Science*, 1(4):339–359.

Martin, Joan (1994) The organization of exclusion: Institutionalization of sex inequality, gendered faculty jobs and gendered knowledge in organization theory and research. *Organization*, 1(2):401–432.

Martin, Joan, and Meyerson, Debra (1997) Women and Power: Conformity, Resistance, and Disorganized Co-Action. In: R. Kramer, and M. Neale (ed.) *Social Influence in Organizations*, Newbury Park CA: Sage.

Martin, Patricia Yancey (1996) Gendering and evaluating dynamics: Men, masculinities, and managements. In: D. Collinson, and H. Jeff (ed.) *Men as Managers, Managers as Men: Critical Perspectives on Men, Masculinities, and Management*, London: Sage, 186–209.

Martin, Patricia Yancey (2001) 'Mobilizing masculinities': Women's experiences of men at work. *Organization* 8 (November):587–618.

Martin, Patricia Yancey (2003) Said and done vs. saying and doing: Gendering practices, practicing gender at work. *Gender & Society,* 17:342–366.

Martin, Patricia Yancey (2004) Gender as social institution. *Social Forces* 82 (June):1249–1273.

Martin, Patricia Yancey (2006) Practicing Gender at Work: Further Thoughts on Reflexivity. *Gender, Work and Organization*, 13:(3):254–276.

McIntosh, Peggy (1985) *Feeling like a Fraud*, Wellesley: Stone Center for Developmental Services and Studies.

Mumby, Dennis K. (1987) 'The Political Function of Narrative in Organizations'. *Communication Monographs*, 54,113–27.

Neiger, Ada (1995) *Nata, l'eroe femminile della verghiana Tigre reale.* In: P. Cordin *et al.* (ed.) *Femminile e maschile tra pensiero e discorso*, Trento: Università degli Studi di Trento, Dipartimento di scienze filologiche e storiche.

Orr, Julian E. (1990) Sharing knowledge, Celebrating Identity: Community Memory in a Service Culture. In: D. S. Middleton, and D. Edwards (ed.) *Collective Remembering: Memory in Society*, Beverley Hills CA: Sage, 169–189.

Pajardi, Daniela (1998) Dall'invidia alla competizione. *Ricerche di Psicologia*, 22(4):53–68.

Papanek, Hanna (1973) Men, Women and Work: Reflections on the Two-Person Career. In: J. Huber (ed.) *Changing Women in a Changing Society*, Chicago: The University of Chicago, 90–110.

Personal Narratives Group (1989) *Interpreting Women's Lives: Feminist Theory and Personal Narratives*. Indiana: University Press, Bloomington and Indianapolis.

Piccardo, Claudia, Varchetta, G., and Zanarini, G. (1990) 'Car Makers and Marathon Runners: In Pursuit of Culture Through the Language of Leadership'. In: P. Gagliardi (ed.) *Symbols and Artifacts: Views of the Corporate Landscape*, Berlin: de Gruyter.

Pitt, Martyn (1998) A Tale of Two Gladiators: 'Reading' Entrepreneurs as Texts. *Organization Studies*, 19(3):387–414.

Poggio, Barbara (2004a) *Mi racconti una storia? Il metodo narrativo nelle scienze sociali*. Roma: Carocci.

Poggio, Barbara (2004b) 'Casting the 'Other': Gender Citizenship in Politicians' Narratives', in *Journal of Language and Politics*, 3(2):323–344.

Poggio, Barbara (2006) 'Editorial: Outline of a Theory of Gender Practices', in *Gender, Work and Organization*, 13(3):225–233.

Polkinghorne, Donald E. (1987) *Narrative, Knowing and the Human Sciences*. Albany: State University of New York Press.

Quinn, Beth A. (2002) Sexual harassment and masculinity: The power and meaning of 'girl watching.' *Gender & Society*, 16(3):386–402.

Rhodes, Carl, and Brown, Andrew (2005) Writing responsibly: Narrative fiction and organization studies. *Organization*, 12(4):167–188.

Riessman, Catherine Kohler (1993) *Narrative Analysis*. London: Sage.

Riessman, Catherine Kohler (2001) *Analysis of personal narratives*. In: J. F. Gubrium, and J. A. Holstein (ed.) *Handbook of Interviewing*, Newbury Park, CA: Sage, 695–710.

Rosenbaum, James E. (1989) *Organization Career System and Employee Misperceptions*. In: M. B. Arthur *et al.* (ed.) *Handbook of Career Theory*, Cambridge: Cambridge University Press.

Schütz, Alfred (1962a) *Collected Papers I. The Problem of Social Reality*. The Hague: Nijhoff.

Schütz, Alfred (1962b) Don Quixote and the Problem of Reality, in *Collected Papers*. The Hague: Nijhoff.

Scott, Joan (1986) Gender: A Useful Category of historical Analysis. *American Historical Review*, 91:1053–75.

Silberstein, Sandra (1988) Ideology as process: Gender ideology in courtship narratives. In: A. D. Todd, and S. Fischer (ed.) *Gender and discourse: The power of talk*, Norwood NJ: Ablex, 125–149.

Sjørup, Karen (ed.) (2005): *European Men Working in Women's Professions*. Denmark: The Danish Research Centre on Gender Equality.

Suleiman, Susan (1983) *Authoritarian fictions*. New York:Columbia University Press.

Swidler, Ann (2001) What Anchors Cultural Practices. In: T. R. Schatzki, K. Knorr Cetina, and E. von Savigny (ed.) *The Practice Turn in Contemporary Theory*, London and New York: Routledge.

Tannen, Deborah (1990) *You Just Don't Understand*, New York: Ballantine.

Tannen, Deborah (1994)

Townley, Barbara (1993) Foucault, Power/Knowledge, and its Relevance for Human Resource Management. *Academy of Management Review*, 18:518–45.

Trice, Harrison M., and Beyer, Janice M. (1993) *The cultures of work organizations*. Englewood Cliffs NJ: Prentice-Hall.

Turner, Victor (1982) *From Ritual to Theatre*. New York: Perfoming Arts Journal Publications.

Vegetti Finzi, Silvia (1990) La mela avvelenata. In: G. Pietropolli Charmet, and M. Cecconi *L'invidia. Aspetti sociali e culturali*, Atti del convegno svolto a Milano il 9 e 10 giugno 1989 Milano: Scheiwiller.

Wagner, Ina, and Wodak, Ruth (2006) Performing Success: Identifying strategies of self-Presentation in women's biographical narratives. *Discourse & Society*, 17(3):385–412.

Weick, Karl E. (1995) *Sensemaking in Organizations*, Sage. Thousand Oaks CA. (trad. it. *Senso e significato nell'organizzazione*, Milano: Cortina, 1995).

Wenger, Etienne (1998) *Communities of Practice: Learning, Meaning and Identity* New York: Cambridge University Press.

West, Candace, and Zimmerman, Don (1987) Doing gender, *Gender & Society*, 1:13–37.

Wharton, Amy, Rotolo, Thomas, and Bird, Sharon R. (2000) Social context at work: A multilevel analysis of job satisfaction. *Sociological Forum*, 15:65–90.

White, Hayden (1981) The Value of Narrative in the Representation of Reality. In: W. J. T. Mitchell (ed.) *On narrative*, Chicago: University of Chicago Press.

White, Kate (1995) *Why Good Girls don't Get Ahead, but Gutsy Girls Do*. New York: Warner Books.

Williams, Christine (1989) *Gender differences at work: Women and men in nontraditional occupations*. Berkeley: University of California.

Williams, Christine (1995) *Still a Man's World: Men who do Women's Work*. Berkeley: University of California Press.

Witten, Marsha (1993) Narrative and the Culture of Obedience at the Workplace. In: D. K. Mumby (ed.) *Narrative and Social Control: Critical Perspective*, London: Sage, 97–118.

Index

186